Social Responsibility in the Global Apparel Industry

◉

Social Responsibility in the Global Apparel Industry

⊙

Marsha A. Dickson
University of Delaware

Suzanne Loker
Cornell University

Molly Eckman
Colorado State University

Fairchild Books
New York

Director of Sales and Acquisitions: Dana Meltzer-Berkowitz
Executive Editor: Olga T. Kontzias
Senior Development Editor: Jennifer Crane
Development Editor: Sylvia L. Weber
Art Director: Adam B. Bohannon
Associate Art Director: Erin Fitzsimmons
Production Director: Ginger Hillman
Associate Production Editor: Jessica Rozler
Copyeditor: Joanne Slike
Cover Design: Adam B. Bohannon
Text Design: Andrew Katz
Page Composition: SR Desktop Services, Ridge, NY

Library of Congress Catalog Card Number: 2007928030
ISBN: 978-1-56367-592-8
GST R 133004424

Printed in the United States of America
TP13

To our students
who ask hard questions,
contribute fresh ideas, and
are endlessly passionate
for the work of
social responsibility.
You make us proud.
Now go out and
change the world.

Contents

Extended Contents

Foreword

It is extraordinary to analyze the evolution in the field of social responsibility (SR) over the last decades. And there are few books that illustrate its complexity, particularly in the apparel industry. Professors Marsha Dickson, Suzanne Loker, and Molly Eckman have delivered a concise yet comprehensive study, *Social Responsibility in the Global Apparel Industry*.

Although many of us believe in the importance of private enterprise and recognize its economic goal of profitability and return on investment, we firmly think that social and environmental performances are equally critical for the sustainability of the business itself. Simply put, corporate social responsibility (CSR) must be an integral part of the business formula. Triple bottom line is the new measurement. Wall Street and financial markets at large have yet to embrace this concept, but the business case has been laid out. Triple bottom line performance assessment will be integrated in a systematic manner in the next two decades. Our values-driven, principles-based movement is redefining business overall and permeating all aspects of society.

But we need informed, committed consumers who reward responsible business when exercising their purchasing power. Then financial investors will follow. Without consumers' buy-in and rewards for responsible business, the concept of CSR will not be sustainable, but just like other movements, it will fade away in the midst of more pressing economic needs by a growing world population.

However, just a look at college campuses, even lower and middle schools across America, provides an insightful perspective. The younger generations are connected and informed. They are writing letters to companies, to government officials, to the media. They are making buying decisions based on principles. They have a vision, and they are voicing their opinions. They are our future consumers, businesspeople, managers, activists, leaders, professors, government officials; they represent the future.

When reviewing the history of the apparel industry in the United States, the authors provide us with a vivid account of stakeholders' initiatives. History repeats itself, and at the beginning of the twenty-first century, it is doing so on a global scale. Our connected world and global economy offer a larger canvas for responsible business. Will our efforts result in securing internationally recognized rights and benefits for the "global worker" in this new century? Will compliance initiatives and CSR programs be instrumental in the eradication of sweatshops? This book examines the evidence of initiatives in the present to consider possible answers to these questions.

Diversity and inconsistency color our efforts worldwide: cultures, languages, political and economic systems, basic human rights, labor rights and freedoms granted—or not granted—to citizens, business models, rule of law, infrastructure setup, security and safety concerns, climate, and natural resources. The list is extensive and interrelated and continues to expand. Potential for conflict is a constant variable. Nowadays, any CSR practitioner must acquire a new set of skills, primarily in conflict prevention and resolution.

More than 16 years ago, I had the privilege to create and implement one of the initial human and labor rights compliance programs in the apparel industry. I have always believed CSR must be an integral part of the business thinking process. It is not an isolated set of criteria but an integrated approach to business. Therefore, from inception, we undertook the painstaking process of educating our associates across the board to influence corporate culture. In general, we all know periods of change and transformation are characterized by conflict, but we stayed the course. And it was not surprising that when our former CEO and CSR champion retired a few years back, our executives, managers, and associates expressed their commitment and support for "our" CSR program. As we stand today, our initiatives have evolved tremendously,

embracing the increasing complexities the authors highlight throughout the book.

As we move forward, we must maximize the undisputable lessons learned. Perhaps our initial monitoring approach in the 1990s—
endorsed by civil society and stakeholders at large—did not deliver the
sustainable improvements we were all hoping to achieve. But it set in
motion a period of disclosure, awareness, education, engagement, commitment, dialogue, collaboration, innovation, and search for sustainable solutions. The latter, we all recognize, requires the involvement of
multiple layers of stakeholders, with the global worker at the center.

The reader needs to remember that the SR field is in its infancy. The
authors, my SR colleagues, and I are committed to carry on our work
to reach new heights, but it is up to the next generation of practitio-
ners to challenge, explore, and innovate. And please keep in mind that
this is not an event but a meaningful journey.

Marcela Manubens
Senior Vice President
Global Human Rights and
Social Responsibility Program
Phillips-Van Heusen Corporation

Ms. Manubens, Senior Vice President of Global Human Rights and
Social Responsibility Program for the Phillips-Van Heusen Corporation, has created and directs the company's program on human rights
and social responsibility worldwide. Since 1996, Ms. Manubens has
participated in the Fair Labor Association, a tripartite initiative to
eliminate sweatshops. She is a member of the Monitoring Committee
and the Audit Committee of the Board.

Ms. Manubens has taught "Human Rights and Multinationals in a
Global Economy" at the School of International and Public Affairs at
Columbia University and "Macroeconomics" at the Business School of
Universidad de Belgrano, Argentina. She has been a lecturer and guest

speaker at national and international conferences. Ms. Manubens has extensive working experience in multinationals.

Ms. Manubens is a member of the Women's Foreign Policy Group in Washington, DC. Ms. Manubens represented U.S. business in the launching of the Global Report on Child Labor by the ILO at the United Nations, and in 2006, Ms. Manubens gave testimony in the United States Congress as an expert witness upon the invitation of the Congressional Human Rights Caucus. Ms. Manubens has been elected as a board member of the Fair Factory Clearinghouse (FFC) and heads its Audit Committee of the Board.

Ms. Manubens was a Fulbright scholarship recipient and a Halsey International Scholarship recipient. She holds an MBA in International Business from the University of Bridgeport and a Doctorship in Economics Sciences from Universidad de Belgrano, Argentina. She also attended the American University, International Service Program.

Preface

This is a book we wish were unnecessary to write. We wish the labor abuses that were found in the apparel industry in the early and mid-1990s were isolated incidents and that the codes of conduct that apparel brands and retailers adopted prevented similar problems from occurring ever again. We wish that the impacts of growing and developing fibers and processing and finishing fibers and fabrics did not cause harm to our water, soil, air, and workers.

This is also a book that many professors and students in the apparel discipline wish were unnecessary. Most people pursuing a career in the apparel industry are keen on designing, promoting, and selling fashion. We have intense interest in better understanding consumers and meeting their functional, psychological, and social needs through beautiful or high-tech garments. We would like to believe that the government or business or social activists are handling the faraway problems associated with production of apparel. After all—we would like to believe—our work as designers, buyers, merchandisers, and sourcing professionals in no way contributes to the exploitation of workers and the environment.

But this book *is* necessary to write. Unsafe factory conditions, long hours, inadequate pay, and use of toxic chemicals are not isolated incidents but widespread, systemic problems throughout the global apparel industry. The efforts brands and retailers have made to uphold workers' rights and protect the environment have had limited success so far, with too few brands and retailers engaged in making significant efforts and too few factories able to eradicate the problems. But that's not all. Although enlightened, committed leadership from top management is important, buyers, designers, merchandisers, and sourcing professionals have a major role in tackling the social and environmental challenges in the global apparel industry. In fact, some of the problems are the direct result of decisions made by professionals in every functional unit in apparel firms.

This is a book that professors and students in the apparel discipline *must* read and study, looking for opportunities to transform our ways of working to support and advance social responsibility. And we need help. *Every* stakeholder involved in the global apparel industry—from consumers to workers, labor unions to governments, investors to advocacy groups—needs to understand the issues, recognize the challenges and opportunities faced in solving them, and look for ways to ensure that workers are treated fairly and with dignity and that the environment is cared for as the precious resource that it is.

This book can be used in a variety of ways. Professors in the apparel field might consider developing an undergraduate course focused on social responsibility in the global apparel industry and use the book as its main text. Alternatively, they may elect to use the book as a supplementary text in a portion of a course focused on the global apparel industry. The book could be used as one of several newly published in the field for graduate-level courses studying current issues and structural concerns in the global apparel industry. Professors in business, sociology, women's studies, international economics, and other disciplines may find the book valuable as an industry sector case when examining business and society, globalization, and international development.

We also hope those already working in the apparel industry will find this book useful. Small apparel businesses not yet fully engaged in social responsibility can use the book as a guide for reference as they begin to adopt socially responsible practices. Large brands and retailers that have limited their activities to adoption of a code of conduct and monitoring can use the book for guidance in expanding stakeholder engagement and communicating their efforts to the public. Exemplary apparel brands and retailers already making strong efforts in social responsibility can use the book to inform their employees, both new and veteran, about the possibilities and continuous improvement necessary to advance social responsibility in the industry. The structure of the industry and the systemic nature of the problems defy the individual actions of single companies and compliance professionals. Not every business will be able to carry out the active engagement we have illustrated throughout the book, but it is important that every business take steps toward greater responsibility and accountability in its global supply chains. The frameworks for thinking about, structuring, and implementing socially responsible actions may be helpful in every scale of apparel business and for industry professionals in every functional area.

To encourage this, the management of apparel brands and retailing firms might give every corporate employee a copy of our book and hold discussions among cross-functional groups charged with creating a more socially responsible organizational culture. Apparel brands and retailers could also provide copies to key vendors so that the management of contract manufacturing facilities around the world can better understand social responsibility—what the issues are, why they are important to address, and how their businesses are needed to find long-term solutions. Our goal in writing this book is to provide a tool for the next generation and current industry professionals to move the global apparel industry forward on social responsibility. While the global apparel industry is the focus of the book, stakeholders associated with other complex, global supply chains—including toys, electronics, and other consumer goods—may find the information presented to be useful in addressing labor and environmental responsibility in their industries.

We may not have written this book without the synergy that was created as we pursued a major grant project. In 2002, we collaborated on a proposal to support post-baccalaureate education about social responsibility in the apparel industry. The proposal was subsequently funded by the U.S. Department of Agriculture's Higher Education Challenge Program.[1] We developed an ambitious list of expected outputs that included developing ten graduate-level, Internet-based courses, case studies, and learning materials. We decided that a textbook on the topic was needed, and so we added this parallel project.

---

[1]Project number 2004-38441-16681, Project director—Marsha Dickson.

Cumulatively, we have over 60 years of experience teaching and researching topics related to the apparel industry, apparel and textiles, consumer behavior, social responsibility, and cultural and design aspects of apparel. As local experts on the apparel industry at our respective universities, we each became involved in the 1990s debates about what actions our universities should take to address the expanding awareness of human rights violations and unfair labor practices used in factories producing apparel printed or embroidered with our universities' logos. We joined campus debates about the issue, presented information about social responsibility in our classes, and held discussions about the ethical and moral issues at hand. We became social activists in our own sphere of influence—our universities.

Marsha Dickson became a member of the board of directors of the Fair Labor Association (FLA), actively participating in the work and decision making of the organization. In fact, she was editing the first draft of the organization's first public report during the summer of 2003 when she recognized the value of writing a text that would illuminate the very difficult work that was unfolding in the headquarters and field offices of apparel brands and retailers that were leading efforts in social responsibility. Dickson knew how much work and resources were being expended, how difficult that work was, and how complex it was to explain the successes and challenges that those working in labor compliance were facing. A textbook aimed at students who would soon enter the industry, and even professionals already working in the apparel industry, was precisely what was needed.

Dickson's membership on the board of directors of the Fair Labor Association uniquely positioned her to participate in and observe the work that was being carried out by the multistakeholder initiative and the apparel brands and retailers leading efforts in social responsibility. Over her years of work with the organization, its participating companies, the FLA board members—including the NGO caucus—and FLA staff all contributed to her knowledge of social responsibility in the apparel industry.

Suzanne Loker's research and teaching has focused on the apparel industry and its emerging trends, including social responsibility. She has worked extensively with industry on both human resource development and technology advancement. Her electronic textbook *The Cutting Edge Guide to Apparel Business* provides small business entrepreneurs information useful in starting and growing apparel businesses, including socially responsible practices. It is available at a free-access Web site, http://instruct1.cit.cornell.edu/courses/cuttingedge. Loker has interviewed a number of apparel entrepreneurs and business executives about their socially responsible practices, and these video interviews are available at http://eclips.cornell.edu.

Molly Eckman became involved in the project as a result of her interest in global trade, the influence of culture on business practices, and writing case studies. She has participated in a variety of research and educational projects aimed at internationalizing curriculum and developing case studies that encourage critical thinking. The challenges facing the apparel industry are complex and will be addressed through innovative ideas and initiatives generated by future apparel executives and managers, many of whom are students in our apparel programs.

As part of the research carried out for the project, we interviewed industry and NGO professionals, interacted with industry associations, read hundreds of reports on the issues, and toured numerous apparel factories around the world. This book project has been exhausting and exhilarating, but ultimately rewarding, as we know the potential this book has for helping change the apparel industry from the inside out by preparing future professionals with the awareness, knowledge, and passion to make it more socially responsible.

Acknowledgments

Writing a textbook on an emerging issue in the apparel industry required extensive support from industry and other stakeholders that are actively pursuing greater social responsibility in the global apparel industry. We have gained immensely from the knowledge of FLA President and CEO Auret van Heerden, who undoubtedly knows more about pursuing social responsibility in the apparel industry than anyone else. Tanida Disyabut, regional manager of the FLA for Southeast Asia, was helpful in connecting us with labor activists in Thailand. Professionals from the apparel brands and retailers leading efforts in social responsibility were completely transparent with their work, opening their doors and the factories in which they contracted for apparel production and allowing us to gain valuable field perspectives on implementing labor compliance and environmental stewardship. We especially thank Bill Anderson, Gregg Nebel, and Barry Tang of the adidas Group; Dusty Kidd, Amanda Tucker, and Caitlin Morris of Nike; Daryl Brown and Bob Zane of Liz Claiborne; Doug Cahn and Nussara Meesane of Reebok; and Dan Henkle and Sumeth Srisangthaisuk of Gap for the contributions they made on behalf of our work. Stephen Frost of CSR-Asia alerted us to emerging issues in China and put us in contact with Hong Kong-based activists. Professor Foengfurad Mungtavesinsuk of Kasetsart University in Bangkok was instrumental in making our trip to Thailand a success.

We are indebted to Doug Cahn now of The Cahn Group, Marcela Manubens of Phillips-Van Heusen, Jorge Perez-Lopez of the FLA, and Lynda Yanz of the Maquila Solidarity Network, all of whom have vast experience with social responsibility, for their review of the entire draft manuscript. Kirk Mayer of Nike reviewed the environmental-related sections of the book. These professionals spent copious amounts of their work and vacation times to read the draft, raise suggestions, and alert us to potential flaws in our thinking because they are passionate about social responsibility and working toward its continuous improvement and sustainability in many arenas. Their suggestions were invaluable. In addition, we made decisions on what to add and change based on their comments and on the recommendations of the following reviewers, selected by the publisher: Jeanie Lisenby, Miami International University of Art & Design and Marjorie Norton, Virginia Polytechnic Institute and State University. However, any errors in the book draft are our own responsibility.

Several graduate students worked with us to develop content that could be included in the book. We are especially grateful to Ayemi Lawani and Kevin Kovaleski of the University of Delaware, and Katie Dombek-Keith and Amy Kinateder of Cornell University. Special thanks goes to Lindsay Lyman-Clarke of Cornell University, who created many of the graphic figures for this book. Members of the international consortium of Educators for Socially Responsible Apparel Business always made us feel that we were pursuing important work. We hope they find the outcome—this book—valuable in their teaching and research.

Of course, we also could not have been successful in writing this book without the support of Olga Kontzias, Executive Editor of Fairchild Books, who was immediately and fully supportive of our proposal. Sylvia Weber, our development editor, was exceedingly patient when we had to give priority to our other work. Her positive comments and gentle editing were appreciated. Our production editor, Jessica Rozler, guided the transformation of our manuscript into a printed text, and for their assistance with the images that enhance the text, we thank art director Adam Bohannon and photo researcher Erin Fitzsimmons.

Finally, our families deserve considerable recognition for their patience and support as we worked on the book. We have left them in charge at home as we traveled around the world, left them in charge of dinner and other aspects of home life as we holed up in our offices to write, and essentially put on hold much of our lives as we worked toward one deadline after another. We look forward to catching up with what we have missed over the last few years.

Chapter 1

What Is Social Responsibility?

◉

Imagine for a few minutes that you are Chen Xiao Mei, a 16-year-old girl living in rural China.* You have lived on the outskirts of a small village all your life. Your family is very poor, living in a one-room house surrounded by a small plot of land where you grow much of the food you eat. It is difficult to afford medicine when someone is sick. You finished your schooling many years ago, having completed only the six years of school that your family could afford. Since then you have helped your mother and father in the fields and with the chickens and pigs (Figure 1.1). You dream that one day you might get married and start a small store that will provide the village people with some of the goods they cannot make themselves. But this is only a dream unless you can find a way to make and save some money to buy the initial stock of goods.

Recently a man has come to your village offering work in the city of Guangzhou, several hundred miles away. He promises good wages and a place for you to live. With the income you make from sewing in the factory, you will be able to save the money you need to start the rest of your life. After discussing this with your parents, you decide that

---

*With the exceptions of Chapters 4 and 6, the stories used to open each chapter are fictional accounts.

Figure 1.1
Work in rural China.

the next time the man returns to your village, you will go with him to take this work. You'll work just two or three years, send money home, and eventually return to the village to start a family and the store.

When you arrive in Guangdong province in southern China and the city of Guangzhou, you cannot believe your eyes. There are so many buildings, cars, and people. This new life will surely be fun! There are so many things you can buy when you begin earning and so many new things to learn about. The man takes you to the factory as promised. You are given a brightly colored smock to wear over your clothes at work and are checked into a dormitory room with seven other girls new to the factory. The man takes your identification papers for safekeeping. It turns out he is the cousin of the factory owner, and he promises you will not need the papers here anyway. You line up for work at 8:00 the next morning, eager to start the work that will change your life.

You are given a pretty easy job at first—trimming the ends of sewing threads that hang from the garment seams. Soon you are shown how to use a machine to sew the hem of a T-shirt. What seemed exciting at first quickly turns to drudgery. How can there be enough people to buy all the pink T-shirts you are hemming? And there is so much noise in the factory with all the machines whirring. Your ears ring at night with the sounds these machines make as you quickly fall asleep, only to be awakened a few hours later to start the next day's shift. Often you work from 8:00 in the morning until at least 8:00 at night. Sometimes the man on the loudspeaker comes on in the evening to tell you that the production must be completed tonight or the factory will have to close and all the employees will lose their jobs. On these days you work until midnight, or whenever the job gets done. Every day you are told the number of shirts you need to hem that day to make a bonus, but it seems like you can almost never reach that number, and the time you did, your paycheck did not seem much bigger. You're not sure how they calculate your pay to check whether it was done accurately. You wonder whom you could ask about this. You've not thought about your dream of opening a shop in your village for some time, but you do think about how nice it would be to have an evening off when you could go to some of the nearby stores and look around at life outside the factory walls.

The factory provides pretty much everything you need. There is a small store where you can buy rice and other ingredients for making a simple breakfast or dinner on the hot plate in your room. Lunch is provided in the factory cafeteria (Figure 1.2). There is always plenty of rice, but the food lacks the spices and flavors you are accustomed to, and sometimes the vegetables taste as if they've gone bad. You are careful to throw them out on those days because if you eat them and get sick, you'll have to miss work to go to the medical clinic or risk having to ask your supervisor for permission to use the toilet frequently during the day. She will be angry because there is no chance you will meet your production quota on those days. You do your best to avoid making your supervisor angry because it is embarrassing when she yells at

Figure 1.2
An apparel factory cafeteria in China.

3

you and the other girls working around you. She calls you a "stupid cow" and says bad things about your family when you break a needle on your machine and makes you take it to the window for a new needle. You know your pay will be a little less next time because you will be charged for the needle. No one seems to care that the needle went through the tip of your finger and it is throbbing and bleeding into the handkerchief you've wrapped around it. You wish there were someone you could complain to about how you are treated.

Living in the factory dormitory isn't bad (Figure 1.3). Your roommates turn out to be from villages near yours, and on days when production is light and you are all dismissed from work early, you share stories about your family and your school days. You all work to keep the toilet in your room pretty clean (this is the first time you have seen such a shiny fixture—the toilet at home was a hole in the ground), but the toilet area gets pretty messy when all of you wash your clothing on the same day. There really isn't much to do when you have days off except try to catch up on the sleep you've missed over the last few weeks.

One time, on your way to the toilet in the factory, you stopped to look at a poster on the wall of the factory. It has the same picture as the label in the T-shirts you are sewing. It tells about some rules the factory is supposed to follow, but you cannot really understand all the words. A supervisor who sees you standing and doing nothing but reading the poster shoos you on your way.

Figure 1.3

A factory dormitory room in China.

Sometimes strangers come into the factory. You know they are coming because before you see them the voice on the loudspeaker tells you. Everyone around you rushes to put on the face masks given to you on your first day of work. No one likes to wear them because they make your face too hot. As the strangers walk around the factory, they ask to talk to some of the other girls. You're relieved when they pass you by. Your supervisor has told you what you have to say if the strangers take you in the other room: You normally work until 5:00 p.m.; your last day off was Sunday; your supervisor is very kind; you are glad to have the opportunity to work here; you wish you could work more overtime so that you could make some more money. You wouldn't dare say anything else. It seems that all the workers in the factory have heard the story of the girl who spoke her mind—she was fired before the day was over. Although this seems to be the worst job in the world, you don't have any idea what you would do or where you would go if you were fired. There is another factory across the street, but would it have work? Would a job there be any better than this one? Will you ever make enough money so that you can return home to open a store?

◉

Why Talk about Social Responsibility in the Global Apparel Industry?

Chen Xiao Mei's life is very much like that of hundreds of thousands of other young women and men around the world who work in factories manufacturing the apparel that we wear. These workers come from rural and urban areas in developing countries that have made export of manufactured goods the strategy for advancing their countries to the next level of economic development and industrialization. This strategy stems from the fact that factories require little capital to equip and can employ a large unskilled workforce. Around the world, workers migrate to cities or the special export processing zones where factories are found. They may come across national borders, such as the migrants from Myanmar who cross the border into Thailand for work, or from just one side of the city they live in to another. Either way, they are likely to encounter unfamiliar situations and even cultural differences.

Although every worker is a unique individual with her or his own values, personality, and family experiences, together these workers have much in common. The wages they earn are low—workers usually need to make more money than they earn on the job if they are to ever get ahead or even get by. They are most often fairly young—in many cases ranging in age from their mid-teens to mid-20s at the oldest—and they are predominantly female—though this can vary greatly if the country offers few work alternative opportunities for men. Few choices are available to them for work, though some may switch factories a few times in hopes of finding one that offers higher pay or more reliable overtime hours or has enough work to keep everyone busy and earning. The workers have usually received little schooling beyond the primary levels required in their countries. In most cases they have never had advice or information about their rights as workers and the obligations their employer has to them as employees. Thus, they often do not know whether laws are being broken, their wages are calculated correctly, or the factory is paying the required taxes to the government that will be used for their social welfare should the factory be closed. Most are not represented by a union.

Social Responsibility in Design, Production, and Sourcing

By introducing you to Chen Xiao Mei, we have illustrated some of the key labor issues related to production and sourcing of apparel products, including:

- Forced labor
- Low wages
- Excessive hours of work
- Discrimination
- Health and safety hazards
- Psychological and physical abuse
- Lack of awareness of workers' rights
- Lack of worker representation for negotiations with management

You probably identified most of these issues as you read Chen Xiao Mei's story; however, you may not have realized that the retention by management of personal identification documents is a form of forced labor because the worker is not free to leave the current place of employment without them. Although Chen Xiao Mei is 16 years of age,

6

we did not list child labor as an issue because 15 years of age is widely viewed as the minimum for regular work in developing countries and many codes of conduct reference minimum legal ages for work.[1] Yet child labor still occurs occasionally in the apparel industry, and with labor shortages in China, it is increasing in that country.[2] Chen Xiao Mei's wages are low, even by standards in her own country. The hours she is required to work frequently exceed the maximum of 60 hours that most codes of conduct allow. Chen Xiao Mei is exposed to equipment that can cause injuries. She is abused by supervisors who do not know that there are better ways to manage workers than by shouting at them. Chen Xiao Mei does not know her rights as a worker nor the labor laws of the country, and she may have been denied her right of freedom of association. The issues listed here are surprisingly similar to ones that have been associated with apparel production work throughout history in many global contexts.

Historical Problems with Labor Standards and Working Conditions

The fact that workers in Great Britain and in the United States were exploited as the apparel industries of these two countries developed during the Industrial Revolution is sometimes offered as an excuse for the working conditions found in developing countries in the twenty-first century. After all, those making this claim say, the United States survived the difficult conditions and look how much better off the country is now.

Indeed, conditions in the nineteenth-century textile mills of Great Britain and the United States were appalling. Individuals testifying to the Sadler Committee in an 1832 parliamentary investigation in England reported having gone to work at six or eight years of age, regularly working for 14 hours per day, and being beaten and having wages disproportionately decreased when they did not arrive on time.[3] The situation would be repeated as the United States further developed its industry, though often with young women, rather than children, who migrated from rural New England to river towns such as Lowell, Massachusetts, to work for the same long hours, very low pay, and in unsafe conditions as their British predecessors. The women behind early attempts to organize workers to demand a better working situation were fired.[4]

The situation for those working in the mass-produced apparel industry in the late 1800s and early 1900s was similar to that described in the textile mills.[5] In small shops run out of immigrants' houses in the Lower East Side of Manhattan, workers toiled for over 80 hours per week with no days off (Figure 1.4). Crowded side by side on whatever perch they could find, workers struggled to sew faster so that the wages they would earn for the total pieces sewn would be enough for food and shelter. Some improvements were seen when production moved to more factory-like settings where workers were less crowded and diseases such as tuberculosis did not spread as easily. However, there were reports that time clocks were rigged to cheat the workers, who were mocked when they complained.[6] But the anger of the immigrant workers grew as they saw their pay reduced to cover the electric power

Figure 1.4
Early 1900s sweatshop.

they used, the chairs on which they sat, and the needles and threads used to make the garments.[7]

The increasing anger of immigrant workers, especially female workers, resulted in action during a period in the early 1900s called the Progressive Era, which included support for women's right to vote, trade unions, and protection for consumers and workers. The Progressive Era peaked in 1909, and there were numerous strikes of women workers across the New York City apparel industry (Figure 1.5).[8] Greenwald provides a synopsis of a 1909 strike involving more than 20,000 women. In a show of humanitarianism and trade unionism, middle-class women who empathized with the workers' plight helped the poor, immigrant women picket.[9] These labor uprisings forced many apparel factory owners to recognize the right of workers to join unions.[10] Following a second major strike in 1910, a new system for workers to submit grievances was established, yet many factory owners continued to disregard the rights of their workers.[11]

Figure 1.5

A strike of garment workers in New York City in the early 1900s.

Workplace safety in all industries went virtually unregulated in the early 1900s. At least one estimate claims that 100 workers in America died daily in a variety of jobs during this period. However, the fire that broke out on March 25, 1911, in the Triangle Waist Company factory, where women's blouses and dresses were made, would remain "for ninety years, the deadliest workplace disaster in New York history."[12] In an area piled with fabric and partially completed garments, the fire found plenty of fuel and spread rapidly. As workers tried to escape the burning building, panic led to blockage of one door, and the workers found other exit doors locked and the freight elevators blocked (Figure 1.6). In desperate attempts to flee the flames, scores of people jumped out of the tenth-floor windows. Just 30 minutes later, 146 people, the majority of whom were women, had perished.[13] The Triangle Waist Company factory fire marked "the crucial moment in a potent chain of events—a chain that ultimately forced fundamental reforms from the political machinery of New York, and after New York, the whole nation."[14]

The people of New York City were outraged by the fire, and marches and demonstrations followed. Over the next few decades, membership

9

Figure 1.6
The aftermath of the Triangle Waist Company factory fire.

in the International Ladies Garment Workers Union (ILGWU), which had formed in 1900, and the Amalgamated Clothing Workers of America (ACWA), founded in 1914, would grow; the ILGWU had 128,000 members by 1917.[15] The substantial union presence coupled with increased government regulation of the workplace led to improved conditions across the U.S. apparel industry for decades following the Triangle Waist Company factory fire. Some media attention in the late 1970s identified and lamented continuing labor problems in the United States[16]; however, it was not until the mid-1990s that people across the country were alerted to how pervasive the labor problems in the industry were.

Contemporary Problems with Labor Standards and Working Conditions

Widespread news reports in the 1990s expressed outrage at the lack of fair labor practices in the United States and in offshore apparel factories. In 1995, the public was informed that 70 Thai women had been found locked in an apparel factory in El Monte, California, held as indentured workers to repay their passage to the United States. Some workers reported not being let out of this factory compound for seven years.[17] Child labor found in a Central American factory where Kathie Lee Gifford's apparel line sold by Wal-Mart was produced brought labor issues to light for many Americans in 1996 and 1997.[18] In the 1990s, reports from activist groups, especially the National Labor Committee, a New York City-based labor group headed by activist Charles Kernaghan, exposed exploitative conditions in major brands' subcontracted factories in China.[19] Liz Claiborne was accused of paying only subsistence wages and forcing workers to work 84 hours a week in a factory in El Salvador.[20] Wal-Mart reportedly paid contractors for workers earning as little as 10 cents an hour to make its products in various locations around the world.[21]

In other examples of problems in the United States and its territories, factory owners in the Sunset Park area of Brooklyn were accused of exploiting Chinese immigrants who regularly worked 7 days a week in 12-hour shifts.[22] Federal class-action lawsuits were filed against 18 well-known brands and retailers for having garments produced in the U.S. territory of Saipan under poor and unfair conditions. The lawsuit was filed on behalf of 50,000 workers, who alleged that they were producing branded goods in sweatshop conditions (Box 1.1).[23]

As some companies and organizations announced initiatives to address working conditions in the factories making name brand apparel and footwear, media coverage of labor abuses seemed to subside. Using the terms "apparel" and "sweatshop" to search LexisNexis headlines and lead paragraphs of general news in major papers produced 473 news articles during 1996 and 1997; the same search for 2000 and 2001 revealed only 230 articles. However, despite lessened media coverage, abuses continued, as the following selected examples reveal.

In a tragedy too similar to the Triangle Waist Company factory fire in New York in 1911, the Chowdhury Knitwear and Garments factory in Bangladesh burned in 2000, leaving 51 dead, including 8 workers who were reported to be between the ages of 10 and 14. Another fire

Box 1.1. Saipan Lawsuits Allege US Firms Are Tied to "Sweatshops"

LOS ANGELES—Thousands of Asians have been lured to the US territory of Saipan to make clothing for American companies, only to be beaten, forced into getting abortions and made to live under guard in cramped, rat-infested quarters, according to lawsuits filed yesterday.

Saipan was described by one lawyer as "America's worst sweatshop," where more than 50,000 Asians have been recruited with promises of good wages to make clothing tagged "Made in the USA."

Three lawsuits seek more than $1 billion in damages for conditions they claim have persisted for the past decade in the 13-mile-long tropical isle in the Central Pacific.

The lawsuits are the first legal attempt to hold US retailers accountable for alleged mistreatment of workers by subcontractors under the federal Racketeer Influenced and Corrupt Organizations Act, attorneys said at news conferences in New York City and Los Angeles.

Describing the workplaces, a plaintiffs' lawyer, William Lerach, said in Los Angeles that they "make medieval conditions look good."

Two class-action suits were filed in federal courts in Los Angeles and Saipan. A third was filed in San Francisco state court by the groups Global Exchange, Sweatshop Watch, Asian Law Caucus and the Union of Needletrades, Industrial and Textile Employees.

Among the 18 companies named are The Limited, Wal-Mart, Sears, The Gap, Tommy Hilfiger, the May Company, J. Crew, Oshkosh B'Gosh, Associated Merchandising, Cutter & Buck Inc., Gymboree Manufacturing, Lane Bryant Inc., Warnaco and Dayton-Hudson Inc., which owns Marshall Fields.

Of the companies named, Nordstrom, Warnaco, Tommy Hilfiger, J.C. Penney, Wal-Mart, Oshkosh B'Gosh and Dayton Hudson Corp. insist they hire subcontractors that strictly follow US labor laws. Other companies said they had no comment or did not return calls.

According to the lawsuits, 32 Saipan factories force people to work up to 12 hours a day, seven days a week, and threaten them with beatings and verbal abuse if they refuse unpaid overtime to meet quotas set by factory managers.

Workers' passports are confiscated upon arrival, they are not allowed to leave the factory compound, and their social activities are strictly monitored, Lerach said.

The factories—mostly owned by Chinese, Japanese and Korean subcontractors—stamp their clothing with "Made in the USA" and are able to sidestep duties, tariffs and quotas imposed on imported clothing.

In the fiscal year that ended in October, the Saipan factories shipped an estimated $1 billion in wholesale clothing duty-free to the US mainland, saving more than $200 million, Lerach said.

Pamela Rucker, spokeswoman for the industry group National Retail Federation, said whether it is misleading to use a "Made in the USA" label is a matter for the Federal Trade Commission and truth-in-labeling laws to regulate.

Saipan is part of the Northern Marianas, an island chain seized by US troops from Japan in World War II that negotiated a commonwealth relationship with Washington. The deal left control of immigration and minimum wages in local hands, and exempted Saipan's exports from US duties and quotas.

SOURCE: Associated Press (1999, January 14). "Saipan lawsuits allege US firms are tied to 'sweatshops.'" *The Boston Globe*, p. A10.

at the KTS Textiles factory, also in Bangladesh, that made garments for less well-known manufacturers based in the United States killed 84 workers.[24] In both cases, workers had been paid very low wages, worked excessive hours, and found locked doors when they tried to escape the burning building. The presence of multiple factories operating in residential tenement buildings, which offer no fire prevention, escalated safety risks in Bangladesh.[25] In 2003, Sean "P. Diddy" Combs's apparel line, Sean John, made headlines when workers from a Honduran factory alleged that they produced the trendy wear in sweatshop conditions.[26]

There are more recent examples of labor problems and working conditions in apparel factories as well. In 2005, *Dateline NBC* broadcast a story on the poor conditions found in Bangladeshi factories producing goods for Wal-Mart, Kmart, and Sara Lee. These problems were occurring despite the codes of conduct many apparel brands and retailers had adopted as required labor standards and working conditions and were found posted on the factory walls. Additionally, factory management had assured the buyers that workers were fairly paid, human rights were respected, and the working conditions in the factory were safe and healthy.[27] The National Labor Committee released a report on wage abuses found in a factory making New Balance footwear in China.[28] Another factory in Bangladesh was reported to use children to sew garments for Hanes and Wal-Mart.[29] Although most factory abuses seemed to have moved overseas, despite more frequent use of codes of conduct and monitoring of factories, problems with labor standards and working conditions continued in the United States and apparel-exporting countries.

Global Context of Problems with Labor Standards and Working Conditions

Problems with labor standards and working conditions in the apparel industry are still a reality at the turn of the twenty-first century and are global issues. The production of American-branded clothing is scattered all over the world—many brands no longer own factories, and brands and retailers contract most of their production. How and when did this transformation occur?

As trade unionism expanded in the New York City garment industry in the 1920s and 1930s, apparel contractors in the city found themselves in a competitive situation where higher union wages affected their ability to earn bids. Many factories shifted production facilities to neighboring states, including the northeast region of Pennsylvania where labor costs were lower.[30] The garment unions expanded into the area, but "the union would come to find that the growth of the runaway industry in Pennsylvania represented just one stop in a large pattern of sweatshop migrations."[31] The apparel industry in the southern United States grew rapidly after World War II until the early 1970s. Here there was an abundance of white female workers in rural areas ready to work for low wages and an absence of unions to push for higher wages. As well, the civil rights movement changed the opportunities for black workers in the 1960s and provided an expanded pool of labor for the apparel industry in the South. In the 1970s, the California apparel industry that had begun in the 1920s increased in size and influence. A notable influx of immigrant labor provided a large and inexpensive base of workers[32] and, similar to the southern United States, the California apparel industry was generally not unionized.

According to Edna Bonacich and David Waller, "the Far East was to the southern United States what the South was to the Northeast: an opportunity to cut costs."[33] A few early apparel importers worked with suppliers in Japan, then Hong Kong and Taiwan in the 1950s and 1960s. By the 1970s, the distinction between apparel manufacturers and retailers began to blur as retailers such as the Gap, which had previously served as the distribution link between manufacturers and consumers, took on the design of products and became direct importers of Asian apparel.[34] Many apparel manufacturers, which were increasingly competing with retailers, found it to be disadvantageous to own factories, and they increasingly focused on the core competencies of design and marketing their name brands. To save money and allow more flexibility in product specialization, production shifted from owned facilities in the United States to contracted production, first with suppliers in the Southeast Asian countries of Malaysia, Indonesia, and the Philippines. As China opened its doors to world trade, production shifted there and to such countries as Thailand, Pakistan, Bangladesh, Sri Lanka, India, and Honduras. A trade regime that attempted to protect the domestic apparel industry of the United States and other developed countries by establishing country-specific export quotas, the Multifibre Arrangement (MFA) pushed outsourced production to a wide range of countries throughout the 1990s and the beginning of the twenty-first century as buyers looked for countries with available quota. During this time, production would reach to virtually every corner of the world, and such countries as Madagascar, Uganda, Vietnam, Cambodia, Laos, El Salvador, and Peru saw orders for garment production increase. Yet a phaseout of the MFA eliminated quantitative restrictions (i.e., quotas) on imports in 2005, and the global apparel manufacturing base began to consolidate to a smaller set of countries and regions as buyers shifted production to manufacturers that could produce larger volumes of apparel. China would continue as a major production site, and other countries in Southeast Asia, South Asia (particularly India), and the Caribbean Basin and Central America were expected to retain notable amounts of production for U.S. apparel manufacturers and retailers.[35] Bangladesh and many of the countries in Africa that had benefited from the MFA as apparel brands and retailers were forced to order from a broader range of countries were expected to lose production.

The production shifts in search of lower wages and the protective trade regime that dispersed production into numerous countries resulted in global supply chains with multiple layers and geographical locations. In 2005, apparel was imported into the United States from 154 countries[36] and individual apparel brands and retailers sourced products and production of goods from many countries and many suppliers. For example, in 2003, Nike reported sourcing production from over 1,100 suppliers located in 54 countries.[37] In 2005, Gap worked with over 2,000 suppliers in 50 countries spread around the world.[38]

Figure 1.7 illustrates the complex apparel supply chains that developed with changes in industry organization and structure. The diagram shows the various partners that contribute to production and distribution of apparel from the textile materials production through consumer purchase. *Brand* is a term that includes apparel manufacturing companies that either produce their own products in their own factories, contract out production to domestic or offshore factories that they do not own, or a combination of both. Brand is a more accurate descriptor than apparel manufacturers because by the 1990s several large companies, Nike and Liz Claiborne, for example, adopted business models that focused on design and marketing, and included contracted production and no factory ownership. Looking horizontally at the figure, note that brands can purchase fabric directly from textile mills or work with agents that represent contractors, work directly with full-package contractors that handle all aspects of production, or work with

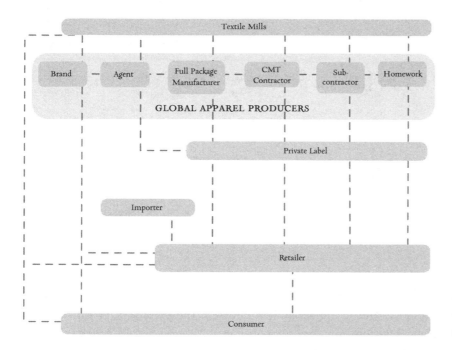

Figure 1.7
Overview of the complex organization of apparel supply chains.

cut-make-trim (CMT) contractors that only cut and assemble garments, to complete one or more of the design, production, and distribution steps in apparel production. Looking vertically, note that brands sell to retailers or directly to the consumer. The blurring of brand and retailer strategies that has evolved is depicted in this diagram; brands and retailers both contract design and production directly and sell to consumers by working with agents or contractors. Retailers sometimes purchase finished goods from importers. Finally, the diagram shows private label—that is, owning and distributing a trade name or brand name unique to a firm only in its own retail stores. Private-label production was pioneered by major retailers with basic goods that had consistent selling patterns such as polo shirts and underwear. To increase the value to their production activities, contractors also pursue private-label activity, benefiting from the design and marketing revenues as well as from the profit from retail markups. Even brands sometimes design and merchandise private-label garments for retailers.

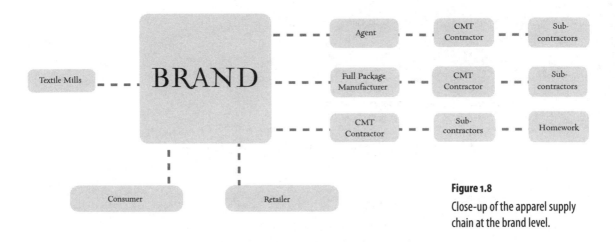

Figure 1.8
Close-up of the apparel supply chain at the brand level.

Figure 1.8 zooms in on the various partners involved in the production of brand-name apparel to illustrate the variety of possible supply chain relationships. Brands contract with agents, full-package manufacturers, and cut-and-sew contractors to produce garments depending on the style, fabric, sewing operation requirements, and distribution plan. Imagine this scenario occurring in dozens of countries and with hundreds of CMT contractors and the complexity of global apparel production becomes clear. This complexity requires vigilance over many suppliers in many nations and affects the ability of companies attempting to be socially responsible.

◉

Environmental Responsibility

Although labor issues have received the most attention from apparel brands and retailers over the last decade, environmental issues are emerging as the next important social responsibility area firms will be expected to address. The major environmental impacts of the production and use of textile fibers and apparel are in:

⊚ Energy used in laundry and needed for production of materials
⊚ Use of toxic chemicals that can harm human and environmental health during growing, production, and processing of textiles and apparel
⊚ Release of chemicals in wastewater during production, dyeing, finishing, and laundering
⊚ Solid wastes during production and at disposal[39]

Unfortunately, these impacts are hard to measure and are usually hidden costs. Until the 1990s, there was little discussion about environmental impacts of apparel production and use or many other consumer products. National environmental laws governing businesses in each country were the standard, though level of protection and its enforcement varied. The little progress made toward greater environmental protection took place in large international forums of government, business, and nongovernmental organization (NGO) leaders such as the 1992 Rio Earth Summit. The United Nations' World Commission on Environment and Development resulted in the 1987 *Our Common Future* report, and the 48-member Business Council for Sustainable Development authored the 1992 report *Changing Course*. As in human rights and labor, we as consumers assumed that environmental conscientiousness was a right rather than a privilege, one that "others" were taking care of and we could enjoy. The rise in fuel costs, increasing debate over global warming, and escalating "organic" offerings across many food and fiber products brought the reality that each of us is paying environmental costs every day with each product that we purchase and action that we take.

Initiatives that address environmental responsibility as part of social responsibility have evolved somewhat differently than labor and human rights initiatives. In the United States, regulations of environmental impacts from growing, processing, and dyeing textile materials were established over the last half of the twentieth century despite strong corporate lobbying against any legislation or for lower standards.[40] Enforcement strategies were focused at the business level, establishing a base level of expectations for every textile and apparel manufacturing business. The legislated regulations and enforcement worked relatively well to move apparel and other industries in the United States toward recognizing and embracing a base level of compliance in environmental issues. Unfortunately, this was not the case in all other countries, particularly developing countries. Environmental regulations either are so low they do not protect against environmental degradation or are not enforced. Either way, the environmental standards of textile and apparel offshore production from developed countries are left to individual businesses and their Western business partners to establish and uphold.

◉

The Triple Bottom Line

Although businesses, including apparel and textile businesses, generally adopt environmental practices according to the law, relatively few incorporated environmental stewardship into their corporate vision before Paul Hawken provocatively presented the problem in his 1993 book, *The Ecology of Commerce*. He argued that the rewards for businesses needed to be transformed from producing the lowest-priced product to a new business reward model that embraced social and environmental responsibility by identifying and paying for their costs up front. What he described has been called by John Elkington the triple bottom line—the winning business strategy that measures corporate performance by social, environmental, and economic practices (or people, planet, profit) and conscientious behavior toward the planet and its inhabitants:[41]

> We require a market economy that rewards the highest internalized cost, an economy in which business prospers when it is responsible both socially and ecologically. We need business to thrive by exceeding regulatory standards rather than by challenging or circumventing them. Businesses should literally compete to be more ecological, not only on moral or ethical grounds or because it is "the right thing to do," but because such behavior

squarely aligns with their bottom line. In short, we must design a marketplace that obviates acts of environmental destruction by making them extremely expensive, and rewards restorative acts by bringing them within our means. If we do this, environmental restoration, economic prosperity, job creation and social stability will become equivalent.[42]

Hawken called for the business system to be revamped so that pollution, environmental degradation, and nonrenewable energy consumption are taxed and replace income and property taxes charged to individuals. He argued that such a radical change is needed to move environmental stewardship and social responsibility from individuals and individual acts to part of the business process, paying for the now unaccounted burden on our environment and its inhabitants. Some large (e.g., Patagonia and Timberland) and small businesses (e.g., Maggie's Organics and Chaco) took note quickly, wrote environmental plans and codes, and began integrating both environmental stewardship and social responsibility into their mission, vision, and business strategies. Business schools began offering courses and immersions in socially responsible business practices, including environmental stewardship. Today, the triple bottom line is talked about, is valued in word and deed, and is beginning to show its benefits in business philosophy and orientation, consumer purchasing and use, and ultimately reductions in environmental impacts and improvement of working conditions around the world.

At the same time, debate about labor standards and working conditions, and broad environmental issues such as global warming, fossil fuel as a nonrenewable resource, organic production of food and fiber, and water quality has become mainstream. In 2007 former Vice President Al Gore won an Academy Award for *An Inconvenient Truth*, a documentary about global warming, and then shared the Nobel Peace Prize with a UN panel of scientists, establishing the debate among citizenry as well as legislative and international circles. Politicians, businesses, organizations, and individuals are publicly declaring their level of carbon use and offsetting this use by payments and contributions to renewable energy sources. Demands for environmental responsibility and stewardship, along with social responsibility, are consolidating in the apparel industry and other industries.

◉

Now Is the Right Time to Increase Social Responsibility

There is clearly an upswing in public opinion that apparel brands and retailers, along with those that manufacture textiles and apparel, must do something to protect people and the environment. Yet many people have rationalized the conditions found in apparel factories in developing countries, claiming that:

⊙ Jobs under these conditions are a necessary step in development. The United States went through the same steps and had equally bad conditions. If stricter labor standards are required, this will curtail trade from the country and slow down or derail its development and the subsequent improvements that would otherwise eventually come to workers.[43]

⊙ These jobs are better than nothing. In fact, more jobs like this should be developed so the country can advance even further.[44]

⊙ The pay is not really that low when taking into account national economic differences. In fact, most multinationals pay higher-than-average wages than workers could earn in other jobs.[45]

⊙ Efforts toward social responsibility are just attempts at protectionism. Proponents are attempting to take away some of the advantage developing countries have in order to reinvigorate the apparel industry in the United States.[46]

⊙ We cannot impose our Western values about work and childhood on other countries and their citizens.[47]

⊙ U.S. apparel brands and retailers do not own the factories, and any single factory has numerous customers. How can a particular brand or retailer be expected to solve these problems at geographically dispersed factories with culturally diverse people who are not even their direct employees?[48]

- It costs companies too much to implement labor reform. If apparel brands and retailers are forced to implement stricter labor standards, retail prices will have to be raised so that companies can still earn the profits required from their investors.[49]
- The collaboration among factories, governments, trade unions, and civil society organizations necessary to pay workers a living wage that covers their basic needs is too ambitious to effectively implement at this time.[50]

Excuses to ignore environmental impacts have been widespread in the media as well, and you probably have heard some like these:

- There really isn't a global warming crisis.
- It is impossible to calculate the cost to our environment of textile processing and production, consumer energy use for laundering and care, and textile disposal in landfills.
- The best way to lessen the environmental impact of apparel and textiles is conservation. Consumers should buy fewer, higher-quality garments.

But for every claim that increased social responsibility is not possible in the global apparel industry, there are counterclaims and examples of apparel brands and retailers, apparel and textile manufacturers, multi-stakeholder organizations, and civil society groups that have taken impressive steps to improve the situation for workers and the environment around the world. This book presents the best practices that companies have been developing over the last 10 to 15 years to ensure that the impact their business has on workers and the environment is positive. You will find a handful of companies, including the adidas Group, Liz Claiborne, Nike, Gap, Philips-Van Heusen, Timberland, Levi Strauss & Co., Patagonia, and others, used frequently as examples. For the most part, these apparel brands and retailers are well known, and there is a reason they have emerged as leaders in socially responsible apparel production and sourcing. As Sandra Waddock and Charles Bodwell explain, "Many brand name companies have suffered significant reputational damage from lack of attention to important issues related to corporate responsibility and have made changes."[51] For some businesses (e.g., Patagonia), socially responsible practices emerge from the company's basic business philosophy. As Waddock and Bodwell point out, however, "there are still many companies for whom responsibility management and external accountability (other than financial accountability) remain a distant and even unidentified target."[52] We hope by the time we write the second edition of this book, many more apparel companies will have taken responsibility within their global supply chains.

Simon Zadek, president and CEO of a U.K.-based organization called AccountAbility, agrees that now is the time for apparel brands and retailers to address issues of social responsibility. Zadek describes four stages that social issues relevant to the apparel industry go through as they mature, gaining increased credibility and exposure:

- Latent
- Emerging
- Consolidating
- Institutionalized

In the Latent Stage, evidence of a societal issue, such as the problems with labor standards and working conditions or environmental impacts from textile manufacturing, is brought to the awareness of the activist community and some nongovernmental organizations. Because factual evidence is weak or not clear-cut, the business community generally dismisses or ignores the issue. As further factual and detailed evidence about the issue is gathered, awareness of the societal issue among political groups and the media expands and deepens. However, because data are still somewhat inconclusive, only leading businesses begin to experiment with solutions in the Emerging Stage.

Issues may not develop much beyond the point of latent or emerging, but if they do, they will develop to a Consolidating Stage, perhaps as a result of litigation and increasing demands for government regulation and legislation. In this stage, a set of business practices emerges around the issue, voluntary standards and initiatives are established, and collective action occurs. In the final Institutionalized Stage, some business norms become part of legislation and what were once seen as "best practices" become a regular part of business excellence. [53]

Through content provided in the remainder of this book, we will demonstrate why we think the issues associated with labor standards, working conditions, and the environment in apparel production have begun to enter the Consolidating Stage and may quickly reach the Institutionalized Stage of issue maturity—see whether you agree. The time for social responsibility in apparel production and sourcing is now. As an issue consolidates and is institutionalized, it becomes increasingly risky for a company not to take responsibility. Consider the potential impacts of not managing responsibility. Consumers will choose not to purchase a company's product because of its reputation for using sweatshop labor or its lack of environmental sensitivity. Investors will choose not to invest in the company and talented prospective employees will choose to work for companies with a better reputation for responsibility management. [54]

◉

The Challenge That Lies Ahead

Increasing social responsibility in global apparel supply chains is not easy, nor is the right path always easy to discern. This book addresses the complexity that surrounds the decisions, evaluates the shortcomings of some current policies and practices aimed at improving workers' lives and reducing environmental impacts, and considers new strategies that are being pursued to ensure improvements are made in the future. Social responsibility is explored as it relates to workers in factories throughout the global supply chain and to the environment. Although many apparel companies are currently pursuing socially and environmentally responsible strategies, these companies and ones that have yet to begin still have much work ahead. There is expanded interest in both social and environmental responsibility during production and distribution of apparel by businesses, NGOs, and consumers that raises our expectations for increasing numbers of best practice examples in apparel production and sourcing in the future.

Socially responsible apparel production and sourcing requires proactive effort. We ask that you think imaginatively about possible strategies to improve working conditions and labor and environmental standards in the global apparel industry. As an emerging area of business action, innovative socially responsible practices and policies are being developed daily. There is a need for professionals from across the industry and from affected stakeholder groups to join the effort. You may currently work in the industry or plan to begin work for an apparel brand or retailer in the near future. Your involvement in this effort is needed for its success. Lend your knowledge, experiences, and creativity to help make the global apparel industry one we can all be proud of and in which those involved can thrive. Waddock and Bodwell explain it this way:

> Some managers today resist managing responsibility. . . . Managing responsibility includes everything from doing nothing (or worse, doing the wrong things) to the full integration of responsibility into a range of processes across the organization. At either extreme company management has made a decision, consciously or unconsciously, on how to deal with labor, the environment, integrity, and other issues that involve impacts on and relationships with key stakeholders.[55]

Expressed in layperson's language, those involved in the industry are either part of the problem or part of the solution. In this book we present an ideal scenario of social responsibility for today and the future. Not every apparel brand and retailer will be able to implement every single action we describe in this book, but every business can take steps to continuously improve social responsibility. Likewise, every individual can be involved. Consider what role you can play in finding and implementing strategies for increased social and environmental responsibility in apparel production and sourcing. It's not just clothes we're talking about—it's people's lives and natural resources.

~

Chapter 2

~

Social Responsibility, Human Rights, Sustainability, and the Responsibility of Companies

◉

Ross is a university freshman. While walking through the student center on campus, he happened to see a poster encouraging students to attend a meeting for those interested in learning more about sweatshops in the apparel industry. Ross is curious about the issues related to sweatshops. He has read about controversies surrounding apparel production, such as concerns that merchandise sold in university bookstores may be made with sweatshop labor. And yet Ross understands that the apparel industry has much to offer countries that are striving for economic development. This sounds like a complicated issue, and Ross looks forward to attending the informational session and learning more about possible alternatives to sweatshops.

Instead of answering his questions about sweatshops, however, the meeting only confused Ross further. First of all, speakers at the meeting who described the various reasons behind why sweatshops exist in the apparel industry seemed to view the issues as black and white, and their suggestions for eliminating sweatshops seemed simplistic. Ross believes that there must be gray areas concerning such a complex issue as sweatshops, especially in the global arena. However, the complexities were not addressed in the meeting. In addition, the speakers used many terms, such as social responsibility, that Ross has heard in connection with sweatshops, but the terms were not defined. Ross is uncertain as to how he can get involved to help eliminate sweatshops because not only are the issues complicated, even the lingo is confusing to him.

We use the term social responsibility in the book title and throughout its chapters, and yet we might have chosen to use the terms corporate social responsibility, environmental responsibility, sustainability, labor compliance, or human rights in our writings. In Chapter 2 we explore these terms, define social responsibility, and explain why we chose to use it as the umbrella term for this book. In doing so, we link social responsibility to concerns about human rights, fair labor practices, the environment, and concepts of sustainability. We also outline a set of guiding principles provided by the United Nations (UN) Global Compact that can be used by apparel brands and retailers as they attempt to increase their social responsibility. Finally, we introduce the theory of Total Responsibility Management. These concepts, principles, and theory provide frameworks for devising, studying, and assessing company efforts in social responsibility.

◉

Definitions of Social Responsibility

The term social responsibility has been widely used in business management, and business textbooks have incorporated numerous definitions of it. Social responsibility first appeared in the business literature in the 1950s. Howard Bowen was the first to use the term, which he defined very broadly as "the obligations of businessmen to pursue those policies, to make those decisions, or to follow those lines of action which are desirable in terms of the objectives and values of our society."[1] In the 1960s, potential beneficiaries of social responsibility were expanded beyond companies and their key decision makers to include society as a whole. In addition, the emerging leadership role taken by several large companies was recognized and that was the reason that some adopted the term corporate social responsibility.

The interests of a broader range of groups throughout supply chains were the focus of social responsibility in the business literature in the 1970s, also taking into account such stakeholders as consumers, communities, and the nation.[2] A variety of terms—business ethics, corporate citizenship, corporate accountability, and sustainability—were used interchangeably to describe social responsibility during the 1980s and 1990s, even though we now recognize that each involves a different aspect of the original term. Business for Social Responsibility (BSR), an organization whose goal is to assist businesses in achieving social responsibility, proposed that in order to achieve social responsibility, companies must integrate practices into every aspect of their operations, maintaining that businesses should be "achieving commercial success in ways that honor ethical values and respect people, communities, and the natural environment" and include "a comprehensive set of policies, practices and programs that are integrated into business operations, supply chains and decision-making processes throughout the company."[3]

We have chosen social responsibility as an umbrella term that includes other terms such as corporate responsibility, environmental stewardship, human rights, and community economic development. It does not limit its focus to corporations or labor issues or environmental stewardship. Rather, it embraces all of the social issues surrounding the relationships between workers and small and large businesses, the health and safety of workers, environmental sustainability, and communities and economic growth.

Definitions by Apparel Educators

The definitions of social responsibility we found in the business literature were very general and had little specific application to business activities within the apparel supply chain. Early references to the term in the field of textiles and apparel were also general, recommending that businesses adopt an orientation toward customer satisfaction by meeting societal expectations and balance global citizenship with fair profits.[4] Mary Littrell and Marsha Dickson provided the most specific definition, maintaining that "social responsibility places major emphasis on day-to-day actions within a business as related to product sourcing, employee treatment, and working conditions."[5] Yet the definition did not cover the diverse activities and challenges faced in global apparel supply chains. In fact, these early definitions did little to assist a business professional faced with improving the social responsibility of her or his company.

To develop a comprehensive definition that could guide the apparel industry, Marsha Dickson and Molly Eckman asked apparel educators to define "socially responsible apparel/textile business"[6] and we use this research as a starting point for defining social responsibility. According to the views of the 74 professors and graduate students responding to this question, socially responsible businesses consider the entire system of stakeholders associated with apparel supply chains, including production workers, sales help, and consumers, and the entire product life cycle from the inception of raw materials and components to product design, use, and discard. Educators' definitions of the term were organized into three dimensions of the concept to form the Model of Socially Responsible Apparel and Textile Business (Figure 2.1).

The first dimension is the orientation or focus of the business on people and the environment. Socially responsible businesses are primarily concerned with the welfare of people both as individuals and in larger societies in a variety of settings: at work, in the home, and in larger communities. Socially responsible apparel businesses are also concerned with the physical environment. For example, one educator explained that "a socially responsible textile and apparel business makes decisions that value and protect the well-being of people and the environments (natural and built) in which they live" and another offered, "Socially responsible businesses conduct their business in a manner that is compatible with maintaining the environment and treating all

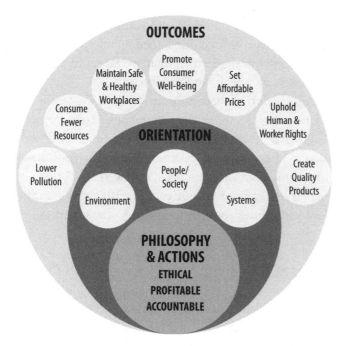

OUTCOMES

Maintain Safe & Healthy Workplaces

Promote Consumer Well-Being

Set Affordable Prices

Consume Fewer Resources

Uphold Human & Worker Rights

ORIENTATION

Lower Pollution

People/ Society

Create Quality Products

Environment

Systems

PHILOSOPHY & ACTIONS

ETHICAL PROFITABLE ACCOUNTABLE

Figure 2.1

Dickson and Eckman's Model of Socially Responsible Apparel and Textile Business.

persons concerned with the business in a fair and equitable manner." Ultimately, being a socially responsible business requires a systemwide focus on the interactions of people, processes, and the environment involved in the production, marketing, consumption, regulating, and disposing of apparel products. The specific issues form the orientation portion of the model and include resource consumption, pollution, consumer well-being, human/worker rights, safe and healthy workplaces, and product affordability and quality.

The second dimension of social responsibility in the textile and apparel industry is the philosophy and actions of a business "that balances ethics and morality with profitability, which is achieved through accountability-based business decisions and strategies."[7] This dimension includes what the socially responsible apparel/textile business aims to achieve, the actions taken to achieve those goals, and the degree to which social responsibility is integrated into daily decision making and company policies. In Figure 2.1, socially responsible apparel businesses are depicted as ethical, profitable, and accountable for their actions. As one educator articulated, the philosophy and actions of a socially responsible business involve "decisions, media and advertising, strategies, and production that strengthen human welfare and the physical and social environment in which we live globally."

The third dimension of social responsibility in the textile and apparel industry relates to outcomes of the actions businesses take. The desired outcome expressed by educators was for people and the environment to be positively affected or at least not harmed by business decisions and activities. One educator described it like this: "A socially responsible business is one that when confronted with a problem (whatever it may be) does something about it to improve the situation."

Perspectives of Industry and Nongovernmental Organizations

A definition of social responsibility needs to be specific enough to be useful and also to reflect how the term is used in the "real world." When apparel businesses and their stakeholders (e.g., workers, civil society organizations, labor unions, consumers) do not share the same expectations, finding solutions that all parties agree are socially responsible may be difficult. Thus, we expanded the Model of Socially Responsible Apparel and Textile Business to incorporate the views of those directly or indirectly involved with social responsibility in the apparel industry by interviewing professionals employed by major apparel brands and retailers about their responsibilities, interest, and expertise in social responsibility and environmental stewardship. Heads of nongovernmental organizations (NGOs) and labor organizations that promote worker rights in global supply chains were asked for the same information.

Emerging themes from these interviews aligned with Dickson and Eckman's model in that social responsibility was oriented toward both people and the environment and the systems that link them. Industry professionals confirmed the importance of a worker-centric view of social responsibility. One industry professional described the necessary focus on workers as follows:

Sometimes it is very difficult to define [social responsibility] for a company itself. Maybe it's better to go out and ask the stakeholders what their expectations are. . . . We started specific worker dialogues because here you realize this is a group of people who are less outspoken; have not the strongest voice compared to certain campaign organizations. So therefore, I think it is important to get information from the worker directly.

A worker-centric orientation requires companies to act in culturally appropriate and internationally informed ways. As one industry professional explained, this means to "understand, not just the local customs and the local laws, but to a certain degree the expectations of the people who work in those overseas factories." These new additions to Orientation and Philosophy and Actions sections of the model are displayed in our Expanded Model of Socially Responsible Apparel and Textile Business in Figure 2.2. We continue to use "social responsibility"

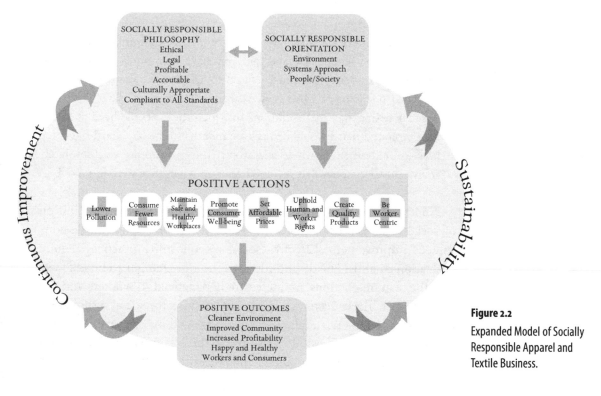

Figure 2.2

Expanded Model of Socially Responsible Apparel and Textile Business.

rather than "corporate social responsibility" because there are so many good examples of small, noncorporate company actions and because "social responsibility" encompasses all of the subterms used for these actions.

Industry professionals also expanded the list of business actions in their definitions of social responsibility. For example, one NGO professional explained that social responsibility required a company to comply with international labor standards and best practices delineated by the International Labour Organization (ILO). Another industry professional explained that "social responsibility for us is pretty simple. It's doing the right thing at the right time. Letting your conscience be your guide and adhering to all laws without exception."

Industry professionals also pointed to how accountability in business can lead to positive outcomes for people associated with the supply chain. One industry professional described the following:

> I made my first trip to a country . . . where there were a lot of people who lived in dormitories, which I found to be absolutely reprehensible. . . . I went to the powers that be and said "you have six months to correct this or we're out of here." . . . And I refused to listen to the excuses that these particular dormitories, while they were less than I would have liked, they were far better than the conditions in which these people lived at home. . . . I promised that I would be back six months to the day, and I did come back . . . and we saw a whole new world. The dormitories were absolutely equivalent to the ones that my children used when they were in school.

Another new theme embodied the constantly evolving definition of social responsibility toward increasing levels of responsibility: continuous improvement. Effective social responsibility practices require evaluation of efforts made and identification of changes to be made so that the resulting actions are increasingly beneficial to workers and the environment. These ever-increasing expectations for social responsibility pressure companies toward leading-edge actions. The rising expectations for social responsibility also mean those companies that are not making progress may soon find themselves the target of activism. One labor organization professional explained the possible actions activists will take as expectations for social responsibility increase.

> This is a very important moment and it's still not clear where companies are going to stand on [social responsibility]. We're going to be looking at, over the next three years, really seeing whether some of these companies who are purporting to be committed and leading edge in corporate responsibility—whether they are really willing to step up to the plate and ensure that these practices are policies throughout their whole company and supply chains. We're going to be looking for that at the same time as trying to continue to put more pressure on the bottom feeders.

Social Responsibility and the Environment

Apparel educators and industry and nongovernmental organization professionals incorporated concerns about the environment when defining the concept of social responsibility. The recent upsurge in discussion of environmental issues occurring in the apparel industry may reflect general interests related to Vice President Al Gore's efforts to educate citizens about global warming and to "organic" products of food and fiber. Likewise, the European Union's (EU's) new requirements for registering and regulating chemicals, the program for Registration, Evaluation, Authorization, and Restriction of Chemicals (REACH), which went into effect June 1, 2007, may be contributing to increased emphasis on the environment. REACH requires documentation of health risks for more than 30,000 chemical substances and a search for safer alternatives. The American Apparel and Footwear Association anticipates that the import of many apparel and footwear products into the EU will be affected by this legislation.[8]

In general, developing countries' environmental regulations fall short of those in the United States, and the ability to enforce the regulations is challenging. We have been informed of growing concern about the environment in China, where large volumes of textiles, apparel, and footwear are produced. Recently the government of China slapped the Dongguan Fu'an textile mill that prints and dyes fabrics with a very large fine and extra sewage processing fees equivalent to nearly US$1.5 million for not following environmental protection requirements.[9] Printing and dyeing fabrics places China's textile industry as the country's sixth-largest producer of wastewater, and only 7 percent of that water is recycled.[10] The remaining 93 percent flows into the country's water systems. Industry professionals will increasingly be required to address situations in production of apparel that adversely affect the workforce and the environment (Figure 2.3).

Figure 2.3

Some dyes used in textile production are off-limits under new environmental regulations.

Social Responsibility and Sustainability

The term sustainability has frequently been used as a synonym of social responsibility. Although there are many definitions of sustainability, we view the two terms social responsibility and sustainability as distinct but related concepts when associated with global apparel production and sourcing. Social responsibility is an umbrella term that covers responsible practices related to labor standards, human rights, and the environment. Sustainability, on the other hand, signifies improving, building upon, and overall achieving responsible practices that are maintained over the long term. Sustainability is the ultimate goal of successful socially responsible practices. It improves the lives of workers and those in their communities and countries and the health of the environment in which they live for the future. To achieve sustainability, companies must first make a commitment to initiate social responsibility activities and then examine these activities to determine their impacts, refining and improving the activities to achieve the desired impacts. Only after taking those steps are companies able to achieve sustainability.

As an example in the area of labor standards and working conditions, apparel brands and retailers have adopted codes of conduct detailing their expectations for suppliers regarding topics like child labor, wages and overtime, and factory conditions, and many are monitoring factories against these codes. They are also evaluating whether codes of conduct and monitoring have had impacts on improving working conditions. Unsatisfied with the results of these activities, some apparel brands and retailers are exploring ways to work with factory management to ensure that their human resources practices and policies maintain fair and safe working conditions. Other companies are considering carefully the economic impact of shifting production among suppliers and supplier countries. In another example, footwear producers such as Nike are experimenting with less toxic glues to assemble footwear.

The goal of environmental sustainability also focuses on the long-term effects of our actions and maintaining the environment for future generations by taking responsibility for it. In the apparel industry, many companies have concentrated their efforts on the choice of environmentally friendly materials and production processes that have low toxic chemical use and waste. Recently the importance of total energy use, including transportation costs for production and distribution as well as end-of-life options such as recycling, redesign, and biodegradable disposal, has been articulated and integrated into business strategies.

Social Responsibility and Human Rights

Another term that arises when we discuss social responsibility is human rights. In fact, when Reebok developed its program to address the conditions of work in the production of apparel and footwear with that brand name, the company labeled the program "Human Rights." The more commonly used label is compliance or labor compliance. Doug Cahn, Reebok's Vice President for Human Rights from 1991 through 2006, explains that choice in Box 2.1. So what are human rights and how do they relate to social responsibility?

Box 2.1. Human Rights at Reebok: A Reflection

Reebok began its association with human rights in 1988 when Amnesty International invited the company to be the sponsor of its Human Rights Now! World Tour. The tour, which featured Peter Gabriel, Bruce Springsteen, Sting, and other top musical artists, brought messages of freedom and justice to millions of people in 23 cities on four continents. That message inspired Reebok executives to make human rights a core value for the company and to establish the Reebok Human Rights Award program to honor young human rights defenders. During its 17 years, the award program recognized 84 recipients from more than 38 countries.

Long before it was common industry practice to examine workplace conditions in factories, the company's association with human rights created a platform for it to take a hard look at its own human rights impacts. In 1991 and 1992, for instance, Reebok was already drafting and beginning to implement a code of conduct to guide its business relationships with the footwear factories in Asia that made its products. As the anti-sweatshop movement took hold in 1993 and beyond, Reebok was regularly praised for having thought through how internationally recognized human rights standards could inform this aspect of corporate behavior.

Being "connected" to the human rights community meant that company officials were routinely exposed to perspectives of human rights advocates. There was no need for formal stakeholder dialogues in a company where the business calendar included regular contact with key human rights leaders. Being "connected" meant that Reebok benefited in three tangible ways. First, the company was able to anticipate many human rights concerns and respond to them before harm was done, including the harm of potentially embarrassing public disclosures. Second, the company was able to

---

engage in enhanced learning through open communication. Learning resulted in the development of leadership programs that further reinforced the credibility and trust of key human rights leaders. Third, Reebok was able to partner with nongovernmental organizations without the same stigma that other companies had in the late 1990s and early 2000s to engage in collaborative projects of mutual benefit.

Reebok's human rights engagement was not limited to managing conditions of labor in the factories that made the company's products. There were other quiet and not-so-quiet activities as well. In the decade beginning in 1990, the company appealed to the Indonesian head of state to release prisoners of conscience, attempted to engage the Chinese premier to enforce labor standards and respect human rights, pushed the industry to eliminate child labor in soccer ball production in Pakistan, and communicated about human rights to investors, business partners, and consumers, to name a few. Employees took enormous pride in their company's willingness to educate large audiences about human rights, tackle global problems by examining its own impacts on them, and confront the potentially conflicting needs of workers, factories, and brands. Importantly, a human rights mandate kept the company focused where it should be—on the people, primarily the factory workers, who made the company's products. This singular focus on the rights of workers drove innovation in worker communication and worker representation schemes that continue to challenge conventional thinking about compliance, corporate responsibility, and supply chain management.

There were risks of such a policy, as well, to be sure. The Indonesian government threatened raids on factories making the company's products upon learning that an East Timorese student activist had won the Reebok Human Rights Award. Another award recipient decided not to accept the honor after a few activists convinced her at the last minute that she could accomplish more by criticizing corporate outsourcing policies than highlighting her own cause. Both incidents passed with little or no long-term negative consequences. In fact, if there was any long-term repercussion, it was that these incidents strengthened corporate resolve and sharpened the company's determination to find yet better ways to communicate the dramatic stories of young human rights defenders around the globe to ever-larger public audiences.

Reebok's entry into the world of human rights may have been unusual or even unique, but the lessons for companies that reflect on their global impacts are not.

SOURCE: Copyright Doug Cahn. Doug Cahn is principal of TheCahnGroup LLC, a consultancy dedicated to sound business practices that are consistent with society needs and stakeholder expectations. He led the human rights program at Reebok International Ltd. for 15 years.

In 1948 the Universal Declaration of Human Rights (UDHR) was approved by the United Nations as an international minimum standard for protection of individual basic rights and freedoms. The declaration stated that:

> Human rights are fundamental principles and standards that enable individuals everywhere to have freedom to live in dignity. All human rights are universal, interrelated, interdependent and indivisible.[11]

Since the approval of the UDHR, these rights have become accepted as the foundation for international law as practiced by governments. But beyond governments, businesses, organizations, and even individuals have the responsibility to recognize and uphold human rights in their everyday work and community lives. The UDHR describes human rights in 30 separate articles that can be organized into four main areas:[12]

- Equality—Prohibition of discrimination on the basis of race, color, sex, language, religion, political beliefs or affiliations, national or social origin, property, or birth
- Life and security—Rights to life, liberty, and security, and the right to be free from slavery or torture; a just legal system; and equal protection under the law
- Personal freedom—Rights protecting personal privacy for family, home, thought, religion, opinion, and property ownership
- Economic, social, and cultural freedoms—Right to Social Security, to work, equal pay, to form and join unions, to rest and leisure, and to adequate health care and well-being

The UDHR was designed to address individual rights in general, in the variety of contexts in a civil society—at home, at work, and elsewhere. The scenarios found in Boxes 2.2 and 2.3 help make the connection with human rights and business practices for social responsibility.

Box 2.2. Human Rights Scenario 1

The following scenario for understanding human rights was developed by the United Nations Systems Staff College. As you read the scenario, the UN asks you to consider the following points:

⊙ What are the human rights issues raised by this story?
⊙ How is the practice likely to affect women working in the factory?
⊙ How will the local community react to this practice?
⊙ How should the human resource manager respond in this case?

A successful apparel company based in Mumbai has recently appointed a new manager of human resources to ensure that there are good labour practices in its own workplace and in its supplier factories. The code includes a non-discrimination clause that specifically refers to gender, maternity and marital status. The company sources and supplies finished clothing lines to major brands in Europe, North America and Japan. As part of her orientation, the new manager is quickly dispatched to one of the company's largest supplier factories to review code compliance and other human resource issues related to the production of a new line of apparel. While there she asks some women workers various questions about the recruitment process. At this point she learns that when female employees are hired, they are subject to mandatory pregnancy tests, the results of which are recorded.

When she discusses this matter in confidence with the factory owner, she also learns that pregnancy tests are carried out on a quarterly basis once the women are in employment. Anyone who tests positive is immediately given notice. The factory owner explains that all other garment factories in the state have similar policies.

SOURCE: UN System Staff College. "Human Rights and Business Learning Tool." Available at www.unssc. org/web1/programmes/gc/Default.asp.

Box 2.3. Human Rights Scenario 2

The following scenario for understanding human rights is adapted from one developed by the United Nations Systems Staff College. As you read the scenario, the UN asks you to consider the following points:

- What are the human rights issues raised by this story?
- How would you respond initially to the NGO?
- What kind of help or advice could you offer the supplier?
- What other immediate actions would you take?

You are an apparel buyer for a retail company and you are responsible for developing and managing relationships with a wide range of suppliers. As part of your supplier approval process, all producers must certify that a number of key labor conditions are met including that no child labor is used in the production of their goods.

You are approached by a local child rights NGO with news that one of your principal apparel suppliers has been found to have children working in a subcontractor factory it sources textiles from. The NGO is prepared to take this piece to the press stating that your company is benefiting from child labor.

When you raise this matter with the supplier, they explain that the supply chain for textiles is highly complex and that the fibers used in these products are usually sourced from several different countries, including countries where it is considered to be perfectly acceptable for children to assist their parents on the farm.

SOURCE: UN System Staff College. "Human Rights and Business Learning Tool." Available at www.unssc.org/web/hrb/Default2.asp.

Note that in all of these resources, human rights issues are considered within a business context. Human rights are a key part of the social and environmental responsibilities of business. These issues cannot be separated; a business cannot act responsibly in personal interactions with employees without acting responsibly with its organization, employee expectations and benefits, and approaches to operations.

◉

Guiding Principles

Much of the work apparel brands and retailers did to address labor problems that were found in apparel factories was pioneering because there were no guidelines or how-to instructions that company executives could consult for models. For example, in the 1990s, various activist groups and the international media exposed serious labor problems in Nike's global supply chains. Imagine how Dusty Kidd, the Vice President for Compliance at Nike from 1996 to 2006, felt when CEO Phil Knight asked him to head up a new branch of the company addressing these problems. Kidd recalls the following.

I felt fine with the challenge and was really excited about the chance to do three things that I would in all likelihood never be able to do again:

1. Be given the potential to have a direct impact on the lives of people who otherwise might not have anyone truly looking out for them. This has always been my biggest motivation and it has driven our staff from day one.

2. Start a new discipline for a global company. Knight and then-President Dr. Tom Clarke gave me carte blanche to hire anyone in the company who wanted to work for me, no matter what their current position. I got all the resources necessary to do the job right. And I was before the board of directors on a regular basis briefing them on challenges and successes, and getting their unqualified support.

3. Be given the potential to contribute to the questions and answers around the issues of corporations and their responsibility in the larger world. There will probably never be one answer to the basic question of what we are responsible for, and how we should be held accountable, but through Nike's participation in various fora—friendly and otherwise—we have been able to contribute to that conversation and take a lot away from it.[13]

Although Kidd had considerable support from Nike, beyond the members of his new team there were few resources to which he could turn for ideas of how to proceed. Had it been a few years later, he might have used the UN Global Compact for initial guidance.

The UN Global Compact was approved in 1998 as a voluntary initiative to address human, social, and environmental rights in the business environment. The initiative brings together companies, labor and civil society groups, and various UN agencies to support ten principles categorized under human rights, labor, the environment, and anticorruption. The ten principles that companies are asked to imbed in their global business activities are outlined in Table 2.1. The principles stem from four key universal agreements:

- The Universal Declaration of Human Rights (UDHR)
- The International Labour Organization's Declaration on Fundamental Principles and Rights at Work
- The Rio Declaration on Environment and Development
- The United Nations Convention Against Corruption

The language of the principles moves beyond the more general standards of the four universal agreements to clearly lay the responsibility for upholding these principles in business. In this way, human rights and social responsibility meet—both are the responsibility of business in the business sphere and the responsibility of government in national and international spheres and of individuals in their everyday lives. The UN Global Compact's voluntary membership approach encourages businesses from around the world to join and provides a variety of resources on its Web site for development, initiation, and benchmarks for businesses' human rights programs. However, the voluntary nature of the UN Global Compact also reflects its limitations. As explained on the UN Global Compact Web site:

> The Global Compact is not a regulatory instrument—it does not "police," enforce or measure the behavior or actions of companies.[14]

Table 2.1. Ten Principles of the UN Global Compact

Human Rights	
Principle 1	Businesses should support and respect the protection of internally proclaimed human rights.
Principle 2	Businesses should make sure they are not complicit in human rights abuses.
Labor Standards	
Principle 3	Businesses should uphold the freedom of association and the effective recognition of the right to collective bargaining.
Principle 4	Businesses should uphold the elimination of all forms of forced and compulsory labour.
Principle 5	Businesses should uphold the effective abolition of child labour.
Principle 6	Businesses should uphold the elimination of discrimination in respect of employment and occupation.
Environment	
Principle 7	Businesses should support a precautionary approach to environmental challenges.
Principle 8	Businesses should undertake initiatives to promote greater environmental responsibility.
Principle 9	Businesses should encourage the development and diffusion of environmentally friendly technologies.
Anticorruption	
Principle 10	Businesses should work against all forms of corruption, including extortion and bribery.

SOURCE: www.unglobalcompact.org.

Some advocacy organizations expand on this limitation, criticizing the UN Global Compact because it does not include standards related to hours of work and wages, does no monitoring, and is not transparent about company progress.

Although the Global Compact is not perfect and the ten principles would not have informed Kidd of exactly what Nike should do, they would have provided him with some guidance about what the company should strive to achieve as a result of the new division's efforts. Additional assistance would have been provided by the theory of Total Responsibility Management, though like the UN Global Compact, it was not developed until after several companies took the reins in developing social responsibility programs.

Underlying Theoretical Framework: Total Responsibility Management

The theoretical framework of Total Responsibility Management is helpful for understanding the various ways that an apparel brand or retailer can pursue its obligations to society and the environment and fulfill the obligations outlined in the UN Global Compact. Sandra Waddock and Charles Bodwell developed the framework based on case study research with a number of different multinational firms. Total Responsibility Management is an emerging system of practices and principles and provides guidance for a company wanting to develop processes and goals for social responsibility.[15] Some apparel brands and retailers are currently carrying out a few or many of the activities described by the framework.

The three interdependent main components in this framework are as follows (see Figure 2.4):

- Inspiration—Vision setting and leadership commitment
- Integration—Changes in strategies and management practice
- Innovation—Assessment, improvement, and learning systems

These three components represent the complexity and depth of commitment required by a company interested in implementing social responsibility practices and policies. Let's look at each component in more depth.

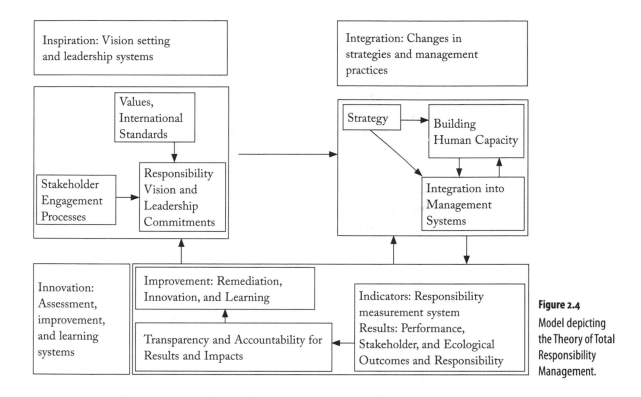

Figure 2.4
Model depicting
the Theory of Total
Responsibility
Management.

Inspiration: Vision Setting and Leadership Commitment

For a company to enhance its social responsibility, it must have a vision for what it endeavors to achieve and gain commitment from the company's leaders. Within this component of Total Responsibility Management, companies make conscious decisions about what they value. It is essential that the company's top management believe in the vision of social responsibility that is being pursued.[16] For large companies with hierarchical management and various levels of top management, commitment of management at each level is necessary. If a president or CEO is committed to pursuing greater social responsibility, the vice president for sourcing and other areas will follow the lead of the senior executive. The research of Waddock and Bodwell shows that without demonstrated commitment, it is unlikely a company will put its vision into operation. Top-level commitment will allow the needed resources to be directed to developing, implementing, and administering an effective program. Essentially, the vision for social responsibility must become part of the organizational culture of the firm.

A survey of 164 buying and sourcing professionals from the largest apparel and footwear companies in the United States supports the influential role of top management commitment to corporate social responsibility. When top management was perceived as being more supportive of socially responsible buying, buying and sourcing professionals indicated that they gave greater consideration to human rights issues when making buying decisions.[17]

Stakeholder Engagement

Engaging with employees, customers, and other groups of individuals who influence or are influenced by the business aids a company in establishing a vision for social responsibility. This process is called stakeholder engagement, and it is fundamental for improving social responsibility. For example, Liz Claiborne holds organized meetings with stakeholders in Hong Kong and southern China that involve the company's human rights representatives working with social welfare groups by discussing the difficulties workers face.[18] Similarly, representatives from the adidas Group and Nike meet with students and faculty on university campuses across the United States to understand their concerns with the production of products bearing their university logos. Other examples of stakeholder engagement are less formal, such as when a compliance executive picks up the phone and calls a customer or activist who has voiced dissatisfaction with the company's practices to talk about solutions.

Stakeholder engagement is a logical way for a company to understand the needs of the groups that are affected by its business or are in the position to influence it. Stakeholder groups can provide valuable information to management to help them improve the company's level of social responsibility. However, carrying out this sort of communication can be difficult. Imagine the stress Gildan Activewear experienced when the Fair Labor Association (FLA), a multi-stakeholder organization that focuses on improving working conditions in factories around the world, demanded that as a condition of the company's continued membership in the organization, its executives sit down and talk with the Maquila Solidarity Network (MSN). The MSN is a Canadian-based worker rights group that had filed a formal complaint with the FLA and led a very public campaign against Gildan for violating worker rights for freedom of association at one of the company's factories in Honduras.[19]

Stakeholder engagement is also difficult when some stakeholder groups have demands that may seem unreasonable when balanced against the needs of other stakeholders. For example, at a 2006 NGO forum hosted by the FLA, a business strategist for Puma outlined the company's sourcing policy in relation to its overall business strategy. A later panelist, an individual representing a European activist organization, commented to the audience that one of the factors interfering with Puma becoming more socially responsible was the company's goal for business growth. Yet to not include growth in profits or sales would almost certainly lead to considerable dissatisfaction among members of another important stakeholder group for Puma—investors. This is not to say that investors' needs should be prioritized over those of workers. Instead, this example illustrates the complex balancing act that must be carried out by companies as their executives consider the wide-ranging needs of their stakeholders.

Stakeholder engagement is a critical process for companies as they establish and continuously realign a vision for social responsibility that aligns with societal expectations. Engaging with stakeholders reflects the "social" part of social responsibility. As explained by Waddock and Bodwell, "by engaging in a dialogue process to improve stakeholder relationships, a company will be better prepared for problems when they arise—and more likely to be able to avert many altogether."[20] However, stakeholder engagement requires staff that is knowledgeable and able to discern what is required of the company if it is to use the gathered information to become more socially responsible.

Foundational Values

The minimum expectations a company sets for being socially responsible are referred to by Waddock and Bodwell as foundational values. Because workers making the product are so important to the success of the apparel brand or retailer, their human and worker rights are fundamental to a company's foundational values. However, using laws to determine ethical behavior is inadequate because the laws may represent only minimal moral standards.[21] Social responsibility to workers in global apparel supply chains is based upon four core labor conventions described in the International Labour Organization's Declaration on Fundamental Principles and Rights at Work.[22] These four worker rights principles are also found in the UN Global Compact along with others related to human rights that are based on the Universal Declaration of Human Rights and the environment, which stem from the Rio Declaration on Environmental and Development.[23]

The ILO's four core labor conventions are widely viewed as minimum requirements for social responsibility.[24] There are also conventions related to hours of work, wages, health and safety, and the employment relationship. These labor conventions form the basis of many company's codes of conduct. Codes of conduct are frequently used to express a company's values.[25] For example, the code of conduct adopted by Phillips-Van Heusen Corporation contains elements related to the ILO's four labor conventions. The code had initially been developed in 1991 and was strengthened to align with ILO conventions when Phillips-Van Heusen endorsed the FLA's code of conduct. You can compare the text related to the forced labor principle that is used by the ILO and by Phillips-Van Heusen in Table 2.2. Determination of whether a company's code of conduct is aligned with the ILO's principles may require a lawyer's close review. However, the Phillips-Van Heusen text lays out clearly for customers and other interested stakeholders the company's values on the core labor convention regarding forced labor.

Table 2.2. Comparison of ILO Convention on Forced Labor
and Phillips-Van Heusen Standard

International Labour Organization Forced Labour Convention, 1930 (No. 29)	Phillips-Van Heusen Code on Forced Labor
This fundamental convention prohibits all forms of forced or compulsory labour, which is defined as "all work or service which is exacted from any person under the menace of any penalty and for which the said person has not offered himself voluntarily."	We will not be associated with any vendor who uses [any] form of mental or physical coercion. We will not do business with any vendor who utilizes forced labor whether in the form of prison labor, indentured labor, bonded labor or otherwise.

SOURCE: Excerpts quoted from the ILO Subjects Covered by International Labour Standards retrieved on December 14, 2006 from www.ilo.org/public/english/standards/norm/subject/index.htm and Phillips-Van Heusen Corporate Responsibility, World Action at www.pvh.com/CorpResp_WorldAction.html.

Establishing foundational values such as the one regarding forced labor provides a basis for enforcement. In 2005, the FLA conducted an unannounced audit of a factory used by Phillips-Van Heusen in Vietnam. The audit revealed that the factory was not maintaining adequate hiring and employment records to prove it was not using forced labor. Phillips-Van Heusen provided a plan for correcting the problem to factory management, who responded by implementing a new system to ensure the needed documents were in place.[26]

In addition to setting the minimum expectations for social responsibility, some apparel brands and retailers have established foundational values that may be difficult for them to reach, thus stretching their capabilities.[27] For example, the adidas Group standard regarding freedom of association and collective bargaining asks vendors in China and some other countries with nondemocratic unions to make extra effort to ensure workers are appropriately recognized. Their code states that:

Business partners shall recognise and respect the right of workers to join and organise associations of their own choosing, and to bargain collectively. *Where law specifically restricts the right to freedom of association and collective bargaining, the employer must not obstruct alternative and legal means for independent and free association and bargaining. In any case the employer shall implement systems to ensure good communication with employees* [emphasis added].[28]

Again establishment of fundamental values aids companies in fixing problems. That the adidas Group was making progress on freedom of association is evident from a 2006 FLA audit of a factory in China that was found not to have a written policy on freedom of association. The adidas Group required the factory to establish such a policy and develop a system to improve worker-management communication. By 2007, a policy had been established and factory management had implemented an open-door policy and mounted suggestion boxes around the factory to ensure workers expressed their concerns to management.[29]

The principles from the UN Global Compact also provide guidance for a company wishing to develop foundational values regarding the environment based on the Rio Declaration on Environment and Development. As seen in Table 2.3, Principle 7 of the UN Global Compact calls on businesses to prevent environmental damage from occurring and is illustrated by the adidas Group's effort to reduce the environmental impact of their business operations.[30] Expanding on the company's values regarding the environment, the adidas Group sustainability report states that:

Looking after the environment is essential if we are to preserve living conditions today and for future generations. Managing environmental issues has also become a critical success factor for business. Environmental awareness drives innovations and resource savings, leading to efficient production and reduced costs.[31]

Table 2.3. Comparison of Global Compact Principle on the Environment and the adidas Group Mission Statement

UN Global Compact Principle 7	adidas Group Mission and Values
Businesses should support a precautionary approach to environmental challenges. . . . The key element of a precautionary approach, from a business perspective, is the idea of prevention rather than cure. In other words, it is more cost-effective early action to ensure that irreversible environmental damage does not occur.	Our vision is for everyone in the Group and the supply chain to share a common set of values and to follow responsible business practices. As well as improving working conditions in suppliers' factories, being responsible also means . . . reducing the environmental impacts of our operations.

SOURCE: Quoted from About the Global Compact, Principle 7 www.unglobalcompact.org/AboutTheGC/The TenPrinciples/principle7.html including statement from the Rio Declaration and adidas Group Mission and Values www.adidas-group.com/en/sustainability/mission_and_values/default.asp.

Integration: Changes in Strategies and Management Practices

Companies pursuing Total Responsibility Management integrate the vision, values, and commitment of leaders into day-to-day business operations. As part of the company's strategy, the vision and values for social responsibility play a part in dictating the company's future goals and how it will achieve these goals. Ultimately, the vision and values for social responsibility play an important role in determining how the company conducts business.[32] For companies pursuing Total Responsibility Management, the business strategy will reflect that aim. For example, NK Apparel in Bangkok, Thailand, a large apparel manufacturer producing goods for adidas and Under Armour, considers social responsibility, high quality, reliable delivery, and profit as cornerstones of the company's strategy for becoming a world-class manufacturer.

53

Building Human Resource Capacity

Even though goals for social responsibility often focus on workers or environmental situations, building an organizational culture for Total Responsibility Management starts with employees at headquarters. Waddock and Bodwell maintain that education and an appropriate reward system are fundamental for operationalizing a company's vision for social responsibility. In addition, the company needs buy-in from employees throughout the supply chain.[33] The leadership of the company needs to communicate the company's values to its employees and assign resources to support the educational effort.[34]

A company might educate its workers about the importance of a social responsibility vision with specialized training materials, training courses, and regular internal communications.[35] At Liz Claiborne, all new employees receive a short training course on the company's values for social responsibility. Other companies' efforts to educate employees may be less comprehensive and less formal. A former employee of one major retailer described that when she started work at the company, she was required to sign a document that she had received a copy of the company's code of conduct. The code was never again mentioned to the employee.

To encourage employee actions and decisions that support social responsibility, changes in the reward structure guiding employee raises and promotions is essential.[36] Apparel buyers have always been evaluated on the profits their decisions bring the company. A company pursuing greater social responsibility may begin to weigh how that profit was achieved by the extent to which it supported or was in conflict with the company's vision and values, including those concerning social responsibility that may increase expenses. Low prices may be less important than working conditions and environmental impacts.

Finally, a company's efforts in social responsibility must also include the needs of its corporate employees, not just workers for overseas contractors making the company's products. As Dan Henkle, Senior Vice President for Social Responsibility for Gap, explains, "If you want to be a socially responsible company, you have to take care of your 150,000 employees first and foremost."[37] To several apparel brands and retailers, the difficulty headquarters' employees face in balancing work and life is a social responsibility concern.

Integration into Management Systems

In the mid- to late 1990s, as apparel brands and retailers leading the industry's efforts in social responsibility grappled with how they were going to ensure their codes of conduct were being followed, major brands such as Nike and Reebok developed compliance or human rights divisions that would monitor factories and develop strategies for improving conditions. In some cases, executive positions such as Vice President for Compliance or Vice President for Human Rights were created to ensure that the companies' vision and values for social responsibility were appropriately carried out. With divisions of up to 90 people assigned to implement company codes of conduct and develop plans to correct problems found, leaders in social responsibility efforts have made notable progress in finding out what problems are occurring in their factories and developing strategies to address those. As an example, Gap Inc. monitored 98.7 percent of its factories in 4,438 separate inspections conducted during 2005. Although the retailer used over 2,100 factories to produce its garments that year, by having corporate representatives in the factories, it was able to identify where breaches of the company's Code of Vendor Conduct had occurred.[38]

Although the creation of compliance divisions with the sole purpose of supporting the company's vision and values for social responsibility illustrates how companies can integrate social responsibility into management systems, social responsibility can be further integrated across other functional units. For example, sometimes inspections made by employees of a compliance division are supplemented by inspections made by product development or quality control employees who visit factories regularly throughout the year. Nike employees in these product-focused positions conduct what the company refers to as SHAPE audits that provide an understanding of a factory's safety, health, attitude of management, people, and environment situation.[39]

By seriously considering company codes of conduct and integrating social responsibility activities into management systems, apparel brands and retailers have collected large amounts of data that generally identify the most pervasive labor problems occurring in the factories producing their products. They also have a wealth of knowledge on which corrective actions were successful and which were not. A next step being examined by many leading companies is how to further integrate social responsibility into their buying and sourcing offices so that suppliers making notable efforts to improve working and environmental conditions are rewarded and company practices such as negotiations of price do not undermine the efforts of compliance divisions.[40]

Figure 2.5
Well-positioned foliage can have a cooling effect.

Practices regarding the environment must also be integrated into company management systems (Figure 2.5). For example, the adidas Group is working to reduce the company's environmental impact at the product design stage. As explained in the company's sustainability report, the adidas Group's:

. . . approach is to seek to design out polluting materials and processes and increasingly to adopt sustainable materials instead. [The company has] a number of initiatives in place:
• Material selection policy
• Sustainable cotton research
• Recycled rubber
• Eliminating PVC and
• Control and monitoring of restricted substances.[41]

Innovation: Assessment, Improvement, and Learning Systems

A third component of Total Responsibility Management involves a process of continual learning as companies measure progress toward social responsibility, evaluate the results of their work, and develop new ways of tackling problems for further improvement.[42]

Indicators: The Responsibility Measurement System

How does a company know it is making progress toward its vision and values for social responsibility? Some sort of measurement must be taken. Traditional financial measures such as gross margin and return on investment have provided valuable input to management but financial measures alone are inadequate for determining progress in social responsibility. Apparel brands and retailers prioritizing social responsibility may measure success against what has been referred to as the "triple bottom line" of economic, social, and environmental performance.[43]

Apparel brands and retailers have begun creating measurement systems that identify the extent that factories are complying with company codes of conduct. These ratings can then be used to guide sourcing decisions. For example, Wal-Mart uses a color-coded scheme: green for factories found to have only minor violations, yellow indicating the presence of more serious "medium-risk" violations, orange assigned to factories with high-risk violations including child labor, and red signaling a supplier that is permanently banned from producing products for Wal-Mart.[44] In addition to measuring factory compliance with codes of conduct, companies can develop tools for measuring how well they carry out stakeholder engagement.[45] A number of companies, including Patagonia and the adidas Group, are using life cycle analysis to evaluate the energy costs and environmental impacts of products, including design, materials, production, distribution, care and maintenance, and end-of-life activities.

Determining what needs to be measured and the appropriate indicators for measuring it are central to Total Responsibility Management. In early 2008, the Global Reporting Initiative released its guidelines for the apparel sector that provide specific details of the type of information apparel brands and retailers need to collect and report to their stakeholders.[46]

Innovation, Improvement, and Learning Systems

Total Responsibility Management does not end once a company has developed measures and collected data about its performance. The socially responsible company uses the data to evaluate how it has done and develop plans to further improve performance in the future. Information about performance shared within the company generates a sense of pressure for better outcomes. By working to remediate the problems found when monitoring factories, apparel brands and retailers strive for better performance. Waddock and Bodwell stress the importance of the self-assessment process because it actively involves employees and stakeholders in finding solutions. Since practices and policies for being a socially responsible company are created every day as new problems are discovered and attempts are made to solve them, Total Responsibility Management "approaches mean an iterative process of improvement over time rather than a single initiative that is implemented and then ends."[47] As Auret van Heerden, President and CEO of the FLA, often explains, "social responsibility is a process, not an event."[48]

Transparency and Accountability

As well as affecting the internal environment for increased responsibility, a socially responsible company transparently shares the information externally through company reports to its stakeholders. By being open and candid about how the company has performed in social responsibility and where it has fallen short, a company can develop more trusting relationships with activists and others pressuring for better performance. This transparency provides a means for a company to be accountable for its actions and impacts.[49] In fact, some apparel brands have prepared annual social responsibility reports and then turned them over to key stakeholder groups to include comments on what has been done well and what needs continued work. For example, while commending Gap for taking responsibility for the workers making the company's products, a group of stakeholder representatives pushed the company for much more:

This report touches on Gap's response to the expiration of the Multifibre Arrangement (MFA)—a significant shift in the global supply system that can have devastating consequences in some developing economies. We encourage Gap to share more information about its approach, while continuing to work with others to mitigate the impact of this shift.

As Gap's new compliance database becomes operative, we expect future reports to provide additional specific and aggregate data to assess factory performance while relating the data to systemic issues. We would like to see a future report highlight the state of the U.S. garment industry. We encourage Gap to broaden the scope of its reporting to address the full range of issues covered by the Global Reporting Initiative (GRI). We look forward to comparable reports from other companies.[50]

Clearly there is much work to be done by Gap and other apparel brands and retailers seeking to improve in the area of social responsibility. Apparel brands and retailers that have led efforts in social responsibility are now in the process of reflecting on what has been learned over the last decade in order to identify ways to improve, ultimately developing policies and practices that are sustainable for the long term.

◉

The Challenge That Lies Ahead

In order to craft policies and business practices for social responsibility, apparel brands and retailers, NGOs, labor activists, and other stakeholders all need to agree about what they are trying to accomplish. Dickson and Eckman's Model for Socially Responsible Apparel and Textile Business, with its three dimensions of orientation, philosophy and actions, and outcomes, provides a foundation for understanding social responsibility. Industry and nongovernment organization professionals emphasize the need for accountability. They stress the necessity to incorporate workers' views when developing practices and policies for social responsibility. Finally, they address the need for continuous improvement, ultimately making the concept of social responsibility a dynamic one. With a definition of social responsibility in hand in an Expanded Model for Socially Responsible Apparel Business, we link social responsibility with environmental concerns, sustainability, and human rights.

The ten principles of the UN Global Compact and the universal agreements on which they are based—for human rights, labor, the environment, and anticorruption—are useful as guidance for companies wishing to enhance social responsibility, as is the theory of Total Responsibility Management. Total Responsibility Management involves companies explicitly stating the values that underlie policies and practices, measuring and reporting how the company lives up to these values, and assessing how it can make further improvements for the future. Apparel brands and retailers leading the way in social responsibility have been observed to practice many of the activities associated with inspiration, integration, and innovation. It would be difficult for companies to practice all the possible activities that are outlined in the theory of Total Responsibility Management, but it is important for all companies to do as much as they can. Understanding the concepts of social responsibility, human rights, and sustainability coupled with knowledge about the UN Global Compact and theory of Total Responsibility Management provides a framework for implementing and assessing social responsibility.

Chapter 3

Cultural, Economic, and Political Dimensions of Social Responsibility

◉

Ahmet is an employee of a textile manufacturer located in a suburb of Istanbul, Turkey. Working for a textile mill was the natural choice for him when finishing school, as generations of his family in Turkey had produced and sold textiles. In addition, textiles have historically been an important industry in Turkey, which for centuries held a strategic position along the Silk Road (Figure 3.1). (The Silk Road refers to an historic system of caravan routes that stretched from China to the eastern Mediterranean Sea. Along these caravan routes the trade of textiles, spices, and other products connected countries and cultures throughout Asia for centuries.) Ahmet could have chosen to work in a large modern factory located several miles from Istanbul in an export processing zone; however, this would have required him to take a long bus ride each day to reach the factory and to work with people who are not familiar to him. Instead, he chooses to work for a company that operates a textile mill in his neighborhood within walking distance of his home and where many of the employees are neighbors and friends.

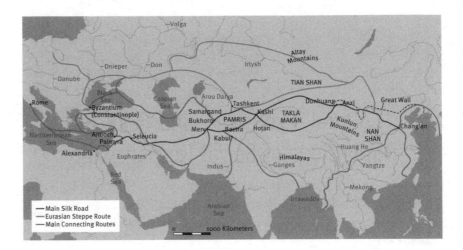

Figure 3.1
The historic Silk Road.

Some of the practices in the factory are those that have been followed in Turkey for many generations and reflect cultural traditions. For example, most of the workers in his textile factory are men, who maintain and tend the modern machinery of textile production. The few women who do work in the textile mill have been placed in quality control or perform other less mechanical tasks. So, Ahmet feels comfortable, as he can work mainly with other men. Women more often work in factories that manufacture apparel, although there are now fewer apparel factories in Turkey, because apparel production is moving to countries such as Morocco and Vietnam, where wages are lower than in Turkey.

The same family has owned the textile factory for generations, and like Ahmet, they are Muslim. He enjoys working for the family because many of their company policies follow the teachings of Islam. For example, the teachings of Islam encourage Muslims to give back to their communities. As such, the factory owners donate a significant amount of money each year to educational and cultural programs as well as to efforts to beautify the neighborhood. In addition, employees are given time off to worship several times a day in a small mosque on the factory grounds. Similar to most factories in Turkey, the cafeteria at Ahmet's factory adheres to the dietary restrictions of the Muslim religion. Also similar to many factories in Turkey, the cafeteria provides a full meal every day at no cost to the employees. This free cafeteria service became commonplace in Turkish factories, as fathers would not allow their daughters to work there otherwise; it would be improper for a conservative Muslim girl to go out in public to purchase lunch. Although employment of women made cafeteria service essential to factory employers, men such as Ahmet benefit from this practice.

Some of the policies, however, are violations of Muslim tradition. For example, the factory operates on Friday, the day of worship for Muslims, and is closed on Saturdays and Sundays. Such policies were introduced when Mustafa Kemal Atatürk, who is considered to be the founder of the modern Turkish republic, served as its first president from 1923 until 1938. Atatürk is much admired in Turkey for having instituted government reforms in an effort to align Turkey with European countries, with which he hoped to increase economic ties and thus enhance his country's economic development. Ahmet does not mind such "Western" practices because this has been the norm in Turkey for more than 80 years, since the founding of the republic. In addition, Ahmet is aware of Turkey's efforts to become a member of the European Union (EU) and thus many Turkish businesses' tendency to adhere to European business practices. Besides, most of the textiles that his factory produces are shipped to apparel factories in Morocco to be assembled for the European market. Consequently, the factory owners are expected to adhere closely to manufacturing laws established by the EU, such as number of hours employees may work, safety measures in the factory, and practices that protect the environment.

Ahmet likes his job and his colleagues. He believes that the factory owners are ethical people who adhere to the teachings of his religion and in some cases forego potential profits in order to enhance the lives of the workers and the standard of living in the community. He is worried, however. He has heard that changes have been made to trade rules by an organization that enforces such rules around the world. He does not really understand how an organization (such as the World Trade Organization, or WTO) can control trade all around the world or what a reduction in quotas means, but he is told that these changes mean fewer guaranteed markets for Turkish textiles. He hears also that changes in the trade rules might mean that China will make more textiles. Rumors among workers at his factory suggest that Chinese workers are paid much less than Turkish textile workers are and some live in company-owned dormitories far away from their villages, family, and friends. These practices make Chinese textiles less expensive than Turkish textiles. When Ahmet asked one of the factory owners about these rumors, she assured him that Turkish textiles are much superior to those from China in quality and design and thus are very competitive with what is being manufactured in China. But he remains concerned that consumers around the world might buy fewer textiles from Turkey. If fewer people want to buy the textiles that he makes, will the factory owners have to lower their prices in order to compete? If so, how will the factory owners be able to afford generous contributions to the community and fair treatment of their employees?

Ahmet also hears that the Turkish government is offering subsidies to businesses if they establish manufacturing facilities in eastern Turkey to encourage economic development there. The subsidized facilities are attracting immigrants who come from surrounding countries seeking work in the factories. These workers are not experienced at textile production but are willing to work for a wage that is lower than his. The textiles that are produced there are cheaper than those made in his factory and may be more price-competitive with those produced in China. Given all of these cultural, economic, and political issues, he wonders how long his job in the textile factory in Istanbul will last.

The apparel industry is global, meaning that the economic, political, legal, and cultural systems of countries involved in the production and trade of textiles and apparel are dependent upon one another. In this chapter, we will examine how economics, politics, laws and policies, and culture influence social responsibility. As Charles Hill suggests, "to understand the economic prospects of a nation and to appreciate its place in international business, we must also understand the interplay between the political, economic, legal and cultural systems in that country."[1] Social responsibility requires recognizing that decisions not only have economic implications but cultural and social consequences as well. The rapid and extensive globalization of the apparel industry has led to concerns about country-specific social, environmental, and developmental implications of corporate activities in the production and sourcing of products. That is why it is important that managers consider the complex consequences that may result from business decisions. As an example, a U.S. apparel brand needs to consider the impact that its decision to source textiles from China rather than Turkey might have on the lives of workers such as Ahmet. In addition, when managers work for businesses whose activities span various geographical and cultural environments, they quickly learn that:

> . . . what is considered normal practice in one nation may be considered unethical in others. Because they work for an institution that transcends national borders and cultures, managers in a multinational firm need to be particularly sensitive to these differences and able to choose the ethical action in those circumstances where variation across societies creates the potential for ethical problems.[2]

In the international landscape of global production and trade in the highly competitive apparel industry, social responsibility cannot be managed effectively by individuals alone. Rather, the United Nations Research Institute for Social Development suggests that the quality of social responsibility initiatives depends upon institutions such as organized religions and the political environment in which businesses operate.[3] Corporate managers as well as policymakers must consider carefully the implications that their decisions have on social responsibility efforts worldwide.

Throughout history, textiles have been a major trade commodity. Owing to the intrinsic value of textiles, they have long served as mediums of exchange and as resources for accumulating wealth. Trade routes, such as the historic Silk Road that developed to enable the transport, buying, and selling of textiles and apparel, have facilitated not only the exchange of goods but also the sharing of culture and political philosophies. The prominent position of textiles and apparel in this process of trade and exchange continues today.

The apparel industry plays a significant role in today's global economy. Textiles and apparel comprise approximately 7 percent of the world's exports, and the United Nations' Industrial Development Organization estimates that in 2000, approximately 26.5 million workers were employed in textiles and apparel production worldwide.[4] Consumers in Western Europe and North America purchase approximately two-thirds of the US$1 trillion in apparel sold worldwide each year, while Asian consumers account for a quarter of the sales.

The economic importance of apparel trade, as well as the role of low-wage labor in its production, has prompted politicians and governments to become involved in molding the industry, particularly through international trade agreements[5] such as those implemented under the World Trade Organization. As a result, political, economic, and social forces are shaping a new world order in which traditional national boundaries are less relevant for the global production and marketing of textiles and apparel.[6] Let's look at specific cultural, economic, and political dimensions that influence social responsibility.

◉

Cultural Dimensions of Social Responsibility

One outcome of the new world order may be that cultures are converging and common behaviors related to both the production and consumption of products are emerging. Although some general behaviors are becoming increasingly similar across cultures and markets are globalizing, at the same time, cultural identity and devotion to local cultural traditions remain strong in many societies.

Definitions of Culture

Many definitions of culture have been developed and vary widely from the very general to the more specific. In fact, in 1952 anthropologists A. L. Kroeber and Clyde Kluckhohn compiled a list of 160 definitions of culture, indicating the diversity in the interpretation of the concept.[7] A definition of culture that is applicable to both groups of people as well as to organizations such as apparel businesses is:

> The integrated patterns of human knowledge, belief, and behaviour that depends upon the capacity for learning and transmitting knowledge to succeeding generations; the customary beliefs, social forms, and material traits of a racial, religious, or social group; the characteristic features of everyday existence shared by people in a place or time; the set of shared attitudes, values, goals, and practices that characterizes an institution or organization (a corporate culture focused on the bottom line); the set of values, conventions or social practices associated with a particular field, activity, or societal characteristic.[8]

In an effort to define culture for the purposes of business applications and to examine how culture influences ethical decision making, Katharina Srnka gathered definitions of culture from anthropology, psychology, and sociology. Based upon these numerous definitions, culture may be described as "a complex phenomenon rooted in the ideas and values shared by a group."[9] Srnka suggests that four levels of culture exist, as summarized in Figure 3.2. These four levels of culture are political, religious, and economic forces; national identity; professional and industry norms; and organizational, family, or clan value systems.

This perspective of levels of culture illustrates that various cultural influences on social responsibility permeate all echelons of a society and that the influences range from the very broad (e.g., beliefs about universal human rights) to the very narrow (e.g., individual decision making). Further, ethical decision making is shaped by one's attitudes and values, which, in turn, are influenced or even determined by culture.[10]

Culture has implications for global apparel production, and its influence is pervasive in the numerous countries around the world in which it takes place. In the global apparel industry, managers interact with people from a wide spectrum of cultures who have different

Figure 3.2
Levels of culture:
A marketing perspective.

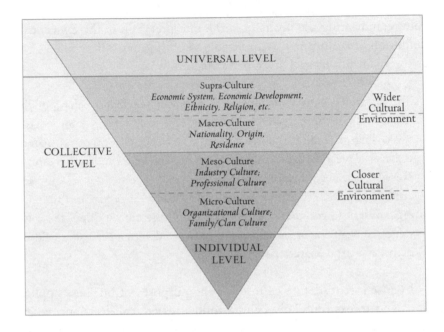

Figure 3.3
A place of worship on factory grounds in Thailand.

political and economic philosophies as well as values, religions, and ethical beliefs (Figure 3.3). Therefore, when engaging in ethical decision making, it is important that managers avoid ethnocentrism, the belief that one's own culture is superior to others' cultures, and instead adopt cultural empathy to accommodate how differences among countries influence both society and business.[11]

Impacts of Culture on Practices in the Work Environment

Conducting business in a global environment is challenging because cultures differ and may clash. Both national culture and organizational culture shape the work environment. National culture encompasses the values and resulting behaviors that are shared by individuals within national boundaries.[12] Organizational culture encompasses values and behaviors that are shared by members and that guide a firm.

National culture is influenced by colonization, trade, migration, mass media, and religion, and incorporates the following components:

- Values (what is important)
- Norms (expectations concerning behavior)
- Institutions (structures of society that communicate values and norms)
- Artifacts (material culture including the processes by which they are produced and the meaning assigned to them)
- Rituals (set of activities preferred in a fixed sequence and repeated)
- Customs (ways of doing something)
- Laws (norms that are officially sanctioned)

National culture has important application to the business setting because it shapes organizational culture.[13] One paradigm that is frequently used to analyze the impact of national culture on individual behavior and that has implications for conducting business globally was developed by Geert Hofstede.[14] He suggests that cultural differences among societies or nations may be described through the measurement of four dimensions. A composite national score for each of these four dimensions enables predictions about how workers behave and how business managers in that society make decisions and operate. The four dimensions include the following:

- Individualism/collectivism—The degree to which a society is collectivist versus individualistic. Turkey is a collectivist society, whereas the United States is individualist. Therefore, Ahmet's expectation that his employer will look after him is not only a reflection of his religion but also of the closely knit social network that is characteristic of a collectivist society. This collectivist mentality elicits Ahmet's loyalty to his neighborhood, friends, employer, and country. Australia and Great Britain, similar to the United States, are individualistic, whereas countries such as Indonesia, Taiwan, and South Korea display collectivistic tendencies.

- Uncertainty avoidance—Whether a society is comfortable with risk or threatened by uncertain situations. Turks tend to be more risk-averse than are Americans. Uncertainty avoidance may have led Ahmet to seek a job in the textile industry where generations of his family have flourished as well as to take a job in the familiar surroundings of his neighborhood rather than risking employment in a new, distant export processing zone. Uncertainty avoidance may explain at least partially Ahmet's concern about the new trade rules and their impact on the future of the Turkish textile industry and his job. Japan and Argentina are among countries that tend to avoid uncertainty, whereas China and Great Britain are societies more comfortable with uncertainty and risk taking.

- Power distance—The level of acceptance of inequality among members of a society. Power distance is somewhat stronger in Turkey than in the United States. As such, relatively high power distance may explain Ahmet's acceptance of the privileges of the factory owners as well as of Ahmet's dependence upon his employers. Countries such as Mexico and China display high power distance, whereas Australia, Great Britain, and Germany score relatively low on power distance.

- Masculinity/femininity—The extent to which the values of a society are feminine (e.g., emphasis on quality of life, relationships, service, sympathy for the unfortunate) or masculine (e.g., emphasis on assertiveness, achievement, profit, acquisition of money). When compared to Turkey, the United States tends to be a more masculine society. Clearly the generosity and service to their employees and neighborhood on the part of Ahmet's bosses as well as the importance of relationships at the factory are reflective of both the Islamic religion and a culture that scores relatively low in masculinity. Japan scores high in masculinity, whereas South Korea tends to be a more feminine society.

Table 3.1. Cultural Distance Scores for Identified Countries

Country	Individualism	Uncertainty Avoidance	Power Distance	Masculine/ Feminine	Cultural Distance from the United States
Australia	90	51	36	61	7
Great Britain	89	35	35	66	13
Canada	80	48	39	52	15
Germany	67	65	35	66	33
India	48	40	77	56	57
Argentina	46	86	49	56	61
Brazil	38	76	69	49	69
Turkey	37	85	66	45	73
Japan	46	92	54	95	74
Hong Kong	25	29	68	57	74
Taiwan	17	69	58	45	81
Mexico	30	82	81	69	82
China	20	30	80	66	83
Indonesia	14	48	78	46	87
South Korea	18	85	60	39	88
Singapore	20	8	74	48	89
United States	91	46	40	62	

Adapted from Hofstede, G. H. (1980). *Culture's consequences: International differences in work-related values.* Beverly Hills, CA: Sage Publications.

Table 3.1 presents two sets of information concerning cultural distance among the countries represented. Scores for individualism, uncertainty avoidance, power distance, and masculinity indicate the degree to which that cultural dimension is representative of a particular country. Scores range from o (the dimension is least representative of that country/culture) to 100 (the dimension is most strongly representative of that country/culture). Second, cultural distance scores in the far right column indicate relative differences in culture between the United States and represented countries. A lower cultural distance score indicates greater similarity to the United States. Scores on these four cultural dimensions help global companies determine how to approach business, for example, how to shape labor practices and policies to complement the cultural characteristics of the workforce.

Complementing Hofstede's perspectives on culture, Harry Triandis identifies three characteristics of culture that are important in identifying similarities and differences among nations: complexity, looseness, and individuality.[15] The level of complexity of a society refers to how simple or complex the thinking of its members is. Examples of simplistic thinkers are members of communist countries, whose thinking is guided by political philosophies; fundamentally religious societies, who base decisions on religious doctrines; and businesspeople who think only of profits with no regard for social responsibility. Loose cultures tend to be heterogeneous groups in which people are accepting of those who deviate from cultural norms. Tight cultures, on the other hand, tend to view issues as black and white and to be more simplistic in their thinking than are loose cultures. Social groups that tend to be simple and tight also tend to be collectivistic (Asia, Africa, and South America), where individuals sacrifice self-interest for the best interest of the group and tend to be loyal. Individualistic societies' (Northern and Western Europe and North America) members are responsible for creating their own self-identity and are less concerned about group membership and stable relationships. Western societies tend to be individualistic, loose, and complex, which is very different from Islamic and African societies, which are typically simple, tight, and collectivist, according to Triandis. These cultural characteristics have implications for perceptions of social responsibility issues. Independents emphasize working hard and striving to achieve, whereas collectivists reveal affective qualities of empathy and altruism in their work and home lives.

As businesses globalize and collaborate across cultures, the greater the differences among countries and cultures in terms of complexity, looseness, and individuality, the more difficult it will be for them to work together successfully, and the more differently they may view issues of social responsibility. For example, collectivists may be more likely than independents to be sensitive to the plight of factory workers as a group and supportive of socially responsible policies in the workplace that have the potential to benefit not just individuals but all of the workers collectively (Figure 3.4).

Similar to a national culture, an organizational culture is composed of members who share values, behave in ways that conform to guidelines or policies reflecting company norms, participate in rituals, and use specialized vocabularies. As we have seen, Ahmet was drawn to work for a company whose values, behavior, and rituals were familiar to him. Organizational culture in industrialized countries, however, may vary from that of businesses in developing countries because of differing behavioral norms and values across cultures.[16] For example, would a textile worker or even a mill manager in the United States

Figure 3.4
Workers taking a break together at a factory in Thailand.

understand the organizational culture at Ahmet's factory? Certainly the way in which personnel in textile mills interact in Turkey is very different from the interactions among employees in a U.S. mill.

In addition, because national culture and organizational culture often guide business practices, what is considered to be ethical and socially responsible in one culture or in one nation may be perceived very differently in another. Creating work environments that address the varying needs of employees and making socially responsible business decisions requires managers to be sensitive to cultural differences and to consider the social implications of their economic actions.

The necessity for cultural understanding is particularly acute in today's apparel industry because of the cross-cultural partnerships that developed in response to the increasingly competitive business environment. From the end of World War II until the late 1980s, a majority of these partnerships formed because the businesses operated in countries that shared similar economic and political philosophies.[7] That is, businesses in communist bloc countries with centrally planned economies, in which the government made decisions about products to be produced and distributed based upon the needs of the government, tended to collaborate with one another (e.g., the former Soviet Union and Cuba). The same was true of those in countries with free market capitalistic economies in which production and distribution decisions were determined by supply and demand based upon the wants and needs of consumers (e.g., the United States and Canada). These shared philosophies simplified the processes necessary for successful collaboration, making cultural differences among trading partners less acute.

Since the 1990s, the apparel industry has experienced rapid globalization as a result of the dissolution of the communist bloc as well as China's increased participation in world trade, in addition to great advances in transportation and communication technology. As a larger number of diverse countries have become involved in the production and trade of textiles and apparel, cultural understanding and sensitivity are increasingly vital and challenging to the health and success of the industry, participating firms, and employees. Operating successfully in a global and multicultural environment requires "purposeful preparation as well as sustained learning."[18]

Success and social responsibility in the global apparel industry may depend upon the ability of company employees to execute their skills while at the same time adapt to new cultural environments. Although globalization of the apparel industry has reduced some cultural barriers to production and trade, the business practices of some firms may be influenced by the culture and the situation. As such, perspectives on human rights such as protection of children, prevention of discrimination against women, and provision of fair wages may vary across cultures.[19] Some social implications for the apparel industry are discussed below.

Protection of Children

Elimination of child labor is a goal of a number of international organizations, including the United Nations and the International Labour Organization (ILO). The ILO is a strong moral force concerning labor standards around the world. Child labor refers to workers who are under the age of 15. Although the ILO strives to prevent and eliminate all forms of child labor, the organization has defined and is focusing upon the worst forms. Of immediate concern are the following practices:

- The sale and trafficking of children
- Debt bondage and serfdom and forced or compulsory labor, including forced or compulsory recruitment of children for use in armed conflict
- The use, procuring, or offering of a child for prostitution, for the production of pornography, or for pornographic performances
- The use, procuring, or offering of a child for illicit activities, in particular for the production and trafficking of drugs as defined in the relevant international treaties
- Work, which by its nature or the circumstances in which it is carried out, is likely to harm the health, safety, or morals of children[20]

Some attempt to justify child labor, including the use of children to produce apparel products, on cultural differences and the context of the workplace. Yet there are counterarguments for these justifications. For example, in the process of socialization, children may be taught skills, such as embroidery and weaving, which are deeply embedded in their culture, as seen in the Middle East rug-making trade (Figure 3.5). However, children who are unable to work on complex designs are often given the dullest and most repetitious tasks that do not support learning.[21]

Figure 3.5

A child weaving a rug.

Most cultures value formal education as an important preparation for children to attain better jobs and a higher quality of life. In wealthy nations, restrictions are placed on children's contribution to the formal economy in an attempt to ensure that children are educated, and a public education system allows virtually all school-age children to attend. In less developed countries, formal education is often unaffordable, but no less important for the long-term growth of the countries. Ironically, when child labor is ended, adults' wages should be high enough to cover educating their children.[22]

Some argue that a child may provide a critical or only source of income for a family;[23] however, children would not have to work if their parents were paid enough to support their families' needs. Furthermore, children often work under debt bondage, thus not earning a wage.[24] In addition, some argue that making apparel products may be a safer means to help support their families than are other options for children, including drug trafficking or prostitution, and it is true that care must be taken to assure that children denied employment can go to school.

Elimination of Discrimination against Women

The workforce in the global apparel industry is largely young women who are "low skilled" or "unskilled," minorities, and immigrants. These young female workers often do not know their rights and are particularly vulnerable to abuse such as sexual harassment and threats by supervisors because they fear retribution such as losing their jobs if they complain.

In an attempt to protect female workers, and male employees as well, many apparel brands and retailers that source goods from less developed countries require specific ethical practices from their suppliers. For example, women may be given "light" work that allows them to stay off their feet when pregnant (Figure 3.6). It is not uncommon for U.S. businesses to have policies that specify working hours that are shorter and working conditions that may be safer than those legally sanctioned in the countries from which they are sourcing goods. Unfortunately, these policies are not always enforced. In addition, contractors may deny workers the right to form trade unions, which would strengthen workers' efforts in demanding rights for safe working conditions, training, and promotion.

Figure 3.6
A pregnant factory worker is provided a less strenuous task.

Minimum Legal Wage versus Minimum Living Wage

The governments of many countries that export apparel have established minimum legal wages for workers. A minimum legal wage is the lowest amount as established by a legal authority that can be paid to an employee. Minimum wages were initially set by governments to ensure that workers around the world were able to meet their basic needs; however, over the years they have been used to attract foreign investment. For example, in 2007 Honduras lowered its minimum wage in order to compete with Nicaragua.[25] Examples of minimum wages in countries that are actively involved in apparel production are presented in Table 3.2; note the variation by country of minimum wages as well as the criteria by which minimum wages are set.[26] In addition, earning a minimum wage is often not sufficient to enable workers to support their families and help them emerge from poverty.

Social activists contend that rather than paying workers a minimum legal wage, businesses should provide a living wage. The Center for Reflection, Education and Action (CREA) defines a living wage as one that supplies enough income to provide a worker and family with the basic needs and money to participate in culturally necessary activities and to set aside for a better future.[27] Certainly a living wage is more ethical than is a minimum legal wage. Yet, although various multi-stakeholder organizations working to improve the working conditions in the apparel industry, such as the Fair Labor Association and the Worker Rights Consortium, agree that providing a living wage is an important goal, there is little agreement as to how to implement it.[28] How to calculate a living wage was initially a problem and still remains complex. A living wage is unique to each country because perceptions of what is "necessary" and "acceptable" is culture-specific and influenced by the level of development of the country. CREA has conducted studies calculating the living wage in various cities in Mexico, Indonesia, Haiti, and El Salvador, using data on prices of goods to develop a purchasing power index. However, there are problems beyond calculation that prevent a living wage from being implemented. Current pricing practices would have to be changed, as would the distribution of income between factory owners and workers. The Joint Initiative on Corporate Accountability and Workers Rights is attempting to address these concerns in a pilot project.[29] Until there is more agreement on how to implement it, apparel brands and retailers are unlikely to enact a living wage policy. At the least, however, apparel brands and

Table 3.2. Minimum Wages and Criteria for Setting Minimum Wages in Selected Apparel-Producing Countries for the Year 2000

Countries with a National Minimum Wage Minimum Wage	Countries with a Minimum Wage Set by Industry, Skill Level, or Geographic Location Minimum Wage (Criteria for Setting Minimum Wage)	Countries with No Minimum Wage Minimum Wage (Criteria for Setting Minimum Wage)
Brazil US$81/mo	Bangladesh US$12.25–76/mo (industry, occupation, skill level)	Macau none
Colombia US$5.07/day	Cambodia US$40/mo for apparel sector only (sector)	Malaysia none
Hong Kong US$599/mo (except for domestic workers)	China US$12–39/mo (province, autonomous region, municipality)	Singapore none
Israel US$675/mo	Costa Rica US$266/mo (occupation)	
Peru US$100/mo	Dominican Republic US$120.75/mo (size and type of industrial activity)	
South Korea US$1.27/hr	El Salvador US$4.81/day (geographic area, industrial activity)	
Taiwan US$476/mo	Guatemala US$3.16/day (industrial sector)	
Turkey US$291/mo	Honduras US$3.34/day (geographic area and industrial score)	
	India US$.24–2.09/day (state, industry, skill level)	

(continued)

Table 3.2. Minimum Wages and Criteria for Setting Minimum Wages
in Selected Apparel-Producing Countries for the Year 2000 (*continued*)

Countries with a National Minimum Wage Minimum Wage	Countries with a Minimum Wage Set by Industry, Skill Level, or Geographic Location Minimum Wage (Criteria for Setting Minimum Wage)	Countries with No Minimum Wage Minimum Wage (Criteria for Setting Minimum Wage)
	Indonesia US$15.12–33.72/mo (geographic area)	
	Mauritius US$13.9/wk in export processing zones (industrial sector)	
	Mexico US$3.02–3.24/day (geographic area, occupation)	
	Pakistan US$38/mo (unskilled workers only)	
	Philippines US$5/day (geographic region)	
	Sri Lanka US$29–37.3/mo (garments) US$21.7–29.7/mo (footwear) (industrial sector, skill level)	
	Thailand US$3.58–4.18/day (geographic region)	

SOURCE: Adapted from: U.S. Department of Labor (2000). *Wages, benefits, poverty line, and meeting workers' needs in the apparel and footwear industries of selected countries*. Washington: U.S. Department of Labor Bureau of International Labor Affairs.

retailers need to ensure that workers making their products are paid no less than the legal minimum wage.

Almost as important to the welfare of employees and almost as costly to employers as wages are benefits provided to workers, such as health insurance, unemployment insurance, and retirement funds. In many developed economies, provision of employee benefits is legally required for full-time workers and is enforced by governmental agencies. As well, some codes of conduct have provisions for employment relationships. Even in developed countries, however, employers sometimes avoid providing benefits by hiring part-time employees who do not qualify for benefits. Unfortunately, in many apparel-producing countries, there are no laws requiring the provision of employment benefits or the laws are not enforced. In such countries, socially responsible businesses and contractors must be relied upon to provide a living wage and benefits to workers.

Impact of Migration on Cultural Aspects of the Workplace and Issues of Social Responsibility

National boundaries are becoming less important in the production and trade of textiles and apparel, in part due to migration of labor. Significant numbers of men and women worldwide leave their homes, villages, and cultural traditions behind as they search for a better life for both themselves and their families.[30] They may choose to seek higher wages elsewhere, or they may be forced to leave their homeland because of national disasters such as famine, violence, or persecution. The workforce in apparel factories in China is primarily young females, many of whom have migrated from rural areas and villages.[31] They are attracted to factory work by the opportunity for economic freedom through employment and earning a salary. In addition, some may view working at a factory as a method to escape arranged marriages that are still traditional and subsistence living that is still typical of rural areas of China. Although the Chinese government's labor laws restrict the workday to 8 hours a day and 44 hours per week, these laws are frequently disregarded. It is not uncommon for employees in China to work 12-hour shifts seven days a week.[32] In spite of these harsh conditions, more and more Chinese are leaving agricultural jobs in rural areas and migrating to cities in search of a factory job. Additionally, both the persecution and violation of human rights at the hands of the Myanmar government as well as the economic crisis in that country have forced workers to seek employment and a safer environment for their families in Thailand.

Workers' homelands as well as their adopted countries feel the effects of labor migration. The countries they leave often experience a loss of the energy, enthusiasm, and skills of their young workforce, which can reduce a country's production output as well as taxable income. Their newly adopted country benefits from an influx of young laborers who are sometimes highly experienced and motivated; however, cultural differences among factory workers may result in a more complex, sometimes volatile work environment in which the integration of workers from a variety of cultures and races may be challenging.

The migrants themselves may experience unanticipated difficulties in their new working environment, such as discrimination, inconsistent employment, lack of employment contracts, and unfair or delayed payment of wages. The ILO confirms that migration and the resulting mix of cultures in the workplace may be generating increased racism and xenophobia worldwide,[33] thus challenging efforts toward social responsibility.

◉

Economic Dimensions of Social Responsibility

Two concepts widely used in development economics and organizational science—vicious circles and virtuous circles—are helpful for understanding the interplay and outcomes of decisions made by governments, businesses, and others. A vicious circle occurs when various decisions and policies reinforce one another to yield progressively negative results. In contrast, a virtuous circle is created when decisions and policies combine to result in positive outcomes.[34]

Vicious Circle

The process of producing and sourcing apparel in the global economy may be described in economic terms as a vicious circle because of fierce competition and the labor-intensive nature of production. This circle begins with consumers who make purchase decisions based on price—the lower the better in many cases. In turn, apparel brands and retailers seek low-cost production sites in developing countries and move production to those sites in order to cut costs and be price-competitive (see Figure 3.7). In an effort to increase employment as well as the production and sale of export products, governments in these countries strive to keep wages low and at times minimize regulations that increase production costs. In this vicious circle scenario, countries and their suppliers view issues of social responsibility in terms of increasing costs of production, thereby placing a country at a disadvantage when competing globally for production work. Thus, as we have depicted in Figure 3.7, the vicious circle in pursuit of the lowest cost resembles a downward spiral leading to a race to the bottom, and in the process diminishing opportunities for workers to enhance their level of living and discouraging employers from addressing issues of social responsibility.

Whichever term is used—downward spiral or race to the bottom—breaking the circle is difficult. The result is that approximately 50 percent of textile exports and 75 percent of apparel exports come from developing countries and most employment in the industry is concentrated in countries such as China, Pakistan, Bangladesh, Mexico, and Cambodia that do not always uphold worker rights.[35] If a government believes that producing apparel products for export is critical to

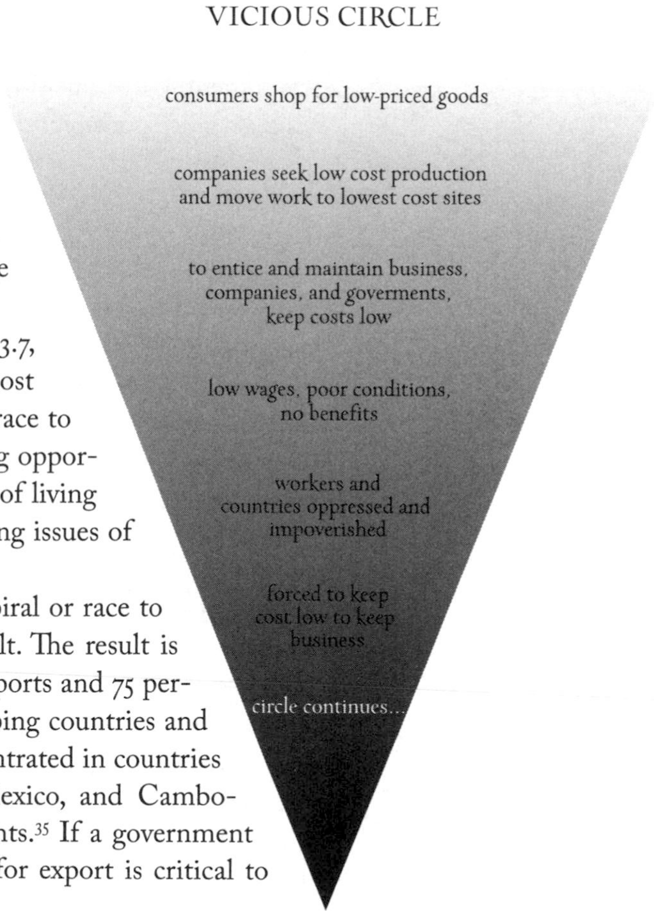

Figure 3.7
Vicious circle.

VICIOUS CIRCLE

consumers shop for low-priced goods

companies seek low cost production and move work to lowest cost sites

to entice and maintain business, companies, and goverments, keep costs low

low wages, poor conditions, no benefits

workers and countries oppressed and impoverished

forced to keep cost low to keep business

circle continues...

that country's economy, and the government employs large numbers of workers, officials may not impose or enforce laws and policies, including those that support social responsibility. Government officials also may not encourage practices such as monitoring that protect workers, as these activities may increase costs of production and decrease the competitiveness of their products in the global market. This lack of enforcement and monitoring may be particularly true for some smaller countries in which apparel production and exports are critical to the economy. For example, 80 percent of total exports from Bangladesh, Haiti, and Cambodia are apparel and textile.[36] When people have little freedom to express their views, few opportunities to organize, and little power to influence government policy, the vicious circle is likely to continue. One way to break the vicious circle is for businesses and government to document the benefits to business that result from pursuing social responsibility.[37]

Virtuous Circle

In contrast to vicious circles, virtuous circles are based upon collaboration among members of the supply chain who each focus upon doing the right thing, in other words the socially responsible action, within their sphere of influence (Figure 3.8). For instance, a virtuous circle may include collaboration among agricultural entities that provide raw materials; factory owners that produce fibers, textiles, and apparel; union leaders who represent workers; retailers who source products; consumers who purchase the products; universities that educate future industry executives; and governments that create laws and policies that impact the workplace.

When consumers value the workers creating their apparel and are willing to pay more for apparel, members of the supply chain are able to build connections with one another directed toward social responsibility. The circles of positive results have the potential to benefit all involved. A virtuous circle has the potential to offer consumers products they can feel good about. Businesses can increase productivity among

VIRTUOUS CIRCLE

Figure 3.8
Virtuous circle.

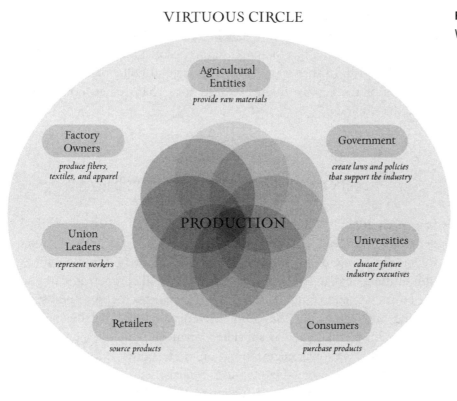

production workers, which provides increased revenues to support the creation of product innovations and better marketing tools, which in turn increases market share. Expanded market share then leads to reduced costs through economies of scale and the circle continues. However, the virtuous circle does not stop there.

When workers are paid a living wage, their children go to school and more services are required from professionals such as teachers, health-care providers, lawyers, and accountants, which in turn generates more jobs for the children when they complete their education. When workers are free to unionize and when businesses and governments are focused upon doing the right thing, working conditions improve, and wages and benefits to workers increase. When standards of living increase, people are better able to give back to their neighborhoods and communities, enhancing the quality of life. Therefore, doing the right thing has the potential to become profitable as well as beneficial to all. In that way, a virtuous circle or collaboration among members of the supply chain can lead to a chain of economic and social development.

◉

Political Dimensions of Social Responsibility

It is often difficult to separate economic considerations from political perspectives; indeed, economic development is often dependent upon the political system operating in a society. Increased internationalization of the global apparel industry has intensified competition among the businesses and countries involved. If a country focuses upon supporting and enhancing the competitiveness of national businesses, government policies such as subsidies, financial incentives, and strategies for international negotiations on trade policy either for freer trade or for more protective measures reflect this orientation.[38] These strategies do not, however, always support social responsibility.

Subsidies

Many countries offer a variety of subsidies to support aspects of their industry that enable national businesses to be more competitive on the world market. As examples, cotton subsidies in the United States help to keep the price of U.S. cotton low on the world market and employment subsidies in China keep labor costs low. Therefore, such subsidies enhance the competitiveness of U.S. cotton and labor-intensive goods manufactured in China compared to products from countries where governments are not providing subsidies for such goods.

Financial Incentives

Governments may provide financial incentives to businesses that operate in export processing zones. These zones often offer benefits such as exemption from regulations and taxes to apparel manufacturers and other businesses located in these zones and engaging in commercial or industrial export activities.[39] Developing-country governments are increasingly pressured to develop export processing zones and offer financial incentives in order to attract potential investors who sell to apparel brands and retailers. Some export processing zones have central human resource departments that screen all applicants. Discriminatory practices in hiring can have far-reaching effects under these systems, especially when workers are fired from one supplier, perhaps for attempts to organize a union, and then "blacklisted" or denied employment at any other supplier in the zone. In these ways, global competition has made socially responsible practices such as good working conditions, job security, and benefits luxuries rather than standard expectations in some countries.[40]

Trade Policies

Because of the economic significance of the apparel industry and the number of people employed in the industry worldwide, politicians and governments have greatly influenced its global operations through international trade agreements.[41] The modern-era trade agreements affecting the apparel industry began with the General Agreement on Tariffs and Trade (GATT), established after World War II (Box 3.1). The GATT was created to free world trade of restrictions introduced during the world depression in the early twentieth century and also to provide a framework for peacefully addressing trade disputes that had the potential to escalate into military confrontations among nations. However, in the 1950s, special protectionist rules were devised within GATT and applied to the trade of textiles and apparel that

Box 3.1. Timeline of Major Events in the Regulation of Apparel Trade

1947 General Agreement on Tariffs and Trade (GATT)

1961 Short-Term Arrangement (STA)

1962 Long-Term Arrangement (LTA) (renewed 1967, 1972)

1973 Multifibre Arrangement (MFA)

1993 World Trade Organization (WTO)

1995 Agreement on Textiles and Clothing (ATC)

were considered to be "exceptional cases" because cheap products from Hong Kong and Japan were disrupting markets in developed countries, including the United States.[42]

The following decades saw the introduction of additional protectionist trade measures for apparel products, including the Short Term Arrangement Regarding International Trade in Cotton Textiles and the Long Term Arrangement Regarding International Trade in Cotton Textiles (LTA). When businesses circumvented restrictions on the trade of cotton by moving production to countries not covered by the Short Term Arrangement and to materials other than cotton (i.e., wool, man-made fibers), developed countries pushed passage of the Multifibre Arrangement (MFA).[43] Under the MFA, trade of a wider range of fibers (cotton, wool, and synthetic fibers) from a larger array of developing countries to markets in developed countries was restricted to protect industry and jobs in developed countries from low-cost imports. Ironically, an unanticipated outcome of MFA was the increased globalization of the apparel industry; as one country's quota of export products was filled, production was moved to another country or was shifted to another product category for which the quota had not been filled. As a result, a new range of countries in regions around the world got involved in the global production of textiles and apparel. Evidence of this is the emergence of the apparel industry in countries in Southeast Asia, Central America, and Eastern Europe, some with long traditions in the industry and others as newcomers to apparel production, which requires little capital investment, little equipment, and few skilled workers. Another unanticipated outcome of the MFA was the impact of quotas on world production of textiles and apparel. Although developed countries sought quota restrictions on imports (i.e., restrictions on the weight, yardage, value, number, etc.), exporting countries came to view quotas as "guaranteed market" access, formalizing the specific amount of goods that they were allowed to ship to markets in developed countries each year.

Thus, although great strides were being made in freeing trade of many products through the GATT, the trade of textiles and apparel was excluded from liberalization and increasingly controlled to protect domestic markets in developed countries. This all changed when, as part of the agreement concluding the Uruguay Round of Multilateral Trade negotiations, GATT members devised the Agreement on Textiles and Clothing (ATC). The ATC formalized efforts to reduce the protectionist regulation of apparel trade through the phaseout of MFA quotas over a ten-year period ending January 1, 2005.

Trade Agreements and Workers' Rights

What does the discussion of trade policies have to do with social responsibility? According to Gary Burtless, "of all the debates surrounding globalization, one of the most contentious involves trade and workers' rights. Proponents of workers' rights argue that trading nations should be held to strict labor standards (e.g., freedom of association, prohibition of forced labor)."[44] Further, he proposes that observance of human rights should be required of nations that seek entry into developed countries' markets.

Acting responsibly may require compromise or even sacrifice. For example, adhering to high human rights standards might mean that wealthy democracies will jeopardize a trade pact that could benefit their domestic businesses and consumers. Yet trade policies can be used to encourage social responsibility:

A trading partner that fails to enforce basic protections for its workers can gain an unfair trade advantage, boosting its market competitiveness against countries with stronger labor safeguards. Including labor standards in trade deals can encourage countries in a free trade zone to maintain worker protections rather than abandoning them in a race to the bottom. If each country must observe a common set of minimum standards, member countries can offer and enforce worker protection at a more nearly optimal level.[45]

Cleopatra Doumbia-Henry and Eric Gravel report that a growing number of recently signed free trade agreements have included minimum labor standards.[46] For example, trade agreements the United States has signed with Canada, Mexico, Chile, Jordan, Morocco, Singapore, Bahrain, Australia, and Peru include social and labor provisions. Additional trade agreements are still under negotiation, such as the Free Trade Area of the Americas and bilateral free trade agreements between Colombia, Thailand, Korea, and the United States.

Canada, Mexico, and the United States signed the North American Free Trade Agreement (NAFTA) in 1992 to promote free exchange of goods and services among the three countries. By signing the parallel agreement, the North American Agreement on Labor Cooperation, the three countries agreed to protect, enhance, and enforce workers' rights as well as 11 principles subject to each country's domestic laws. Of concern, according to Doumbia-Henry and Gravel, is that these principles are very general and have weak enforcement mechanisms, and the agreement does not specify minimum standards for domestic laws in each country.[47] Only domestic labor laws are enforceable in other trade agreements with Chile, Jordan, Morocco, and Singapore.

Owing to these challenges, some suggest that labor standards recently included in trade agreements are more "aspirational" than they are enforceable commitments, and the efficacy of the inclusion of labor standards in trade agreements and their effect on socially responsible practices is under debate because the labor standards may not be practiced.[48] Regardless, progress can be marked by the labor provisions included in bilateral trade arrangements. Bilateral trade agreements concluded by the United States and the European Union in the last decade support freedom of association, freedom to participate in collective bargaining, and the prohibition of child labor and forced labor.[49]

Virtuous Circle: Example of Trade Agreement with Cambodia

There are a variety of reasons—poverty, lack of resources, and lack of political will among them—why some developing countries fail to enforce labor standards.[50] However, there appears to be a synergy brought about by free trade and increased trade, which results in economic growth and development that in turn can lead to enforcement of international labor standards and socially responsible practices.

One positive approach to social responsibility in the apparel industry is to provide access to lucrative markets as an incentive to promote human rights and comply with labor laws. Positive trade incentives may be effective tools for encouraging compliance with labor laws[51] and fostering development of a virtuous circle.

The 1999 Textile Trade Agreement between the United States and Cambodia is an example of this approach; it is the first agreement that linked measurable improvements in factory conditions with favorable trading terms.[52] Specifically, the agreement stated that the United States would grant to Cambodia increased quotas for textiles and apparel exports to the U.S. market if Cambodia enhanced the enforcement of its national labor laws and protected apparel workers. For its part, the Cambodian government allowed international monitors from the ILO into factories to document whether improvements were being achieved in labor practices, such as wages; working hours; safety standards; freedom of association; and banning child labor, discrimination, and forced labor. It may be argued that Cambodia had little choice but to agree to the groundbreaking trading terms. The Cambodian government, similar to those of many developing countries, had identified the apparel industry as an opportunity for economic development so desperately needed in the country. Just emerging from a long period of war and political and economic strife, the annual per capita GDP, at U.S. $260, was among the world's lowest. The apparel industry was viewed as a vehicle to economic growth for the country if it could gain access to the U.S. market for their exports.

Many developing countries criticized the agreement between Cambodia and the United States, arguing that the inclusion of higher labor standards was just another form of a protectionist trade barrier.[53] On the other hand, the United States government viewed the agreement as a new tool for encouraging trading partners to adhere to responsible labor standards. U.S. labor unions and NGOs were very pleased with the new precedent of associating trade with labor standards.[54]

Despite criticism of the trade agreement among developing countries, this program was seen as very successful both by the U.S. and Cambodian governments and by Cambodian workers and businesses in Cambodia's apparel sector.[55] Positive outcomes of the agreement include growth in Cambodia's GDP, strengthening of the nation's labor laws and working conditions in factories that could be used as a model for other developing countries, assurance to U.S. brands and retailers that apparel manufactured in Cambodia was done so with fair labor practices, and a resulting increased direct foreign investment that moved garment production into the lead as the largest manufacturing sector in Cambodia.[56] This progress came at a price, however, with strife between labor and management often resulting in strikes that discouraged some direct foreign investment. Additionally, the requirements of monitoring may have driven away some businesses seeking cheaper production and a more submissive workforce.

The United States–Cambodian textile agreement ended in 2005. There is some uncertainty as to whether Cambodia's apparel industry can remain an important engine for the country's economy in the absence of quotas that granted Cambodian manufacturers access to the U.S. market. The question relating to social responsibility is whether "the resulting higher costs of manufacturing will be offset by international retailers willing to pay a premium for a labor-conditions safe haven."[57] In fact, in June 2007, the Cambodian government changed its overtime laws to decrease payment to workers in hopes of attracting greater investment in its garment industry.[58] This action heralds a disappointing change of policy from a virtuous circle to a vicious circle approach in the absence of the United States–Cambodian textile agreement.

The Impact of Businesses and Executives on Policy That Affects Social Responsibility

Internationally recognized business scholars Michael Porter and Mark Kramer concur with the stance of the United Nations by arguing that the greatest impact that a business can have on a society is to contribute to prosperity and economic development.[59] Each company cannot address all of society's ills but can focus on those that are most related to its businesses and those for which each firm has the greatest potential to address effectively.[60] The virtuous circle positions social responsibility activities to encourage innovation and competitive advantage if businesses incorporate social responsibility into their daily operations and view it as an opportunity rather than as "damage control."

To date, four rationales have been used to describe why social responsibility is important to businesses:

- The moral obligation to do the right thing
- Sustainability, which encourages businesses to strive for long-term decision making aimed at maximizing economic, social, and environmental performance
- Targeting social responsibility efforts at social issues that matter most to a business's stakeholders
- Reputation or pleasing external constituencies[61]

Unfortunately, these rationales often result in initiatives that are not always related to the business's overall strategy and that do not necessarily form cohesive social responsibility programs that have effective impacts on society and the business's competitiveness.

Expanding on these rationales, Porter and Kramer propose a framework that encourages the identification of values shared by society and business and building programs of social responsibility shaped by those shared values.[62] Although values are the foundation for building a business plan for social responsibility, values are also fundamental to ethical decision making on the part of individuals. Company-based initiatives directed at social responsibility can be successful only if the individuals in the organization are committed to ethical decision making on a daily basis. The steps to building social responsibility programs include (1) identifying social issues that may be important to society but are not within the realm of influence of the business (shared values), (2) social issues that are influenced by business decisions (value chain social impacts), and (3) factors that are critical to competitiveness for the section of the supply chain in which the business functions (social dimensions of competitive context). Through this categorization process, managers can identify best practices within their realm of influence to elicit social impacts and at the same time develop strategies that are unique (e.g., lowering costs or offering unique products) and provide competitive advantage. Businesses develop an integrated and proactive plan for social responsibility that is effective in generating positive social *and* economic outcomes.

Nike provides one example of how a company can address factors critical to society and competitiveness in pursuit of social responsibility. Over a decade, Nike invested in research and development aimed at decreasing the amount of organic solvents (e.g., glues, primers, cleaners) used in the manufacture of footwear. The company has realized a 90 percent reduction of use of the petroleum-based chemical solvent, replacing it with a more environmentally friendly, water-based chemical. The move made sense to Nike in many ways. For workers, the reduced amount of solvent made it safer to assemble the footwear. Impacts on the environment were lessened as there were fewer chemicals that had to be disposed of. It was good for the company because of cost reductions from the amount of solvent used.[63]

◉

The Challenge That Lies Ahead

In this chapter we have explored various cultural, economic, and political influences on social responsibility. We have examined ways in which the diversity in these dimensions across countries, businesses, and individuals complicates the process of addressing social responsibility in the global apparel industry. Yet at the same time, we have discovered that the outcome of competition in the global apparel industry does not have to be a generation of winners and losers. Rather, there is potential for virtuous circles of collaboration linking not only members of the supply chain but also cultures, economies, and governments such that all may benefit from a socially responsible industry.

Governments can collaborate, using international trading standards to develop and sustain socially responsible practices. Countries of varying levels of economic development and traditions can all be winners by embracing international labor standards, enforcing labor laws, and encouraging business practices that foster social responsibility and a "race to the top." In fact, without government involvement, there are real limits to what apparel brands and retailers can accomplish with their social responsibility programs. Businesses can play a valuable role to improve social responsibility by ensuring employees are culturally literate, understanding the mix of cultures found in countries and even in factories where garments are produced. As well, apparel brands and retailers can foster organizational cultures that are supportive of socially responsible practices. Finally, businesses can design social responsibility programs that are based on shared values and make sense to their core missions. Working cross-culturally and collaboratively, governments and businesses can create a socially responsible global apparel industry.

Chapter 4

Stakeholder Theory
and Social Responsibility

◉

In the late 1800s in New York, a progressive era of reform focused
on protection for consumers and workers and supported trade unionism and the vote for women. It was led by radical immigrants living
in the Lower East Side of Manhattan who shared an ideology that
favored the community and social justice for groups rather than individual rights.[1] In solidarity with the women workers, middle-class
women were also involved in the reform efforts.[2]

The middle-class women who were involved aligned with a pressure group called the National Consumers League of New York that
had been formed in 1891. The group appealed to consumers to demand
products made under safe working conditions and strived for legislation that would make sweatshops illegal (Figure 4.1). The group developed a garment label called the "white label" that factories voluntarily
working to ensure good factory conditions could sew into their garments to spread information among consumers.[3]

PAMPHLET No. 84

FEB. 6 1909

Soc 1580.7.5

(Box on sh)

National Child Labor Committee

INCORPORATED

105 EAST 22D STREET

NEW YORK CITY

CHILDREN WHO WORK IN THE TENEMENTS

LITTLE LABORERS
UNPROTECTED BY CHILD LABOR LAW

NO SATURDAY PLAY-TIME FOR THIS SEVEN-YEAR-OLD SCHOOL-BOY.

AS SHOWN BY PHOTOGRAPHS TAKEN BY

CONSUMERS' LEAGUE, N. Y. CITY

NEW YORK CHILD LABOR COMMITTEE

NATIONAL CHILD LABOR COMMITTEE

FOR THE

Exhibit of Congestion of Population of New York City

MARCH, 1908

Figure 4.1

Example of work done by the National Consumers League.

Despite the highly corrupt nature of local politicians in New York at the time, with bribes a usual way of conducting business,[4] the social reformers of the Progressive Era enjoyed many successes. The New York Women's Trade Union League was founded.[5] Membership in the International Ladies Garment Workers' Union (ILGWU) grew to tens of thousands in the period between 1909 and 1913.[6] Specifically, the local unit of the ILGWU representing 500 members at its inception grew to 20,000 within the course of a few months in 1909.[7]

Major strikes in 1909 and 1910 led to some changes in apparel factories. After a strike of women garment workers in 1909, small- and medium-sized garment-making shops settled with the union, promising to no longer charge for needles, thread, and electricity and recognizing the right for committees to negotiate the piece rates they paid.[8] A strike in 1910 by New York City's cloakmakers (primarily men making men's outer garments) ended with the "Protocol of Peace," which regulated production to take place in more factorylike settings instead of small shops and homes. The Protocol of Peace solidified an alliance between labor and trade unionists and Progressive Era reform groups.[9] It standardized wages, hours, and working conditions across all shops, regardless of size.[10]

But the safety precautions that had been campaigned for in the strikes of 1909 and 1910 were not completely implemented and would not be addressed until the horror of the Triangle Waist Company factory fire of 1911 forced more fundamental reform involving government (Box 4.1). The fire came at the "crucial moment in a chain of events—a chain that ultimately forced fundamental reforms from the political machinery of New York, and, after New York, the whole nation."[11]

The media played an important role in reform immediately after the fire. The *New York Times* and the *World* ran front-page stories speculating on the causes of the fire—particularly focusing on whether doors were knowingly locked while the workers were inside the factory. William Randolph Hearst's paper, the *American*, day after day devoted pages to attacks on the building codes and the bureaucrats who drafted them. The paper repeatedly called for creation of new laws drafted by a panel of experts that would increase safety in factories. No doubt, the

Box 4.1. 141 Men and Girls Die in Waist Factory Fire; Trapped High Up in Washington Place Building; Street Strewn with Bodies; Piles of Dead Inside

Three stories of a ten-floor building at the corner of Greene Street and Washington Place were burned yesterday, and while the fire was going on 141 young men and women at least 125 of them mere girls were burned to death or killed by jumping to the pavement below.

The building was fireproof. It shows now hardly any signs of the disaster that overtook it. The walls are as good as ever so are the floors, nothing is the worse for the fire except the furniture and 141 of the 600 men and girls that were employed in its upper three stories.

Most of the victims were suffocated or burned to death within the building, but some who fought their way to the windows and leaped met death as surely, but perhaps more quickly, on the pavements below.

All Over in Half an Hour. Nothing like it has been seen in New York since the burning of the General Slocum. The fire was practically all over in half an hour. It was confined to three floors the eighth, ninth, and tenth of the building. But it was the most murderous fire that New York had seen in many years.

The victims who are now lying at the Morgue waiting for some one to identify them by a tooth or the remains of a burned shoe were mostly girls from 16 to 23 years of age. They were employed at making shirtwaist by the Triangle Waist Company, the principal owners of which are Isaac Harris and Max Blanck. Most of them could barely speak English. Many of them came from Brooklyn. Almost all were the main support of their hard-working families.

There is just one fire escape in the building. That one is an interior fire escape. In Greene Street, where the terrified unfortunates crowded before they began to make their mad leaps to death, the whole big front of the building is guiltless of one. Nor is there a fire escape in the back.

The building was fireproof and the owners had put their trust in that. In fact, after the flames had done their worst last night, the building hardly showed a sign. Only the stock within it and the girl employees were burned.

A heap of corpses lay on the sidewalk for more than an hour. The firemen were too busy dealing with the fire to pay any attention to people whom they supposed beyond their aid. When the excitement had subsided to such an extent that some of the firemen and policemen could pay attention to this mass of the supposedly dead they found about half way down in the pack a girl who was still breathing. She died two minutes after she was found.

The Triangle Waist Company was the only sufferer by the disaster. There are other concerns in the building, but it was Saturday and the other companies had let their people go home. Messrs. Harris and Blanck, however, were busy and [??] their girls and some stayed.

Leaped Out of the Flames. At 4:40 o'clock, nearly five hours after the employees in the rest of the building had gone home, the fire broke out. The one little fire escape in the interior was resorted to by any of the doomed victims. Some of them escaped by running down the stairs, but in a moment or two this avenue was cut off by flame. The girls rushed to the windows and looked down at Greene Street, 100 feet below them. Then one poor, little creature jumped. There was a plate glass protection over part of the sidewalk, but she crashed through it, wrecking it and breaking her body into a thousand pieces.

Then they all began to drop. The crowd yelled "Don't jump!" but it was jump or be burned the proof of which is found in the fact that fifty burned bodies were taken from the ninth floor alone.

They jumped, they crashed through broken glass, they crushed themselves to death on the sidewalk. Of those who stayed behind it is better to say nothing except what a veteran policeman said as he gazed at a headless and charred trunk on the Greene Street sidewalk hours after the worst cases had been taken out:

"I saw the Slocum disaster, but it was nothing to this." "Is it a man or a woman?" asked the reporter. "It's human, that's all you can tell," answered the policeman.

It was just a mass of ashes, with blood congealed on what had probably been the neck.

Messrs. Harris and Blanck were in the building, but they escaped. They carried with them Mr. Blanck's children and a governess, and they fled over the roofs. Their employees did not know the way, because they had been in the habit of using the two freight elevators, and one of these elevators was not in service when the fire broke out.

Found Alive after the Fire. The first living victim, Hyman Meshel of 322 East Fifteenth Street, was taken from the ruins four hours after the fire was discovered. He was found paralyzed with fear and whimpering like a wounded animal in the basement, immersed in water to his neck, crouched on the top of a cable drum and with his head just below the floor of the elevator.

Meantime the remains of the dead it is hardly possible to call them bodies, because that would suggest something human, and there was nothing human about most of these were being taken in a steady stream to the Morgue for identification. First Avenue was lined with the usual curious east side crowd. Twenty-sixth Street was impassable. But in the Morgue they received the charred remnants with no more emotion than they ever display over anything.

Back in Greene Street there was another crowd. At midnight it had not decreased in the least. The police were holding it back to the fire lines, and discussing the tragedy in a tone which those seasoned witnesses of death seldom use. "It's the worst thing I ever saw," said one old policeman.

Chief Croker said it was an outrage. He spoke bitterly of the way in which the Manufacturers' Association had called a meeting in Wall Street to take measures against his proposal for enforcing better methods of protection for employees in cases of fire.

No Chance to Save Victims. Four alarms were rung in fifteen minutes. The first five girls who jumped did go before the first engine could respond. That fact may not convey much of a picture to the mind of an unimaginative man, but anybody who has ever seen a fire can get from it some idea of the terrific rapidity with which the flames spread.

It may convey some idea too, to say that thirty bodies clogged the elevator shaft. These dead were all girls. They had made their rush their blindly when they discovered that there was no chance to get out by the fire escape. Then they found that the elevator was as hopeless as anything else, and they fell there in their tracks and died.

The Triangle Waist Company employed about 600 women and less than 100 men. One of the saddest features of the thing is the fact that they had almost finished for the day. In five minutes more, if the fire had started then, probably not a life would have been lost.

Last night District Attorney Whitman started an investigation not of this disaster alone but of the whole condition which makes it possible for a firetrap of such a kind to exist. Mr. Whitman's intention is to find out if the present laws cover such cases, and if they do not to frame laws that will.

All Would Soon Have Been Out. Strewn about as the firemen worked, the bodies indicated clearly the preponderance of women workers. Here and there was a man, but almost always they were women. One wore furs and a muss, and had a purse hanging from her arm. Nearly all were dressed for the street. The fire had flashed through their workroom just as they were expecting the signal to leave the building. In ten minutes more all would have been out, as many had stopped work in advance of the signal and had started to put on their wraps.

What happened inside there were few who could tell with any definiteness. All that those escaped seemed to remember was that there was a flash of flames, leaping first among the girls in the southeast corner of the eighth floor and then suddenly over the entire room, spreading through the linens and cottons with which the girls were working. The girls on the ninth floor caught sight of the flames through the window up the stairway, and up the elevator shaft.

On the tenth floor they got them a moment later, but most of those on that floor escaped by rushing to the roof and then on to the roof of the New York University Building, with the assistance of 100 university students who had been dismissed from a tenth story classroom.

There were in the building, according to the estimate of Fire Chief Croker, about 600 girls and 100 men.

Article reproduced as is. SOURCE: 141 Men and Girls Die in Waist Factory Fire. (1911, March 26). New York Times, p. 1. Obtained from www.ilr.cornell.edu/trianglefire/texts/newspaper/nyt_032611_5.html.

extensive media coverage fueled the community of citizens who asserted themselves in strikes and labor rallies and at the polls. A funeral march after the fire brought out 350,000 people, who either marched on the streets or watched in solidarity from the sidewalks. The city was clothed in black mourning dress (Figure 4.2). But just one month after the fire, newspapers were losing interest in the story.

Social reformers continued to expand their efforts after the fire. The executive secretary of the National Consumers League, Frances

Figure 4.2

Protesters marched in the streets of New York after the Triangle Waist Company factory fire.

Perkins, had seen the fire firsthand and led efforts to collect social science research data that would be used to support reform. Many researchers and social workers joined in this and related efforts. Listed as influential to labor reform were "the socialist writers and lecturers, the progressive millionaires and college students, and researchers and settlement house workers."[12]

Labor unions also expanded their efforts after the fire. The Women's Trade Union League argued that the public and its elected officials had failed the workers who perished in the fire and the many union employees who continued to work in dangerous factories. Picketing shop workers were influential to local politics, as were union leaders.

Among various government groups, initially there was considerable shifting of and denying blame for the fire. New York's governor claimed he was powerless; New York City's mayor referred questions to the state's labor commissioner, who referred questions to the city department in charge of building. Finally, a Joint Board of Sanitary Control was initiated and supported by the unions. The board was comprised of multiple stakeholders, including those representing unions and manufacturers, and they monitored working conditions in factories.

A multi-stakeholder Committee on Safety went to the state capital in Albany to lobby the politicians for reform. They proposed their role to be studying factory conditions and proposing new laws to present to politicians. However, astute politicians helped them understand the need to include politicians throughout the process and to establish a committee of legislators that would take on the task of labor reform. This was known as the Factory Investigating Committee.[13] The group visited factories, held hearings, and subpoenaed witnesses (Figure 4.3). Al Smith, a New York legislator who would later become governor, helped the very progressive social reform legislation work through the system.[14] By 1913, a series of new laws had been passed and a newly re-organized Department of Labor was charged with enforcement. David Von Drehle credits the group with producing "a new model for worker safety in American mills and workshops."[15] Over time, local politicians came to understand and value the needs and influence of their own stakeholders who could be either supporters or not when it came time to vote.

Figure 4.3

The Factory Investigation Committee found machinery blocking a fire escape outside the windows on the left in a men's underwear factory.

The New Deal era under Franklin Roosevelt, which commenced in 1933, expanded the role of government by creating legislation on labor standards.[16] Frances Perkins, who had led the National Consumers League, became the first female Secretary of Labor under President Roosevelt.[17] The National Labor Relations Act of 1933 was the first effort to create a national labor code developed by a tripartite group representing industry, government, and labor.[18] The National Labor Relations Act, also known as the Wagner Act after New York's Senator Robert Wagner, established the right to join a union and engage in collective bargaining.[19]

The passage in 1938 of the Fair Labor Standards Act was able to create national labor standards because it dealt with interstate commerce.[20] The Fair Labor Standards Act legislated the minimum wage that was allowable (25 cents at the time), set the maximum workweek at 44 hours, required that time and one-half pay be given for work beyond the standard hours, and banned products of child labor from interstate commerce.[21]

As you can see from the aftermath of the Triangle Waist Company factory fire, social responsibility is dependent on the involvement of a multitude of stakeholders. Stakeholder theory explains how various groups are benefited or hurt by the actions of companies and why those groups must be taken into consideration when business decisions are made.

Although stakeholder theory has emerged only over the last two or three decades, history shows that stakeholder groups historically played a role in improving working conditions. The Triangle Waist Company factory fire in 1911 and social actions during the periods that preceded and followed it illustrate various ways that ordinary citizens, elected officials, union leaders, and other stakeholder groups worked together to ensure greater protection for workers. The international nature of global apparel supply chains makes the situation a little different now, because national boundaries have historically limited efforts to regulate and reform the workplace and efforts by workers to resist exploitation.[22] Nonetheless, examination of how stakeholder groups worked together early in the twentieth century provides us with ideas for collaborations that can be pursued in the present.

◉

Stakeholder Theory

Stakeholder theory accounts for the influence diverse groups have on business and how business influences various stakeholder groups. Stakeholder management and stakeholder engagement are activities addressed in stakeholder theory. Stakeholder theory is often contrasted with a theory of management that focuses on maximizing the value of the firm and that considers shareholders the primary group of concern. That theory is exemplified by the statement by Milton Friedman in 1970 that "there is one and only one social responsibility of business—to use its resources and engage in activities designed to increase its profits . . ."[23] R. Edward Freeman, Andrew Wicks, and Bidhan Parmer express concern with this theory of management, explaining that "at the worst, it involves using the prima facie rights claims of one group—shareholders—to excuse violating the rights of others."[24] They argue that business perspectives focused solely on shareholders foster tunnel vision whereby management sees itself as responsible to only one group. Their preference is to maintain a stakeholder perspective for socially responsible business management rather than a shareholder perspective, fearing that "a view that places morality largely out of the conversation, and that reduces managerial responsibility to making money, is more likely to foster unethical behavior."[25]

Archie Carroll also makes the case for a link between social responsibility and stakeholder theory, arguing that the stakeholder concept "personalizes social or societal responsibilities by delineating the specific groups or persons business should consider in its CSR [corporate social responsibility] orientation and activities. Thus, the stakeholder nomenclature puts 'names and faces' on the societal members or groups who are most important to business and to whom it must be responsive."[26] From a stakeholder theory perspective, corporations cannot think only about shareholders and their profits, but instead must consider the wide-ranging needs of a variety of groups with a stake in their business. In the early twentieth century, when the Triangle Waist Company factory fire took place, apparel factory management seemed to have had the needs of the company owners in mind, but not those of a broader range of stakeholders, such as workers, consumers, and the community.

R. Edward Freeman is credited as being the first business scholar to introduce stakeholder theory and the idea that a wide variety of stakeholders should be considered in managing corporations.[27] Stakeholders are viewed as having cooperative and competitive interests and as possessing intrinsic value, thus meriting consideration in management decisions. The theory focuses on two core questions to guide businesses: "What is the purpose of the firm?" and "What responsibility does management have to stakeholders?"[28] The theory provides guidance for business management in that it "recommends attitudes, structures, and practices that, taken together, constitute stakeholder management."[29]

Stakeholder theory pushes managers to clearly articulate and value the relationships they have with their stakeholders.[30] Max Clarkson explains the importance of achieving this clarity, stressing that "if any primary group perceives, over time, that it is not being treated fairly or adequately, whether it is the employee, customer, or a shareholder group, it will seek alternatives and may ultimately withdraw from that firm's stakeholder system."[31] Withdrawal of key stakeholder groups from the firm's activities can put business at risk of failure. In the early twentieth century, workers and other stakeholders sought alternatives to the exploitative conditions they faced in apparel factories. These stakeholders chose to be out of work on a strike, with hopes of changing conditions for the long run. The examples provided with the historical account of stakeholder action around this fire reflect how dialogue and partnership with stakeholders can both prevent negative occurrences and also correct or manage crises.

Thomas Donaldson and Lee Preston maintain that the greatest value of stakeholder theory is that it provides normative guidance on the firm's moral responsibility to its stakeholders through its corporate management and operation.[32] Stakeholder theory helps answer questions related to global processes and appropriate end products—specifically, "Socially responsible to whom?" and "Social performance judged by whom and by what standards?"[33] Had owners of apparel factories of the early twentieth century given thought to these questions, perhaps they could have addressed the labor and health and safety problems of that era before tragedy occurred.

Who Are the Stakeholder Groups?

What groups should apparel brands and retailers consider as stakeholders? Donaldson and Preston describe stakeholders as "persons or groups with legitimate interests in procedural and/or substantive aspects of corporate activity."[34] Similarly, Clarkson defines stakeholders as "persons or groups that have, or claim, ownership, rights, or interests in a corporation and its activities, past, present, or future."[35]

The terms "primary" and "secondary" are often used to refer to groups of stakeholders with differing relationships or closeness to the business. Clarkson defines primary stakeholders as groups "without whose continuing participation the corporation cannot survive,"[36] such as investors, suppliers, customers, employees, governments, political groups, trade associations, and communities.[37] Had the white label of the National Consumers League of New York thoroughly reflected consumer demands, apparel factories of the early twentieth century that exploited workers might have faced lost sales to competitors that attended to workers' needs.

In addition to primary stakeholders, Clarkson defines secondary stakeholder groups as "those who influence or affect, or are influenced or affected by, the corporation, but they are not engaged in transactions with the corporation and are not essential for its survival."[38] Secondary stakeholders include competitors and the media. New York newspapers filing stories about the Triangle Waist Company factory fire helped mobilize support of community leaders, middle-class citizens, and other stakeholders in efforts to improve working conditions in early-twentieth-century apparel factories.

Although the primary and secondary system of categorization is useful, it is more effective to consider the importance of stakeholder groups as they relate to the social responsibility issues the company is addressing. The U.K.-based organization AccountAbility suggests six criteria for identifying a company's stakeholders, including responsibility, influence, proximity, dependency, representation, and policy and strategic intent.[39] Using the criteria provided by AccountAbility, apparel brands and retailers can consider which groups are stakeholders for such social responsibility issues as labor compliance and environmental sustainability. Let's examine each of the six categories listed above, considering stakeholder groups that were active in the early twentieth century. Keep in mind that groups might be considered as stakeholders for two or more criteria.

Responsibility Stakeholder Groups

Companies have, or in the future may have, financial, legal, or operational responsibilities resulting from regulations, contracts, policies, or codes of conduct with stakeholder groups. In the Triangle Waist Company factory fire, workers were a group for whom apparel factory owners had responsibility. They owed safe working conditions to those workers who came to the factories and made the products the company sold. Currently, apparel brands and retailers enter into contractual arrangements with suppliers who want continued business. Thus, whether they source their products from one factory or 3,000, these suppliers represent a stakeholder category. Although workers assembling apparel or footwear for contractors are not directly employed by apparel brands and retailers, they are covered by the companies' codes of conducts and thus are stakeholders. Apparel brands and retailers could not survive without these workers, who are willing to work day in and day out to manufacture their products.

Influence Stakeholder Groups

Influence stakeholders are groups that have influence or decision-making power. Certainly shareholders are stakeholders because of the influence they have over company policies, corporate governance, and funding—if the company does not achieve certain, usually financial, goals, the leadership is often changed, and some shareholders may divest from the company. Legal authorities influence the company. Pressure groups that campaign for consumers to engage with certain brands or retailers on issues also influence company decisions. Historically, the National Consumers League has applied pressure on apparel manufacturers who treated their assembly workers poorly. The media is another influence stakeholder group that often works in tandem with the various pressure groups to highlight the problems found in factories and the lack of responsibility among apparel brands and retailers.

Proximity Stakeholder Groups

Proximity stakeholders interact most frequently with companies and include internal stakeholders such as management, outsourced employees, local communities, and long-standing business partners. Companies depend daily on these stakeholders who craft regulations and provide supplies and necessary infrastructure. Communities and governments provide companies with incentives to locate their businesses in the community and define the regulatory environment in which the company operates. Communities also provide a base of employees in the area. Communities and governments expect benefits in return for the incentives they provide companies, including tax revenue and philanthropic and employee volunteer contributions to the greater needs of the community's people. After the Triangle Waist Company factory fire, the government of New York was a key partner in passing legislation that would help reform conditions in the workplace.

Dependency Stakeholder Groups

Some stakeholder groups are economically dependent, either directly or indirectly, on a company's activities. This type of dependency is seen when a company is the only employer in a community or is the sole purchaser of a stakeholder's goods. Large communities of immigrants residing in the Lower East Side of Manhattan in the early twentieth century were dependent on apparel factory owners who provided work for the low-skilled masses. As policies for world trade evolved over the last decade and resulted in ever-mobile off-shore production, the dependence of some communities and even countries on the production business provided to them by apparel brands and retailers was again apparent. One need not look any further than communities in North Carolina, Texas, and others across the United States that were devastated as U.S.-based manufacturers shuttered their factories and began outsourcing production around the world.

Representation Stakeholder Groups

Representation stakeholder groups, such as trade union representatives or local community leaders, represent those people or things that cannot adequately represent themselves because they lack voice or a place at the table where decisions are made. In the early twentieth century, newly formed labor unions were extremely influential because they represented workers in negotiations that increased worker wages, eliminated at least some exploitative practices, and required somewhat safer factories. Currently, there are many countries producing apparel where labor unions are either illegal or suppressed. This creates tremendous problems for many young women workers, who, because of their age, lack of experience, and lack of alternative work, often are unaware of their rights as workers and are powerless to influence the conditions under which they work.

Policy and Strategy Stakeholder Groups

Policy and strategy stakeholders are addressed directly or indirectly by companies through their policies and values and can include consumers and local communities. This category of stakeholder also includes activists, academics, and civil society representatives who can provide warning of emerging issues that may present risks to the company. Academic researchers who focus on the issues that a company is attempting to manage are policy and strategy stakeholder groups. In the early twentieth century, academic researchers collected valuable data about working conditions that was then used by policy makers and other stakeholders to craft labor reform legislation. Today the same is true, and researchers are looked to by policy makers for greater understanding of the issues and approaches to potential policies. We now turn to the details of carrying out stakeholder engagement and stakeholder management, bringing in present-day examples to show the current value of stakeholder theory.

◉

Stakeholder Engagement:
Prioritizing Diverse and Conflicting Needs

With all the varied stakeholders associated with apparel production and sourcing, it is not surprising that their needs sometimes conflict. Simply knowing that a wide array of groups have a stake in the business does not provide guidance for the relative importance that should be placed on each of their needs.[40] Stakeholder management can require expending significant company resources, especially when the issues a stakeholder group raises threaten the organization's viability.[41] Donaldson and Preston contend that "the ultimate managerial implication of the stakeholder theory is that managers should acknowledge the validity of diverse stakeholder interests and should attempt to respond to them within a mutually supportive framework."[42] Businesses need to consult with stakeholders in order to gather important information, manage conflicts, improve decision making, build consensus across groups with diverse views, and enhance corporate reputation.[43] Stakeholder engagement provides systems for companies to assess the views of diverse stakeholder groups and respond to their needs. We can begin to understand what stakeholder engagement is by reviewing Box 4.2, which includes text from the adidas Group's annual sustainability report that describes the types of activities that apparel brand carries out with stakeholder engagement.

Box 4.2. Excerpt from adidas Group Sustainability Report on Stakeholder Engagement

Our stakeholders include:

Employees of the adidas Group

Authorizers government, trade associations, shareholders, Board of Directors

Business partners unions, suppliers, workers, service providers

Opinion formers journalists, community members, special interest groups

Customers professional sports people, distributors, retailers, consumers

For many stakeholders, the credibility of our CSR programme rests on two critical elements: our transparency as an organisation and our accountability as a transnational corporation.

We believe that clear, effective and honest communications are the hallmarks of transparency and this is best achieved through active stakeholder engagement and through a public reporting process.

Accountability is about acting on the feedback of our stakeholders: using what is shared with us to make informed choices, and being accountable for the outcomes, and impacts, of our business decisions. . . .

Efforts at Transparency In 2004, we reported on the way our relationships with several critical stakeholders are maturing. In 2005, we continued in our efforts to reach

---

new levels of understanding and transparency, through closer engagement with key stakeholders, in particular unions, and by sharing information on our supply chain. These efforts included:

- Ongoing dialogue and meetings, facilitated by the ILO, with the Play Fair at the Olympics campaigners (OXFAM, the Clean Clothes Campaign and international trade unions).
- Participation in a pilot project to promote two-way communication between employees and management in Romania. Other participants included international brands, German trade unions, international and local NGOs and organisations. . . .
- Participation in a panel discussion and conference which dealt with the topic of worker-management communication and freedom of association. The Frankfurt conference was facilitated by the Clean Clothes Campaign and hosted by the German Union IG Metall, an affiliate of the International Textile Garment and Leather Workers Federation (ITGLWF).
- The execution of an agreement with the University of Wisconsin's administration to audit and evaluate SEA monitoring records for factories that make licensed products.
- Engagements for labour rights training and clarification of local compliance issues with ministries of labour, government agencies, and trade associations in Guatemala, Honduras and El Salvador.
- Engagement with El Salvador NGOs, unions and government agencies to resolve issues with the non-payment of severance compensation to the former employees of Hermosa Manufacturing.
- The completion of a year long project with the local NGO GMIES to monitor water potability at the Chi Fung factory in El Salvador. . . .
- Participation in an ILO training programme with trade union federations in Asia, to openly discuss the impacts of the end of the MFA on our supply chain. . . .

SOURCE: adidas Group (2005). *2005 Social & environmental report—Connected with football*. Available at www.adidas-group.com/en/sustainability/reporting/reports_to_download/default.asp.

Engaging with stakeholders leads to organizational excellence by providing companies with the opportunity:

- To learn and understand the needs and perceptions of their stakeholders
- To innovate on the basis of stakeholders' knowledge and insights
- To develop performance measures allowing stakeholders to assess the company's progress[44]

Cate Gable and Bill Shireman provide a guide to stakeholder engagement. The steps they propose represent an ideal case for companies wanting to fully engage with stakeholders. Apparel brands and retailers just getting started with stakeholder engagement may need to proceed in more modest ways. The methods Gable and Shireman outline were developed with and are utilized by members of a non-profit network named The Future 500, for which they serve as senior consultant and president, respectively.[45] The Future 500 includes professionals from businesses and organizations in the Americas, Europe, and Asia who share knowledge and ideas about implementing stakeholder engagement. Their three-phase method for stakeholder engagement includes an internal preparation phase wherein a leader for the process is identified, a stakeholder team is formed, and the company's performance and stakeholders' perceptions of performance are measured. In a second phase, stakeholders are inventoried and mapped in relation to business objectives and the results are used to develop a plan for engagement. The third phase is when the actual engagement occurs and results are measured and communicated. We will examine each of these phases in more detail, supplementing Gable and Shireman's ideas with those of other organizations and academics.

Phase 1 of Stakeholder Engagement: Initial Preparation

In the internal preparation phase, the company chooses a leader for the stakeholder engagement initiative. The leader is someone skilled in conflict negotiation and able to speak honestly, delivering bad news if necessary. The person is able to see the nuances in issues and perspectives. The leader needs to have an intimate understanding of the business, be well respected by managers across the firm, and be well connected within the company leadership, especially with the chief executive officer. The stakeholder engagement team involves representatives from across the company.

As an initial activity, the stakeholder engagement team establishes a baseline of the company's performance and how the company is perceived. Actual performance and perceived performance will not always match. For example, an apparel brand or retailer may have a procedure on fair labor and do a pretty good job of complying with most components of that procedure; however, they may not communicate the procedures or results to the public. Communication is a critical aspect of stakeholder engagement, and Gable and Shireman warn that "for purposes of measuring public perception, the key question is: Who knows that you have this procedure in place?"[46] A company must be ready to provide credible measures of performance, even if stakeholders perceive the company is doing a good job, or it risks being exposed when stakeholder engagement ensues.

Company performance can be assessed against various standards, including the ILO conventions, local laws, the UN Declaration of Human Rights, Global Compact principles, the Global Reporting Initiative (which has specific guidelines for the apparel and footwear sector), and others. A company's code of conduct also provides a relevant set of benchmarks against which to measure performance. The company measures the extent to which it achieves the standards it has adopted.

Key opinion leaders provide feedback and initial assessment of the company's performance. Shareholders, company executives and suppliers from the workplace, local government and NGO representatives from the community, consumers, and advocacy leaders for labor rights groups are relevant parties for apparel brands and retailers to survey. The initial survey of stakeholder groups rates how the company is doing (from negative to positive) from their perspectives. These ratings are then mapped against each group's ability to influence the business (low to high), such as shown in Figure 4.4. In this figure, stakeholder group C has relatively negative (low) perceptions of the company but somewhat high ability to influence the company's business. The company would want to reach out to this group in order to understand how it might improve in the eyes of its members. As an example, if Wal-Mart were to map the company's stakeholders, the company might map the International Labor Rights Forum in the lower right quadrant because the activist organization has low or negative perceptions of the retailer and relatively high ability to affect the business, as evidenced by an ongoing lawsuit against Wal-Mart for labor abuses.

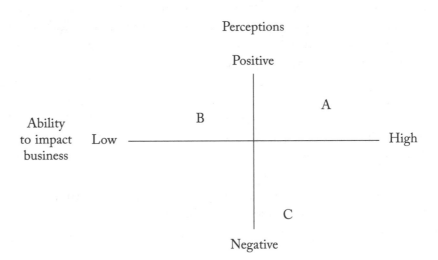

Figure 4.4

Map of stakeholder perceptions and influence.

Simone De Colle suggests a similar type of map that can be used to prioritize which stakeholders are engaged.[47] The grid depicted in Figure 4.5 considers the power the stakeholder holds over the company and interest in the company's activities. The resulting grid displays where the greatest attention needs to be paid. Edith Weiner and Arnold Brown provide ideas for how to rate a stakeholder group's power by considering its:

- Access to media
- Access to government
- Importance to the company's ability to profit or survive
- Authority to determine decisions made by the company
- History of successful court challenges on this/similar issues[48]

For each stakeholder, each of the five factors can be rated from 1 (little to no influence) to 5 (high influence) and added together for a total score.

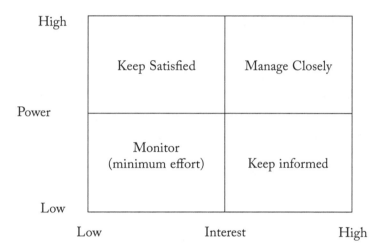

Figure 4.5
Grid for prioritizing stakeholder needs.

An example based on the grid in Figure 4.5 for apparel brands and retailers is the Educators for Socially Responsible Apparel Business, a group of professors teaching in apparel design and fashion merchandising. Because of their high interest in topics of social responsibility and their role in educating future industry professionals, the group is considered a stakeholder by apparel brands and retailers. The group's current relative low power could increase in the future if it mobilizes talented students to prioritize employment with certain responsible companies, though it does not yet have a history of this type of action.

On the other hand, many apparel brands consider the activist organization the Clean Clothes Campaign to be a stakeholder group with relatively high power due to its ability to organize consumers against companies. The organization also maintains a high interest in labor problems in global apparel supply chains. Thus, executives charged with social responsibility for apparel brands spend considerable time engaging with this group's leaders, hoping that by collaborating on the issues, a campaign against the company can be prevented. As well, when a crisis ensues, they may consult with the organization on how to appropriately manage the crisis.

Another consideration when determining which stakeholders to engage with is their proximity to the issues. Even NGOs, which might be thought to agree on issues, may have conflicting views dependent on whether they are grassroots groups located in a country of production or are based in a developed country.

About what issues should companies engage with their stakeholders? AccountAbility recommends that companies engage with stakeholders on "material issues" that can influence the decisions and actions of both stakeholders and the companies.[49] These might include the apparel brand or retailer's compliance to a code of conduct for labor standards or whether and how living wages might be paid to workers.

Phase 2 of Stakeholder Engagement:
Stakeholder Mapping and Strategic Planning

Once a company has worked through the internal aspects of stakeholder engagement, it is ready to move into the second phase of stakeholder engagement. In the Stakeholder Mapping and Strategic Planning phase, the company develops a plan for how it will actually engage with stakeholders.

Future 500 has developed a several-step process for this mapping and planning phase that ties stakeholder engagement activities with business objectives that stakeholders can contribute to if effectively engaged.[50] Initially, the universe of stakeholders must be defined, including their type and geographic location. This can involve a few hundred different groups that might be the type that influences regulations restricting or supporting the company's work, or the type that influences the market, such as the media or consumer pressure groups that work to expand consumer awareness about issues. Another type of stakeholder that might be included is groups that are influential to an apparel company's core business, including suppliers, competitors, and shareholders. In the case of apparel brands and retailers, stakeholder groups are likely to be geographically dispersed. Each stakeholder group is categorized by the extent it can influence business objectives as shown in Figures 4.4 and 4.5. As the database of stakeholders and a stakeholder map are created, thought is given to how the various stakeholder groups interact for greater influence.[51] This idea recognizes that the power of any one stakeholder group can advance considerably when stakeholder groups collaborate.

Once the stakeholders are identified and mapped, the company can define how it will engage with each group. Business for Social Responsibility (BSR) reminds us of the necessity for companies to be ready to *respond*, not just to *listen*, to their stakeholders. The organization suggest that companies ask, "Are we doing this because we genuinely feel stakeholders have something to contribute or is it because we feel we should and think it will be good for our image?"[52] For example, some stakeholders may desire that the company spend considerable time and effort to collaborate with them, whereas others may just want to be informed. Modes of stakeholder engagement generally range from limited interaction to joint collaboration. Projects for stakeholder engagement are planned and prioritized. As a result of the mapping and planning process, stakeholder groups are identified and their relationships are understood, and the role they play in influencing how the business operates is defined. The most appropriate ways to engage with each group in relation to the company's business objectives are then determined.[53]

Phase 3 of Stakeholder Engagement: Execution of the Plan

The third phase of stakeholder engagement encompasses the actual execution of plans. A relatively friendly representative of a stakeholder group is chosen for first contact, and potential areas of common ground are explored. Building relationships with key stakeholder groups takes time and expectations should start small. Although this advice may be very difficult for some companies to embrace, Gable and Shireman promote three effective tactics for stakeholder engagement:

1. Acknowledging the company's faults
2. Apologizing
3. Attributing the positive impacts the stakeholder group has had on the company[54]

This level of stakeholder engagement may make companies uncomfortable because it requires an openness and collaboration to which many are unaccustomed. But this openness and collaboration has the potential of finding common ground with a critical stakeholder group.[55] At the same time, however, stakeholders must understand that it falls to companies to make final decisions on how they will respond to stakeholder requests. Not every stakeholder will be accommodated on every demand. Most companies have limits to what they are willing and able to do.

The adidas Group provides detailed reports of stakeholder engagements conducted by the company's Social and Environmental Affairs program. For example, a June 2005 dialogue focused on developing strategies for training workers on topics such as occupational health and safety and worker representation. The stakeholder dialogue was held at the adidas Group sourcing office in Guangzhou, China, and included representatives from NGOs in mainland China and Hong Kong. An outcome of the stakeholder engagement was a comprehensive action plan for implementing the training [56]

Communication with stakeholders is important in terms of social responsibility and activists because it can be a means for preventing conflict.[57] As stakeholder engagement unfolds, internal reports are used to assess progress. Companies can also consider public reporting of progress made against the standards set with inclusion of how stakeholders were involved. Public reporting allows the company to demonstrate to its stakeholders that the company "walks the talk."[58] The Global Reporting Initiative (GRI) provides considerable detail about what should be included in a social responsibility or sustainability report. The organization's new supplement for the apparel sector provides specific guidelines appropriate for use by brands and retailers. The GRI apparel sector supplement is a comprehensive set of guidelines divided into five areas (economic, environment, social, business integration, and code of conduct) with 50 items suggested for reporting.[59]

How Stakeholders Judge Social Responsibility

To show that the needs of various stakeholder groups are being met, it is important to provide information through monitoring devices and public reporting and enforcement mechanisms. Having a code of conduct reflects that a company is aware of some of its responsibilities; however, its presence does not indicate whether the code has been implemented. Clarkson stresses the importance of presenting performance data that reflect "what the company is actually doing or has done with reference to specific issues . . . If data about an issue are not available, that fact in itself is important in evaluating a company's strategy or posture. When no data are available, that issue is not being managed. . . . Performance data are available whenever a particular stakeholder issue is considered by a company to be of sufficient importance to justify being managed."[60]

Several apparel brands and retailers have been especially transparent about their labor compliance programs for social responsibility. The adidas Group, Nike, Gap, and a few others publish comprehensive social responsibility reports on their corporate Web sites.[61] The reports detail the problems they are finding in their factories around the world and the efforts the companies are making to solve the problems. In addition to those special company-issued reports, companies that are members of the multi-stakeholder initiative the Fair Labor Association, including the adidas Group, Nike, Puma, Nordstrom, Liz

Claiborne, Patagonia, Phillips-Van Heusen, and others, allow the organization to publish actual findings for specific factories it has monitored. Although not going so far as to name the factories, the reports list details about the problems found and how each compliance breach has been corrected.[62] These reports can be a little disturbing to read when you realize even the companies that are taking the lead in terms of social responsibility continue to find numerous gaps in compliance with their codes of conduct. But the greater worry are the companies that are not reporting this type of information—either they do not know what is happening in their factories or have nothing to report about how they are solving the problems. The working conditions in factories producing for less transparent apparel brands and retailers are unlikely to be better than those found in factories where companies are working with factory management to improve conditions. Brands and retailers working together as an industry to continuously improve conditions in factories will eventually achieve compliance aligned with the rights of workers.

Beyond performance on issues of social responsibility, Clarkson proposes "posture" as a means for evaluating the level of responsibility a company demonstrates. Companies decide how they are going to respond to stakeholder and social issues and can be judged on their performance. In his Reactive-Defensive-Accommodative-Proactive (RDAP) Scale, Clarkson links denial or acceptance of responsibility and the extent that the company does what is required by its stakeholders (Table 4.1). What is required may be determined by law or by a company itself when it adopts a code indicating the company accepts its responsibilities to certain stakeholder groups.

The concrete risks to a company behaving in reactive versus proactive ways lies in the heavy fines that may be imposed when existing local, national, or international labor or environmental regulations are broken. To apparel brands and retailers, however, even when laws are not broken, companies found to be reactive or defensive in their response to stakeholder needs run the risk of long-term reputational damage to their brands.[63] In contrast, taking a proactive approach means that the investment is made up front, providing protection from risk of fines

Table 4.1. The Reactive-Defensive-Accommodative-Proactive (RDAP) Scale

Rating	Posture or Strategy	Performance
1. Reactive	Deny responsibility	Doing less than required
2. Defensive	Admit responsibility not fight it	Doing the least that is required
3. Accommodative	Accept responsibility	Doing all that is required
4. Proactive	Anticipate responsibility	Doing more than is required

SOURCE: Clarkson, M. B. E. (1995). A stakeholder framework for analyzing and evaluating corporate social performance. *The Academy of Management Review*, 20(1), 92–117. Table on p. 109.

and preventing damage to reputation. "Success in satisfying multiple stakeholder interests—rather than in meeting conventional economic and financial criteria—would constitute the ultimate test of corporate performance."[64]

As well as judging a company's performance and posture, we can assess effectiveness by examining which stakeholder groups' concerns are considered. Jem Bendell refers to this as stakeholder democracy—in other words, "organizations should be accountable to those they affect—particularly those who are negatively affected."[65] Ronald Clement indicates that corporations respond most to stakeholders that are powerful, legitimate, and with urgent claims. However, he cautions that companies should not ignore demands of "fringe" stakeholders who, although lacking power individually, may band together to pursue legitimate claims.

Some stakeholder groups, particularly NGOs and activists, are increasing their capacity for action through the ability to transmit large amounts of data with electronic communications. The quick and effective communication strategy makes some "fringe" or historically less influential stakeholders potentially more powerful, especially when they are tied to other groups that could potentially be mobilized to act in response to an issue.[66] Stuart Hart and Sanjay Sharma suggest that companies "fan out" to identify the fringe stakeholders and generate innovative responses that preempt their concerns.[67] By engaging activist and community groups, companies may prevent extensive costs associated with resolving conflicts that are illegal or risk their reputations. Additionally, companies can head off negative consumer actions such as negative Web campaigns[68] and even class-action lawsuits. Nike would probably be the first to admit that had the company reacted differently to early allegations of labor abuse, it might have avoided some of the very negative campaigning that went on and continues to tarnish its reputation. By building relationships with stakeholder groups in countries where factories are located, companies can better understand diverse cultures, laws, and languages and overcome challenges they might otherwise face in their operations there.[69]

The ultimate method of evaluating performance on corporate social responsibility, however, is whether the responsibility policies and practices intended to help the targeted stakeholders (e.g., workers, consumers, community, and the environment) are indeed doing so.[70] Some ethical trade and sustainability initiatives are developed by NGOs or large companies and may not meet the needs of the intended beneficiaries. If this is the case, the policies and practices pursued may not be as valuable as initiatives proposed by local stakeholders in the communities and countries where production is located. The key to ensuring that the intended beneficiaries are indeed benefited is to provide stakeholder groups with meaningful participation in decisions that will affect them. Thus, apparel brands and retailers seeking to engage with stakeholders need to involve grassroots stakeholders—such as the workers themselves or groups that can appropriately represent them, community members, or representatives of environmental organizations. A company attempting to offset risk by pursuing corporate social responsibility activities that does not involve critical stakeholder groups may find its efforts undermined by the inability to make a real difference.

◉

The Challenge That Lies Ahead

Stakeholder theory and the concepts of stakeholder management and stakeholder engagement are fundamental to companies pursuing social responsibility. Companies operating from a stakeholder perspective identify groups to whom they are responsible, and attempt to understand and prioritize their needs. The Triangle Waist Company factory fire in 1911 provides an early example of the role that various stakeholder groups, including ordinary citizens interested in reform, labor unions, and politicians, had in improving working conditions and labor standards in the apparel industry. Unfortunately, not all apparel brands and retailers today embrace the stakeholder approach of business management and recognize the important role of workers, consumers, and other groups to the success of their businesses. We have presented a thorough process that companies can follow for engaging with stakeholders that might seem daunting, but the important step is to begin engaging with stakeholders, even in a small way if necessary.

Consumers, investors, and other stakeholders can and should evaluate companies on their efforts in social responsibility, and we have presented tools for doing this. Not every stakeholder will always be able to be accommodated, but an earnest attempt to listen and account for varied perspectives will be viewed favorably and help apparel brands and retailers consider the risks their companies face and make informed decisions. Evaluation requires that the company be informative and transparent in sharing data that can be used to judge company performance and posture in responding to societal needs. The publication of social responsibility reports that compare company performance against labor and environmental standards is a valuable mechanism for evaluating social responsibility and more apparel brands and retailers should publish these. Ultimately, however, the results should be judged on the basis of how they affect the targeted stakeholder group. In the labor area, the best assessment of social responsibility efforts is determined by the impact the efforts have on factory workers around the world.

Chapter 5

Key Stakeholders for Social Responsibility

◉

Terese is shopping for her children's back-to-school wardrobes today.
Her three boys will all need at least a couple pairs of new jeans—
she can hardly believe how fast they wear out good-quality clothes.
Twelve years ago, when she was a college student in North Carolina,
she boycotted one retailer specializing in denim wear because of concerns about the workers who sewed its clothing. There had been a rally
on campus, and some workers from the factory in Central America
talked about how they were treated and how little money they were
paid. But a college classmate of hers recently sent an e-mail saying that
the retailer had put a lot of effort into monitoring the factories it uses
to get rid of child labor and other problems. Surely all the problems
have been taken care of, or at least Terese hopes so. She doesn't have
time to look for information about this, and she doesn't know where
she would find reliable information anyway.

Thinking about how simple her life was 12 years ago, Terese smiles
ruefully. Those were the days. It was easy to be an activist. It seemed so
simple to classify everything as right or wrong. Terese had little else to
worry about then, and with the other students all fired up, it was natural to have passion for the cause of eliminating sweatshops.

Things are sure different now! With all three kids under age nine and a middle-class income, she needs to be careful about what she spends. She tries to stay within a budget for clothing and other family and household needs because saving for the boys' college education and her and her husband's retirement is a big worry. But wouldn't it be awful to buy clothes for the kids that were made by other kids? Where should she go shopping today if she wants to be sure that she is not contributing to the type of labor problems she heard about back in the 1990s? Maybe she does have a few minutes before going shopping that she can use for an Internet search for "social responsibility" or "sweatshop."

Stakeholders have an important role in helping apparel brands and retailers become more socially responsible in the production and sourcing of their products. In this chapter, we introduce a wide variety of stakeholders with specific interests and discuss the organization and goals of groups in these broad categories:

- Workers
- Labor unions
- Governments and intergovernmental organizations
- Advocacy organizations
- Consumer and pressure groups
- Colleges and universities
- Financial markets and investors

Many of the groups we discuss can be described as civil society organizations. The World Bank uses this term to describe "the wide array of non-governmental and not-for-profit organizations that have a presence in public life, expressing the interests and values of their members or others, based on ethical, cultural, political, scientific, religious or philanthropic considerations." These groups are important for delivering social services and implementing international development projects and often complement government action. Included under the term civil society are "community groups, non-governmental organizations (NGOs), labor unions, indigenous groups, charitable organizations, faith-based organizations, professional associations, and foundations."[1] The United Nations has benefited from partnering with civil society organizations that champion the same values as expressed in the UN Global Compact: human rights, labor standards, environment, and anticorruption. These stakeholders bring valuable expertise to the effort to align economic activity with social and environmental needs.[2]

An important type of civil society group is that of nongovernmental organizations, or NGOs. These are nonprofit organizations in the private sector that operate outside of government. NGOs typically carry out service- or development-related activities associated with social, environmental, or political concerns. Many of the organizations we discuss in this chapter can be classified under the broad term of NGO and the even broader term of civil society organization.[3]

⊙

Who Are the Key Stakeholders?

Based on stakeholder theory, it is important for apparel brands and retailers to consider a wide range of people and groups when planning and implementing policies and practices for social responsibility. At times, particular stakeholders may be much more vocal than others. In addition, some stakeholders, such as consumers and workers, may not be organized in ways that make contacting them and understanding their needs easy. Nonetheless, apparel brands and retailers that neglect a key stakeholder group may discover the issues such a group has with the firm's policies and practices in unexpected, public, and harmful ways.

Workers

Social responsibility is oriented toward people at all levels of the apparel supply chain, from workers who assemble products to consumers who buy those same products. A number of the principles of the UN Global Compact are based on universal agreements about human rights and worker rights. Thus, workers who sew or make the products are a stakeholder group of central importance to apparel brands and retailers. Indeed, it is their responsibility to ensure the rights of these workers. Recent riots involving thousands of apparel workers in Bangladesh illustrate the problems that can arise when workers' needs are not addressed. Hundreds of workers took to the streets, protesting low wages and disputes about their payment (Figure 5.1), resulting in workers' deaths and injuries, and vandalized factories.[4] In addition

Figure 5.1

The Bangladesh garment industry has been hit by a series of protests over low wages and poor working conditions.

to the perils faced by workers, apparel brands and retailers with production in Bangladesh undoubtedly suffered shipment delays and loss of inventory. Yet in a remarkable endorsement of the influence of good management, workers from factories with good working conditions defended their factories from being vandalized.

Many workers in the apparel industry are not organized to bargain collectively for their rights. Because production work in the apparel industry often represents the first formal employment for young women or men in developing countries, many workers are unaware of their legal rights in the workplace. Additionally, they are vulnerable because of their young age, high unemployment rates in their communities and countries, and culturally bound hierarchies that define relationships between workers and management and between men and women (Figure 5.2). For these reasons and out of fear that they will be dismissed, workers often feel uncomfortable speaking up when they face problems in the workplace.

Apparel brands and retailers leading efforts in social responsibility make serious attempts to gain information about problems workers are having. Sometimes these problems can be quite simple to address, such as ensuring that the factory cafeteria serves clean and unspoiled foods seasoned to workers' tastes. However, some problems that workers express can be much more serious. In its 2005 Human Rights Report, Reebok shared some of the text messages its field staff around the world had received from workers on a confidential hotline set up for them to report problems in their factories (Figure 5.3). For example,

Figure 5.2 (left)

Workers in Thailand.

Figure 5.3 (bottom)

Reebok encourages workers to text the company's representatives with factory problems.

Peraturan yg dibikin Reebok sangat bagus tapi perusahaan [pt spotec] management, pejabat level chip sampai karu banyak pelanggaran, cuti tahunan dipersulit dll : Reebok standard is very good, but management at [company name from chief to group leader commit many violations. Annual leave is difficult. 我们很相信您！希望您保密！请问我们签的合同书为什么只有厂方有？我们是不是应该也有一份？: We believe you very much. Ho can keep secret our question. Why was a copy of the labor contract we signed with the factory not provided to us? Should we have copy of the contract? Bizler 12 modelhane iscisiyiz ve yilbasindaki yemek paketlerini alma yerine maas zammi konusunda patronla konusmak istedik. Bizimle konusmediklari gibi, bayramda tum iscilere birer yemek paketi daha verildi. Bize verilmedi. Ayrica model haneyi kucuk ve havasiz bir yere tasidilar. Reebok tan geldiginizde bizimle konustuktan sonra personel muduru tarafindan sorguya cekiliyoruz. Disarida gorusebilir miyiz? : The 12 sample workers spoke to the management for a salary increase. Management refused an retaliated by moving the sample department to a room with poor ventilation and fire safety. Whenever you come to visit and talk to us in the production floor, HR manager asks questions about you. Can we talk out of the factory? 你好！我是和通力的员工，我们厂实在是太过分了！上班要我们早点回车间，下班时间跟北京时间慢十多分钟，给我们买的社保还要我们出钱，工资本来就不高，还不知道我们出的钱拿不拿得到，还要过 3个月，请问我是三年的老员工，算一下钱还是不少的，对我们农民的家庭来说是不少的。: Hello! I am worker from [company name] our factory is very bad to us. We must pay for social insurance, our wage is not high Meanwhile we don't know whether we really can obtain the social insurance money back. We are farmer family, the amount is not small for people like us. Size soylemek istedigim su ki, her denetime geldiginizde {Li&Fung ya da Reebok} yaslari 15-17 arasinda olan bazi genc iscileriust kattaki evlerine sakliyorlar. Siz on kapidan girince oniar da yangin merdiveninden yukaridaki patronun evine saklaniyorlar. : The owner hides some minors between 15-17 years old when Li & Fung or Reebok monitors visit the factory. They hide the workers from the fire exit door going to upstairs, where the owner family has a house. REEBOK 2005 HUMAN RIGHTS REPORT 我最 我是上海通尔芬的员工，我们每天都加班到10点11点，又没有加班费，工厂支付的工资很少，工厂实在太苦了。: I am worker from [company name] we worked overtime to 10 PM - 11 PM every day, we were not paid overtime wage. Factory paid us few wage, we are too poor. 我是北京圣瑞的工人，我就是上次你来工厂和你说话的其中一个，我记得你说工厂做你们的订单，你会帮助我们工人解决问题，我由于身体 不好，年前己经辞职了。前两天去工厂要工资，工厂说得我工资不发了。: I am worker from [company name] I am the worker you interviewed in your last visit. I remembered you said factory is doing order for your company, you would help us, worker to solve problem. Due to my poor health I resigned before Lunar ... y approved this. But 2 days ago when I went to factory to as for payment, factory said I would not be paid. 你好，我是和通力的员工，我们不知道为什么从明天开始我们科长姚美... 没有工资，不去要罚款。我要投诉他们。: Hello. I am worke from [company name] we don't know why since tomorrow our supervisor required us to early arrive at 6:30 AM. If we d... if we don't go, we would be fined. I would like to complain. 费小姐，不好意思您没有给您打电话，我手机没有钱了，我是圣瑞制衣的晶平，前几天请您帮忙是我工资的事。到现在... 问问，谢谢您！: So sorry that I did not call you because I used up my pre-paid fee in my mobile. I am [worker name] from [company name]. Few days ago, I called you about m... it. Would you do me favor to help me to ask factory again Thanks. 闵小姐你好，非常感谢！我的工资已经全部拿到我，现在准备去（天津）外商国际制衣厂上班，谢谢你！Hel... not the full payment of the salary, now I am planning to go and work in kming garment factory. Thank you! Hi ms beck gud pm pauwi n rn ako 3 kming uuwi pnbbyaran tlga sm... to d2 ngpprotesta ang mga tao kc bnwsan ang sweldo at dd ang fod alow. Dpat b tigang byran ung levi tax pcensya n wla kc kaming pwdng pgtanongan d2. : Good evening. The fact... he levy tax. It's a little bit uneasy here now and many worke are on protest because the salary have decreased and food allowance is being deducted. Do we really have to pay... ient with us, there is no one here we can ask help from. 请来休息一事，因我们已经三个星期没放假了，每晚加班（包括周日）总... ow on behalf of all workers of [company name], I want to ap 3 weeks, and the overtime every night (including Sunday) are always ... 加始缝制衣厂的员工。我们厂做人权为什么还加12点？请回音 ...ry, our factory is supposed to be applying Human Rights standards, b... work till 24:00pm? please reply. 是七点+五打?上班,打?前 ...d to punch in before 7:15am, but the factory counts the working hours... 有我们伙食费是有个人支付,厂内伙食太差,我们不愿意在厂内 伙食费 : There is another issue about food service in this factory. We n... he food. The food quality is very bad. We don't want to eat i 王先生:我... espite whether we eat or not in the factory each month. 王先生:我... 机,声音太响了,仓库是工作的地方.能否建议把压缩机换个地 h undesirable noises near the 1st floor warehouse. Warehouse is ... u recommend the factory to change the place for the air an po akong ittnong.kailangan po bang bigyan ng memo at warning a... of emergency? Pgblik ko po knabukasan hnd n ako pnpaso ng wori ... t bk : good evening. I have a question. Do I really have to be issued ... ng to work because of an emergency? When I reported back to work k even though I have a medical certificate with me. *Please reply.*

The text messages on the cover are reprinted verbatim from communication received by our human rights field staff during October & November 2005. As you'll see by reading the English translations, these grievances are from workers regarding factory workplace conditions. Our field staff responds to these complaints—and thousands more each year—to seek solutions, protect workers and improve their lives. These messages are evidence of the continuing challenges we face. They are also a clear indication of our success in winning the trust of workers and empowering them to raise issues of concern. Read on to see how we're shifting our efforts from an approach based on factory assessments and food allowance is being deducted. resolve human rights issues themselves in open dialogue.

Reebok

one worker shared that "the owner hides some minors between 15–17 years old when [company name] or Reebok monitors visit the factory. They hide the workers from the fire exit door going to upstairs, where the owner family has a house." Another message read: "Hello! Now on behalf of all workers of [company name], I want to apply [for] rest from your company. Because we have no rest/holiday for 3 weeks, and the overtime every night (including Sunday) are always till 10 or 12 pm."[5] Workers are a very important stakeholder group with which companies should engage.

Labor Unions

The growth of labor unions at the turn of the twentieth century was in part due to government failure to regulate workplace safety. Labor unions generally share an interest in protecting workers' rights and bargaining collectively on their behalf. Because of the vulnerable situation in which apparel workers often find themselves, labor unions can play an important role in protecting workers' rights by providing a safe avenue for workers to express their concerns and a united front in presenting their case to management. That is why freedom of association is an important worker right. Although labor unions may not be directly affected by business policies and practices for production and sourcing, they are legitimate stakeholders because they represent the needs of the workers.

UNITE HERE!, Change to Win, and the AFL-CIO Solidarity Center

UNITE HERE!, the main textile and apparel union in the United States, is the result of a 2004 merger of two other unions in the United States and Canada, the Union of Needletrades, Industrial and Textile Employees (UNITE) and the Hotel Employees and Restaurant Employees International Union (HERE). UNITE was created earlier with a merger in 1995 between the International Ladies Garment Workers

Union (ILGWU) and the Amalgamated Clothing and Textile Workers Union (ACTWU). UNITE HERE! is based in North America and represents 450,000 active members working in the United States and Canada. Its priority is to organize workers employed in apparel and textile manufacturing, apparel distribution centers, apparel retail, and industrial laundries, as well as those employed in the hotel and food service sectors.[6] Because of its focus on workers in North America, UNITE HERE! has had limited impact on social responsibility in the apparel industry, where the vast majority of production now takes place in other countries; however, in its earlier days, UNITE was active in the anti-sweatshop movement.

Often unions like UNITE HERE! work together as members of federations that represent several unions. Until 2005 UNITE HERE! was part of the AFL-CIO; however, it now is part of the Change to Win Federation, which consists of seven affiliated unions representing 6 million workers. Change to Win addresses the needs of American workers, particularly those vulnerable to having their jobs outsourced. The federation advocates for wages that support workers' families, universal and affordable health care, retirement security, and dignity at work. The strategic organizing function of Change to Win provides an opportunity for the seven unions to integrate their programs into large-scale campaigns. Change to Win is working with unions around the world to urge multinational corporations to raise levels of living and respect workers' rights everywhere they work.[7] Success with this global initiative will probably be difficult to achieve because of difficulties encountered when working across national lines; however, it is a laudable goal that would potentially reduce countries' competition with one another and the race to the bottom associated with the vicious circle.

Although UNITE HERE! is no longer a member, the AFL-CIO maintains a Solidarity Center that engages in programs aimed at protecting workers' rights globally. The center assists with organizing campaigns and works with local partners to educate workers around the world on freedom of association and laws protecting their rights.[8]

The International Textile, Garment and Leather Workers Federation

Another noteworthy labor organization supporting workers in apparel production worldwide is the International Textile, Garment and Leather Workers Federation (ITGLWF). The global union is composed of 217 affiliated organizations from 110 countries, including UNITE HERE!. The ITGLWF develops policy guidelines for unions in the relevant industrial sectors and coordinates the activities of its worldwide affiliates. It also compiles relevant information for unions in these sectors and undertakes solidarity actions, supporting workers whose trade union rights have been denied. Especially important to the global workforce employed in apparel production, the ITGLWF provides assistance to unions in developing countries that are trying to educate and organize workers. As well, the ITGLWF is active in the Ethical Trading Initiative, a multi-stakeholder forum focused on improving working conditions in apparel and other industries. Finally, the group lobbies intergovernmental organizations and others to ensure workers' rights are taken into account in international decision making.[9] The ITGLWF is itself part of an umbrella organization called the International Trade Union Confederation (ITUC). The ICFTU collaborates with the International Labour Organization (ILO) and other international agencies to organize and campaign around issues related to worker rights, forced and child labor, quality, the environment, and others.[10]

Labor Unions in Apparel-Producing Countries

Countries vary in their support of labor unions and rights of workers to organize. In China, workers are not allowed to associate freely, given that only one union is allowed in the country and it is run by the government. The All China Federation of Trade Unions (ACFTU) maintains the conflicting responsibilities of representing the interests of government, the Communist party, factory management, and workers. Historically, the ACFTU served as a worker welfare organization that organized social activities for workers in state-owned enterprises[11] rather than addressing basic human and worker rights. The situation in China is changing, however, and the ACFTU is an evolving union that may become more supportive of worker rights in the future.

The Vietnamese government recognizes the Vietnam General Confederation of Labor (VGCL) as the only legal union in the country. Union representatives are commonly appointed by management, which compromises the independence of the union and its ability to address worker concerns.

Although China and Vietnam have countrywide limitations on freedom of association, other countries limit this important worker right in certain regions. For example, in Bangladesh the right to form unions is severely restricted for those who work in export processing zones, where much apparel is produced. The limitation on freedom of association rights is described by the Bangladeshi government as a temporary measure meant to protect investment and employment. In Mexico, "official unions" have close ties with political parties and the government, and they often operate without workers' knowledge that they exist or awareness of who represents worker interests. There are also "white unions" that are tied with companies. Independent unions also exist in Mexico, but because they have a reputation for being very active in pushing for changes in factories, workers who attempt to organize or join an independent union are often fired and blacklisted, preventing their employment in other factories. Ultimately, without the ability to organize freely and join unions, workers are severely restricted in their abilities to defend their rights.[12]

Governments and Intergovernmental Organizations

Governments are key stakeholders for ensuring labor standards and protecting worker rights, given that they are charged with the welfare of their citizens. But governments vary in their interest and actions around social responsibility and its enforcement.

The U.S. Government

During the early 1900s after the Triangle Waist Company factory fire, important legislative action addressed issues in the workplace. In the United States, the National Labor Relations Act of 1933 established worker rights for freedom of association and collective bargaining. In 1938, the Fair Labor Standards Act (FLSA) established minimum working standards for workers engaged directly or indirectly in interstate commerce, including those involved in production of goods bound for such commerce.[13] However, legislation protecting workers is valuable only if it is enforced.

In the United States, the Wage and Hour Division of the Department of Labor (DOL) is granted the responsibility of enforcing the FLSA. The agency has been underfunded and does not have enough labor inspectors to adequately monitor the many factories in the U.S. apparel industry. It was calculated in 2004 that it would take each inspector 58 years to actually visit all the factories assigned to him or her. Over the years, government priorities have prevented additional funds from being used for labor inspections. However, the extensive media coverage that followed Kathie Lee Gifford's connection with child labor and substandard wages in factories making her line of products for Wal-Mart resulted in an increase in the number of inspector positions in the mid-1990s.[14]

Under the Clinton administration, Secretary of Labor Robert Reich increased enforcement of the FLSA, but greater emphasis was also placed on business to monitor itself. A "hot goods" provision of the FLSA allowed the government to confiscate garments made in violation of the FLSA that were shipped across state borders. That meant that goods could be taken from retailers after delivery from factories and payment. It was risky for retailers to be put in this situation because their primary function is to sell products, so the intent was to compel them to monitor their suppliers' activities more closely. Those retailers and brands who volunteered to monitor their suppliers for compliance with the FLSA were put on Secretary Reich's "Trendsetters" list so that the public could support their actions through purchases. However, because many of the Trendsetters were involved in widely reported sweatshop scandals over the ensuing years, it became clear that this entirely voluntary method of controlling working conditions had only limited success.

The Apparel Industry Partnership (AIP) was also formed under the Clinton administration, and President Clinton and Secretary Reich charged members representing businesses, labor unions, and NGOs to find solutions to the labor problems in the apparel industry. The group's ideas were to develop an industry-wide code of conduct and an organization to oversee the monitoring function and the work of member companies, and to inform consumers through a "No Sweat" label which were the socially responsible companies (Figure 5.4). The labor union and NGO representatives pushed for a rigorous system of monitoring compliance with the code's standards. Heated negotiations led some business and labor representatives to depart because of disagreements about wages and how freedom of association would be treated in the code of conduct. As the AIP concluded its work, many involved continued with the new organization charged with implementing the code of conduct and monitoring principles—the Fair Labor Association (FLA). The FLA mission is "to combine the efforts of industry, civil society organizations, and colleges and universities to protect workers' rights and improve working conditions worldwide by promoting adherence to international labor standards."[15] Although the FLA celebrated its tenth-year anniversary in 2006, as the Clinton administration came to an end, so did the Department of Labor's focus on working conditions in the apparel industry.

Over the last 10 to 15 years, there have been other examples of U.S. government efforts to improve labor standards and working conditions for apparel workers both domestically and in offshore factories. Senator Tom Harkin of Iowa has introduced several bills aimed at curbing child labor in overseas production. The Child Labor Deference Act would have banned the import of products made in countries using child labor.[16]

Figure 5.4
No Sweat logo used by Robert Reich.

Help End Sweatshop Conditions for American Workers
Robert B. Reich, Secretary
U.S. Department of Labor

An outcome of this proposed legislation, which was never passed, signals the need for considerable care when legislating working conditions. In Bangladesh, apparel contractors fearful of losing access to the U.S. market laid off nearly 50,000 children 13 and younger. Many of the children were later found to have substituted more dangerous work, including crushing stones and prostitution, for their apparel production work.[17]

More recently, in 2007, Senator Byron Dorgan of North Dakota, along with others, introduced a bill titled the Decent Working Conditions and Fair Competition Act. If passed, the bill would "(1) prohibit the import, export, or sale of goods made in factories or workshops that violate core labor standards; and (2) prohibit the procurement of sweatshop goods by the United States Government."[18] In a statement introducing the bill, Senator Dorgan described sweatshop conditions as "violations of the labor, health, and safety laws of the country where the labor is performed."[19]

Although it will be difficult to enforce at the government level through the U.S. Customs and Border Protection and the Federal Trade Commission, Senator Dorgan's bill introduced a Private Right of Action allowing competitors and investors to sue retailers violating the law. This section provoked considerable discussion among representatives of many brands and retailers, who forecasted that the industry would be brought to a virtual standstill from a flurry of lawsuits should the bill be passed into law. In a written statement for a hearing before a subcommittee of the Senate Committee on Commerce, Science, and Transportation, the American Apparel and Footwear Association cited the many ways in which the industry had worked to improve working conditions and concluded that "while we applaud the goals of S. 367, we disagree with how the legislation proposes reaching these goals. All of [the] time, effort and resources . . . that have been devoted to finding better ways to improve workplace conditions around [the] world would be stifled by the draconian measures proposed in S. 367."[20]

Other National Governments

Senator Dorgan's bill makes it seem that apparel-producing countries have not acted in ways that provide for basic labor rights and good working conditions, and in many cases this accusation may be true. Governments of developing countries are often conflicted as they try to attract foreign investment and trade opportunities while also ensuring protection of workers. As a result, the labor laws of many countries are either lax or are not enforced. In Thailand the legal number of hours of work allowed per week is 84, far beyond the 60 hours that many apparel brands and retailers allow in their codes of conduct. In comparison, Chinese labor laws are considered to be some of the most rigorous in the world, but they are poorly enforced.[21] Nonetheless, the president of the Fair Labor Association observes:

[China is] a country characterized by both widespread non-observance of the labor law and increasing efforts to improve standards . . . Inconsistent enforcement of labor law left certain sectors and groups of workers exposed to abuses and the result has been a series of high-profile accidents and strikes . . . In recent years the government has promulgated two important pieces of legislation that could facilitate the development of democratic structures to represent workers in consultations and negotiation . . . our monitoring results show that China is no closer to the bottom than a number of other sourcing destinations . . . whereas a number of the other key sourcing countries or regions are characterized by defunct or failed systems of regulation, the Chinese government is still actively seeking to improve its system of labor market regulation and labor law enforcement. Most commentators agree that the performance of the Chinese government in this regard has been inconsistent, but there can be no doubt about the fact that the government is determined, and has the political will, to act to improve labor standards.[22]

Newly enacted labor contract law would provide many workers with contracts detailing the terms, conditions, and benefits of their employment. Yet critics caution that without proper enforcement, the law will do little to stop labor abuses.[23]

As an example of the efforts of another apparel-producing country, the government of Cambodia has worked with its apparel industry to compete for brands' and retailers' orders on the basis of good working

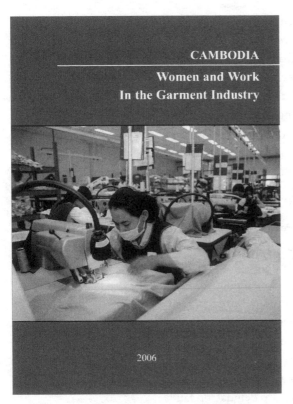

CAMBODIA

Women and Work
In the Garment Industry

2006

Figure 5.5

The Better Factories project
involving the ILO and Cambodia
has produced valuable data on
factory conditions.

conditions and labor standards. A Better Factories Cambodia project was established in collaboration with the ILO in 2001 (Figure 5.5). The project involves monitoring and reporting working conditions in Cambodian factories using both national and international standards.[24] This approach is innovative; however, questions have been recently raised about whether the ILO misrepresented the conditions in its factories and whether ILO inspectors had been bribed by companies to produce positive reports.[25] If true, this issue illustrates the complexity of implementing social responsibility programs in culturally and geographically different contexts.

Intergovernmental Organizations

Beyond national governments, intergovernmental organizations such as the United Nations and the International Labour Organization are also stakeholders attempting to address global problems of working conditions and labor standards. The ILO, based in Geneva, Switzerland, is a UN agency focused on promoting decent work conditions around the world. Founded in 1919, the organization is composed of representatives from governments, business, and labor who work together to form policies and programs benefiting workers. The ILO holds an International Labor Conference every year that representatives attend. During these conferences, delegates from member states, often government officials with labor responsibilities plus representatives of workers and employers, vote whether to adopt new labor conventions and recommendations and discuss labor issues of international interest. When they ratify labor conventions, member states become legally obligated to apply the convention's provisions.

An important accomplishment of the ILO was the 1998 adoption of the Declaration on Fundamental Principles and Rights at Work, which embodies eight conventions related to freedom of association and collective bargaining, elimination of forced and compulsory labor, elimination of discrimination in respect of employment and occupation, and the abolition of child labor.[26] All ILO member states are expected to promote and respect those conventions, whether they have ratified them or not. The labor conventions included under this declaration serve as a foundation for the UN Global Compact and many companies' codes of conduct.

Advocacy Organizations

Another type of stakeholder group that is important in helping apparel brands and retailers understand the needs of workers and the societal conditions affecting workers are advocacy organizations that work closely with workers, women, and other marginalized groups to improve their situations. These groups launch campaigns that advocate for changes in government policy, business conduct, and consumer behavior so they support the needs of workers.

Maquila Solidarity Network

The Maquila Solidarity Network (MSN) advocates for workers' and women's rights, working with groups based in Mexico, Central America, and Asia that are also trying to improve conditions in apparel factories. It advocates for policies and attempts to build capacity of labor rights groups in the regions of interest. The MSN also pursues corporate campaigns and engagement, pushing for greater corporate accountability. For example, a campaign launched in October 2006 targeted Hanesbrands for concerns about how workers were treated in a Mexico factory closure. In another effort made in cooperation with the Ethical Trading Action Group, MSN has developed a Transparency

Report Card that ranks apparel brands and retailers selling products in Canada. The evaluation focuses on labor compliance policies and the companies' transparency in communicating their efforts to the public.[27]

The International Labor Rights Forum

The International Labor Rights Forum (ILRF) is another advocacy organization with an agenda similar to that of the MSN. The ILRF advocates for just and humane treatment of workers around the world. The organization promotes labor rights enforcement by educating and mobilizing the public, as well as through research, litigation, and legislation. In addition, the ILRF collaborates with labor, government, and business groups. The organization led creation of the RUGMARK, a program that has certified over 2 million handwoven carpets as free of child labor, and that might provide a model program for apparel production. The ILRF also was behind the first social clause to be added to U.S. trade legislation through the Generalized System of Preferences, which promotes economic development by providing duty-free access to certain products from designated countries.[28] In 2005, the ILRF made headlines for filing an unprecedented class-action lawsuit against Wal-Mart that alleged the retail giant failed to enforce the labor standards contained in its code of conduct and made false and misleading statements to the public regarding its practices toward labor and human rights.[29] Wal-Mart filed a request that the case be dismissed, but it was still under consideration in 2007.

Other Advocacy Organizations

There are additional advocacy organizations addressing worker rights in a variety of industries, including the apparel industry. For example, the U.S. Labor Education in the Americas Project (US-LEAP) led some of the first campaigns against major apparel brands in the early 1990s, and the organization continues efforts to provide justice to workers.[30] Sweatshop Watch focuses on the apparel industry and currently has a campaign to hold apparel brands and retailers accountable for the conditions under which garments are made.[31]

Other advocacy organizations make labor standards and worker rights part of a broader agenda of economic development or human rights activities. For example, in 2004, Oxfam International joined with the Clean Clothes Campaign (discussed later in this chapter) and the ITGLWF to launch a campaign called Play Fair at the Olympics, which highlights the plight of women sportswear workers who work long hours for poverty-level wages making apparel for the Olympics. A follow-up campaign, Playfair 2008, tackles the Beijing Olympics and the Chinese government's failure to enforce labor laws and worker rights to form independent labor unions.[32] Besides this work, Oxfam International and its 13 affiliate organizations pursue broader goals of "lasting solutions to poverty, suffering and injustice."[33] Similarly, Human Rights First, a longtime advocate for worker rights, advocates for change at the national and international policy level, through the courts and through the media. Their broad interests in human rights involve protecting people at risk, including refugees, victims of crimes against humanity, and others.[34]

Consumer and Pressure Groups

Market-based regulation of labor standards and working conditions relies on consumers to play a key role. Consumer and pressure groups are a type of advocacy organization that spends considerable time educating consumers and involving them in campaigns to influence businesses. Through their purchasing, consumers can influence business behavior, rewarding apparel brands and retailers that adopt socially responsible practices and punishing those that do not. Some commentators go as far as to say that consumers ultimately decide what goods will be produced and sold, referring to this as consumer sovereignty. As Powell indicates, "Everyone who goes into a shop and chooses one article over another is casting a vote in the economic ballot box."[35]

The term consumer citizenship describes the idea that consumers are obligated to contribute to society through their purchases.[36]

The National Consumers League

The National Consumers League (NCL) played a key role in early-twentieth-century labor reform, such as the Triangle Waist Company factory fire, and its efforts have continued into the present. Explaining the important role of consumers, Josephine Shaw Lowell, founder of what was then known as the New York City Consumers League, stated in 1891 that "it is the duty of consumers to find out under what conditions the articles they purchase are produced and distributed and to insist that these conditions shall be wholesome and consistent with a respectable existence on the part of the workers."[37] An early motto of the NCL illustrated consumer responsibilities in the marketplace: "To live means to buy, to buy means to have power, to have power means to have duties."[38] The current mission of the NCL focuses on protecting and promoting social and economic justice for workers and consumers by bringing consumers' perspectives on issues including child labor to government, business, and others. Recent work focusing on corporate social responsibility included a survey tapping consumer perspectives on the topic.[39]

The National Labor Committee

Pressure groups involve and organize consumers to use boycotts, media exposure, and other means to make demands on corporations. In the United States, a pressure group that has notably influenced social responsibility is the National Labor Committee (NLC). Although most Americans may not recognize the name of the organization, many were introduced to labor issues associated with the production of apparel when the NLC waged the high-profile campaign involving Kathie Lee Gifford regarding her clothing line manufactured for Wal-Mart. In defense of workers' rights, the NLC has successfully pressured well-known brands and retailers to improve conditions in their factories. This organization is run by labor activist Charles Kernaghan, who has visited factories around the world, taken video footage of exploitative conditions, and scavenged through factory dumps for evidence of excessively low wages. His work has been featured on national television shows, in major newspapers, and in films created for college campuses.[40] The NLC Web site explains the organization's perspective on global industry and goals, stating that:

> The lack of accountability on the part of our U.S. corporations—now operating all over the world, and the resulting dehumanization of this new global workforce is emerging as the overwhelming moral crisis of the 21st century. The struggle for rule of law in the global economy—to ensure respect for the fundamental rights of the millions of workers producing goods for the U.S. market—has become the great new civil rights movement of our time.[41]

The Clean Clothes Campaign

Among apparel brands and retailers, the Clean Clothes Campaign (CCC) is another well-known pressure group. Based in Amsterdam, the CCC has nine offices across Europe that campaign to improve working conditions in the global apparel industry. Besides pressuring corporations to adopt more socially responsible practices, another key activity of the CCC is to educate and mobilize consumers (Box 5.1). The CCC also works on legal issues related to labor standards and intervenes in cases where workers have been unfairly compensated. In the European Union, the CCC actively lobbies the European Parliament about codes of conduct and social responsibility.[42] The CCC works in solidarity with labor unions and other organizations in efforts to improve conditions for apparel workers, such as with Oxfam International and the ITGLWF on the Playfair 2008 campaign focused on the Beijing Olympics.

Box 5.1. Example of an Urgent Appeal

A-One Factory Closed—Action Still Needed

On June 18, workers from the A-One factory arrived at the factory expecting to find a notice on the gates indicating how their demands had been met. Instead, when the workers got to the gates and saw there was no notice about the workers' demands, and it became known that the factory was to be closed indefinitely, the workers took to the streets to demonstrate.

Following the disturbances, A-One workers, management, and the authorities in the export processing zone where the factory is based engaged in several hours of negotiations, but no agreements were reached. As their demands have not been met, the A-One workers have refused to go back to work, and the factory remains closed.

Your support is still needed to continue to pressure brands and A-One factory management to meet the original demands of the workers as detailed here. Even though the factory is currently closed, the demands to the brands and the factory owner remain valid.

Background: Workers had formed a committee* to represent their interests at the factory in February 2005, but in mid-September, management started to illegally dismiss workers and the representatives of the committee, and workers received death threats. The dismissed workers were not paid the dues owed by the factory management. Workers' demands in relation to wages and working conditions, reinstatement of workers, abusive treatment of workers, and good-faith negotiations with workers' representatives have not been met. Following months of repression by management, during which workers remained peaceful, the A-One factory was targeted repeatedly in the wave of protests that have been taking place in the export-processing zone since mid-May, which are an inevitable consequence of the appalling working conditions and repeated violations of workers' rights in Bangladesh.

*The workers' had formed a Workers' Representation and Welfare Committee, which is the only currently legal form of workers' association in Bangladesh's export processing zone.

Follow-up: The actions suggested including writing letters to the brands sourcing from the factory urging them to request a resolution between the factory management and the workers. The case was settled in February 2008 when the dismissed workers received compensation from the factory's only remaining buyer—Tessival of Italy.

SOURCE: www.cleanclothes.org.

Colleges and Universities

Colleges and universities are stakeholders in the apparel industry because they license use of their logos for sweatshirts, T-shirts, hats, and other items. The rights to make products incorporating a school's logo are licensed to businesses that either produce the goods themselves or contract production. Licensees range from large apparel brands including the adidas Group, Nike, Russell, and VF that produce goods for a number of colleges and universities, as well as small licensees employing just a few persons who manufacture a unique product, often in a U.S.-based shop, for a single university. For the large apparel brands, licensing to colleges and universities is only a tiny portion of their overall business. Besides those licensed to make textile products, there are many licensees authorized to make a multitude of additional products bearing college and universities logos, including seat cushions, golf tees, video games, jewelry, pens, glassware, and small trinkets.

In the early 1990s, a number of activist groups publicized that college logo goods were being made in factories with poor working conditions and labor standards. The campus movement took hold after several students interned at the UNITE office during the summer of 1997, where they explored what college and university administrators were doing to ensure that their licensed apparel was not made in sweatshops. In the spring of 1998, United Students against Sweatshops (USAS) was formed and sit-ins and protests took place at Cornell, Duke, Georgetown, Wisconsin, Notre Dame, and other higher-education institutions (Figure 5.6). These protests pushed many university administrators into adopting codes of conduct and looking for ways to enforce the codes.[43] USAS continues more than ten years later with students and individual faculty, and some campuses joining the fight for workers' rights. As described on the USAS Web site:

We believe that university standards should be brought in line with those of its students who demand that their school's logo is emblazoned on clothing made in decent working conditions. We have fought for these beliefs by demanding that our universities adopt ethically and legally strong codes of conduct, full public disclosure of company information and truly independent verification systems to ensure that sweatshop conditions are not happening.[44]

Figure 5.6
University of Iowa USAS students take part in a silent vigil as they interrupted a meeting with the president of the university.

USAS was formed in part as a protest against the FLA, a multi-stakeholder organization that at the time involved civil society and major brands working together to find solutions to poor labor conditions. The FLA had developed a code of conduct and was developing processes for monitoring factories against the labor standards set out in the code. A handful of major universities had negotiated a deal with the FLA whereby colleges and universities could join the group to access assistance with monitoring factories where their logo garments were produced. Although over 200 colleges and universities are now affiliated with the FLA[45] and the organization is viewed as "the most credible, multi-stakeholder initiative that exists" and a "tremendous tool that provide(s) structure, systems, process, and credibility,"[46] in 1997 students rejected the FLA because they felt that companies could not be trusted in designing and implementing solutions to improve working conditions in factories making their products. They were also compelled to reject the FLA because their union affiliate UNITE! dropped out of the organization, charging there were shortcomings in the FLA's provisions and enforcement.[47]

A notable accomplishment of USAS and its collaboration with scholars, labor unions, and human rights groups was the founding of the Worker Rights Consortium (WRC) in 2000 as an alternative to the FLA. The WRC assists colleges and universities in enforcing their codes of conduct for the production of logo products.[48]

After several years focusing on global issues not as closely related to the apparel industry, USAS was reinvigorated in 2006, when it proposed a new program that would require colleges and universities to have production of logo goods done by factories preapproved for paying living wages and having unions representing the factories' workers.[49] By 2007, the Designated Supplier Program had received support by some universities, but many others were fearful about the details of implementation and the potential for licensees to encounter antitrust violations (Box 5.2).

Box 5.2. Sourcing Licensed Apparel for Universities
Letter from Purdue President about not joining the DSP

December 12, 2006

To Members of the Merchandise, Licensing and Marketing Policy Committee, I am writing in response to the Committee's recommendation following its meeting of November 15, 2006. The minutes of that meeting were transmitted to me on November 27, along with a minority report from two of the members, and background information on the Worker Rights Consortium's Designated Supplier Program. I have thoroughly reviewed all these materials. On December 6, I met with four representatives of the Purdue Organization for Labor Equality, which has advocated adoption of the DSP and has organized a hunger strike in support of that view. In addition, I have discussed the DSP proposal with my senior staff and with executives of peer universities, including some that have made the decision to adopt the DSP.

After consideration of all these inputs, I have decided on behalf of the University to accept the Committee's recommendation that Purdue not adopt the Designated Supplier Program at this time. I agree with the Committee majority's conclusion that the DSP in its present form would require Purdue to adopt practices in one sector of business—the granting of licenses for manufacture of logo-bearing apparel—that it does not use in any other sector. I also agree with the Committee's view that it is not certain that the DSP would achieve its objective of better ensuring that Purdue-licensed apparel was manufactured in compliance with our code of conduct. The consequences of adopting the DSP are not understood at this point, and I cannot commit the University to the program when so much doubt exists.

The specific aspects of the DSP that cause me concern are:

- The requirement that suppliers be neutral about union organization: This is a requirement that does not exist in federal or Indiana law, and it certainly is not something Purdue would stipulate in a contract in any other area of business.
- The living wage provision of the DSP: A living wage is not defined in law, and efforts to develop such a definition have been unsuccessful. I am not persuaded that the WRC can or should determine what constitutes a living wage in the numerous markets and nations where apparel is manufactured.

- Price controls: Under the DSP, the WRC would require that licensees set prices at certain levels in order to assure that living wages could be paid by manufacturers. Price fixing is illegal in most cases, and it is at odds with Purdue's policy of accepting the best, lowest bid in contracting.

While there remains evidence of abuse and exploitation in the global apparel industry, I am not persuaded by the argument that the DSP should be adopted because the current system is not working. First, while the DSP is an alternative to an imperfect system, there is not convincing evidence that it is an effective alternative. Second, while enforcement of university codes of conduct—including Purdue's—for the manufacture of licensed materials has not eliminated labor abuses in the global apparel industry, there is evidence of progress.

Through its membership in the WRC and the Fair Labor Association, Purdue and other universities receive reports alleging violations of codes of conduct. Purdue's Contracting Group works with the two organizations, other universities and the licensing companies to address these issues, mitigate any abuses and bring about resolutions. While it is true that problems persist, it is apparent that these are attributable primarily to global labor conditions and the legal and cultural realities in the more than 75 countries where most apparel is manufactured. It is not apparent that our efforts to enforce the code of conduct are counterproductive or ineffective.

However, I believe we should continue to seek better solutions to this problem. Therefore, I have decided to pursue two courses of action:

1. I would like the Merchandise, Licensing and Marketing Policy Committee to continue to meet regularly and keep me apprised of progress on enforcement of the code of conduct.
2. We have received an invitation to send a Purdue representative as an observer to future meetings of the Designated Supplier Program working group, which is studying implementation of the DSP by the universities that have decided to adopt the program. I have decided to accept that invitation and to ask Doug Sabel, director of the University Contracting Group, to represent Purdue at future meetings. He will report back to the Committee. I believe this step will allow us to become better informed about the DSP and to evaluate any modifications to the program.

While I do not believe the DSP is a viable choice for Purdue at this time, I am prepared to reconsider this decision if changes to the program address my concerns. I also am hopeful that other ideas will come forward as we continue to study this issue.

Purdue is determined to enforce the code of conduct that governs its licensing program. Everyone with whom I have discussed this matter has a sincere interest in protecting the dignity and rights of the people who manufacture the products that bear Purdue's name. Because of the complexity of the issue and the deep feelings involved, it has not been possible to achieve unanimity on the best means of assuring compliance with our code of conduct. However, these differences should not keep us from working cooperatively. The students who have continued a hunger strike for more than three weeks have made a bold statement of their commitment to a solution. Their passion for a better world will be needed as we move forward, and I hope they will discontinue this tactic in favor of a cooperative effort.

Finally, I am deeply grateful to Chairman Dworkin and the entire Committee for their hard work on this complex issue. I look forward to working with you as we continue to pursue compliance with our code of conduct.

Sincerely,
Martin C. Jischke
President

SOURCE: Released by Purdue News Service.

NOTE: Purdue President Martin Jischke sent this memo to the university's Merchandising, Licensing and Marketing Policy Committee. It accompanied his decision to not adopt a Designated Supplier Program being advocated by a group of hunger-striking students.

A "Fair Trade" Approach to Licensed College Gear

One day seven or eight years ago in Bangkok, Joe Falcone began to feel an uncomfortable sensation of futility. The grandson of garment workers, he had been working in Asia's clothing factories for nearly a decade, making certain they complied with labor and environmental laws. The idea was to assure American consumers their apparel and shoes were not made in sweatshops.

But, as Mr. Falcone recalled in a recent interview, he had come to wonder if the laws were strong enough.

He worried whether the manufacturers' compliance ended once his inspection did. And he knew that factories felt incessant pressure from American apparel companies to cut prices, even at the expense of wages and working conditions.

By 2005, Mr. Falcone had turned his disquiet into action. He formed his own apparel company, Counter Sourcing, which found its niche producing licensed shirts for 11 major universities, including Duke and the University of North Carolina.

The company pays 10 percent of its annual sales to factory workers as bonuses, and puts another 7 percent into medical, environmental or educational programs chosen by employees. Those sales reached $150,000 in 2007, Mr. Falcone said.

Last month, Counter Sourcing paid its first bonuses to some 2,700 garment workers at the Pride Group factory in Dhaka, Bangladesh. Each received about $3.50 above the typical monthly wage of $25.

A social-service organization oversaw distribution of the bonuses.

It is no coincidence that Mr. Falcone chose to enter the market for college gear. All those shirts, sweats and hats emblazoned with logos or adorned with mascots constitute a $2 billion annual industry.

The concept of "fair-trade apparel," as Mr. Falcone calls his product line, also taps into the urge of students to make social change and do good even as consumers, whether by patronizing farmers' markets or using renewable energy sources. On campuses across the country since the 1990s, student advocates have particularly pressured administrators and corporations, most visibly Nike, to sell only those licensed items produced without sweatshop labor.

But doing good has proved difficult to define. Mr. Falcone stands at the intersection of a debate over whether and how American consumers and institutions, especially colleges and their students, can use their purchasing power to improve conditions for workers abroad.

To plunge into this discussion can feel like time-traveling to the City College cafeteria of the 1930s, when every left-wing sect had its own alcove and was certain every other sect was wrong.

Mr. Falcone has based Counter Sourcing's approach on the so-called fair-trade model, in which retailers buy directly from local producers for an established, fixed price in stable, long-term commercial relationships. Fair trade, however, has been practiced primarily with either agricultural commodities or handcrafts. There is no set of agreed-upon standards for how it would apply to manufactured goods like Mr. Falcone's.

Zack Knorr, the international campaigns coordinator for United Students Against Sweatshops, criticized Mr. Falcone for using a nonunion factory in Bangladesh while that nation is functioning under an emergency decree.

This objection has been echoed by some members of a coalition of workers' rights groups and university administrators that has been trying, unsuccessfully thus far, to set standards for purchasing licensed apparel; it favors using as suppliers only designated factories that abide by certain wage and working condition standards, and allow employees the right to organize.

Scott Nova, the executive director of the consortium, said Mr. Falcone was too small a customer to exert much positive pressure on factories.

"It's impossible for a single small customer to transform a factory into a fair-trade business," Mr. Nova said. "I'm sure the workers appreciate the few bucks. It's well meaning, but it's not meaningful."

But Shareen Hertel, a professor of political science at the University of Connecticut with a specialty in global social movements, defended Mr. Falcone's efforts; she has signed on to Counter Sourcing's advisory board.

"What Joe's doing, while incremental," she said, "is giving workers some voice. And workers really value having that voice."

Mr. Falcone said the bonuses his company pays to individual workers and the contributions it makes to social services programs for them provide some form of "worker empowerment." And he said that as his company grows, he plans to award equity stakes to its workers, which would give them clout even without a union.

"Everybody is against sweatshops," he said of his critics. "The question is: What are you for?"

Dawn Crim, a special assistant to the chancellor at the University of Wisconsin in Madison, was one administrator persuaded by Mr. Falcone's sales pitch.

"Our chancellor has always said to find the best supplier who makes the best product in a fair way and give him a chance," said Ms. Crim, whose responsibilities include licensing. "We're always on the lookout for a company that can operate in an ethical way."

SOURCE: Samuel G. Freedman, "On Education," *New York Times*, February 13, 2008, p. B5.

Financial Markets and Investors

A final set of stakeholders important to apparel brands and retailers is financial markets and investors because of the power they wield over the firm's corporate governance, company policies and practices, and continued availability of funding. The needs of shareholders have sometimes dominated corporate actions in ways that discourage social responsibility. By seeking to satisfy financial markets, investment groups, and individual shareholders' desires for short-term profits, companies sometimes give socially responsible practices lower priority to avoid possible divestment of funds.[50]

Financial Markets

Financial markets tend to reward firms that have quick growth and that provide investors with expanded earnings. There are mechanisms available, however, that track firms with social responsibility initiatives because the businesses are managing risk while embracing opportunities and, as a result, provide long-term value. If greater use would be made of this sort of information, then the businesses, including apparel brands and retailers, would have more incentive to carry out socially responsible activities.

The Dow Jones Sustainability Index tracks over 300 leaders in social responsibility through a series of criteria and weights that include labor practices, public reporting on social criteria, and eco-efficiency, along with others. Asset managers in 15 countries use the index to manage funds totaling over $5 billion.[51] In London and through its many world offices, the FTSE Group, owned by the Financial Times and the London Stock Exchange, provides financial information for use by asset managers, investment bankers, stock exchanges, brokers, and others for investment analysis, performance measurement, and asset allocation. It maintains the FTSE4Good global, United States, United Kingdom, and European indices, providing information about socially responsible companies that can be invested in or from which funds can be created.[52]

Investment Groups

A string of purchases of apparel brands and retailers made by private equity funds during 2006 and 2007 have fueled fears about investors' lack of support for long-term social responsibility goals. There are at least two ways that private equity funds are used. The first and most threatening to a company's social responsibility activities is referred to as asset stripping, whereby the company's profitable divisions and other assets are sold off. The goals of these funds are to provide private equity fund investors with large and quick payouts. As Allen White explains, these private equity funds "seek to move swiftly to acquire controlling interests in a firm and may impose severe cost-cutting measures that do not comport with long-term value creation measured against typical CSR goals, such as the enhancement of human and environmental capital."[53]

A second type of private equity fund is more promising for companies pursuing a social responsibility agenda. These funds plan to turn around an underperforming company, remaining invested in the company for five to seven, or sometimes even ten, years. They focus on improving management, product, and marketing performance. These private investors seek out certain types of companies, often from the same sector, and their stewardship model allows for the possibility of retaining a company's social responsibility initiatives.

Of major concern, companies controlled by private equity funds may cut costs by reducing staff and terminating training and other human capital development activities associated with social responsibility programs. In an announcement of the pending 2007 purchase of a majority share of Limited Brands, the company indicated that it was reducing its staff by 10 percent.[54] Additionally, because execution of social responsibility takes both direct dollars and staff time, such programs must effectively compete with every other company program and activity. White maintains that:

> Private equity investors are best viewed as agnostic on CSR matters. They are by definition newcomers with neither the institutional memory nor commitments to bring CSR activities to life. If CSR activities add mid-term

shareholder value, they are likely to survive at the firm. If they do not, they probably will not. Of course, many CSR investments are long term by nature. For the general partner of a private equity fund, intangible benefits such as reputation gains and attraction of top talent will likely fall into the category of "nice to have, but will not materialize within the life span of the fund."[55]

Gavin Power of the UN Global Compact believes that investor responsibility lags behind the activities of businesses and all types of investors will have to change their mind-sets from "trading" to long-term socially conscious "investment." Because implementing practices for social responsibility requires considerable resources, apparel brands and retailers pursuing these agendas may be forced to accept smaller short-term social responsibility improvements in exchange for long-term earnings.[56]

Individual Investors

Growth in socially responsible investing (SRI) offers the possibility that individual investors will consider the social and environmental consequences of their investments. With SRI, companies that meet certain standards are identified and invested in by investment firms. These screened funds evaluate publicly traded firms based on social and/or environmental criteria. The five most popular screening criteria are tobacco, alcohol, labor relations, environment, and gambling. Labor relations criteria focus primarily on actual employees of the company rather than on employees of contract factories commonly found in apparel production. A more appropriate screen for human rights that would capture these issues of concern in apparel production was used by funds holding only $11.2 billion in assets as compared with the more popular tobacco screening used by funds holding $124 billion out of a total of $1.7 trillion in assets in screened funds. An environment screen was used by funds holding $28.9 billion.[57] Thus, although SRI seems on the surface to support apparel brands' and retailers' efforts for socially responsible production and sourcing, many funds appear not to screen on relevant criteria pertaining to labor.

Investors interested in human rights may be better off scrutinizing individual companies' records rather than relying on mutual funds' screening. In 2000 on at least nine occasions, shareholders proposed resolutions for their companies to address issues of human and worker rights. However, SocialFunds.org claimed that there was still a long way to go. For example, "a shareholder resolution with Wal-Mart [in 2000] regarding vendor standards for working conditions and workers' rights was challenged by the company, on the basis of it being an 'ordinary business' matter, and omitted by the Securities Exchange Commission because of references to a 'sustainable living wage.'" SocialFunds.com goes on to warn that:

> Human rights will continue to remain a central goal of social investors, achievable through both shareholder activism and screening. But investors will have to remain vigilant to assure that improvements in company practices and codes of conduct become a reality on the ground in China, Haiti, Indonesia, and wherever global outsourcing leads them.[58]

The Calvert Fund is an example of an investment product that does screen for human rights and pays particular attention to global supply chains for apparel and footwear production. The fund takes credit, along with others, for pressuring Gap to publish its first sustainability report in 2003. As explained on its Web site:

> Calvert is particularly concerned about human rights abuses in the apparel and footwear manufacturing industry, which typically produces and sources from developing countries. All too often, companies source from vendors with sweatshop-like and substandard working conditions in their factories. . . . Calvert looks for disclosure of information regarding a company's suppliers, and a corporate commitment to improving working conditions for those who make its products, including codes of conduct and monitoring programs for its suppliers.[59]

Calvert Funds also screens for labor and workplace safety, which encompasses employment practices and international labor relations, especially the fundamental rights recognized by the ILO.[60] As is the case with many screened funds, what remains unclear is exactly what information Calvert Funds uses in its screening process and the extent to which it reliably evaluates apparel brands and retailers on their socially responsible practices. Although funds like the one offered by Calvert are a start, there is probably more information that could be incorporated into these screened funds. As well, more SRI funds need to incorporate the types of criteria relevant to global apparel production and sourcing.

There have been greater advances in socially responsible investing regarding environmental initiatives. The impacts of SRI on environmental practices of firms are supported by the Brown-Wilson Group, which provides global outsourcing services to companies. The group notes a rise in corporate demands for environmentally responsible suppliers, especially among publicly owned businesses, 94 percent of which intend to use environmental standards when negotiating contracts with suppliers. This compares with only 36 percent of privately owned businesses that are planning to do the same.[61] This is an example of how social responsibility for the environment is evolving differently than for workers.

◉

The Challenge That Lies Ahead

Stakeholder groups, particularly workers, labor unions, governments and intergovernmental organizations, advocacy organizations, consumer and pressure groups, and investors, play critical roles in improving working conditions and labor standards in the apparel industry. Yet solving labor and environmental problems in the apparel industry is not the sole responsibility of stakeholders external to the company—the work of apparel brands and retailers is also needed. Some stakeholders would like to impose solutions on business firms without their interference in determining the appropriateness or feasibility of the solution. However, the best solutions will result from collaboration among engaged stakeholders, including company personnel, rather than ones imposed by a single group. Although engagement may sometimes be challenging with certain stakeholder groups, the knowledge and experience brought to the table by the diverse stakeholders discussed here is vast and a valuable resource for apparel brands and retailers wishing to improve social responsibility.

Chapter 6

Codes of Conduct and Monitoring

◉

It's 10 o'clock at night and Charlie Kernaghan is driving around the garment district in Dhaka, Bangladesh. It's well past quitting time for the fabric cutters and seamstresses who started work in the factories at 8 o'clock that morning. But the workers aren't coming out of the gray, decaying buildings, even though they have already worked for 14 hours. (A 6-day, 60-hour workweek is the maximum allowable under Bangladeshi law.) Soon factory managers roll black crepe paper over the windows to conceal the workers toiling inside. By midnight, as work continues, the temperature hovers in the 90s outside and is even hotter inside the factories, forcing the managers to roll the paper back up. They're convinced that no one could be watching at such a late hour. But Kernaghan, director of the National Labor Committee, an anti-sweatshop organization based in New York, is there to observe them. "It's easy to see what's going on," he says. "Ask anyone in the neighborhood and they will tell you."

What's going on is that the workers, who are making clothes that will end up on the racks of large U.S. retailers, including Wal-Mart

Stores Inc., are being forced to work extraordinarily long shifts. "If [their employer] is on a deadline, they will work until two or three in the morning and they'll do it for two or three days in a row," explains Kernaghan.[1]

The first apparel brand credited with developing a code of conduct to set out its rules for labor standards and working conditions is Levi Strauss & Co. The company's leadership was not really surprising, given it had a reputation for being socially responsible, and in 1987, CEO Robert Haas oversaw development of its Aspirations Statement, which defined the shared values meant to guide the company's managers and workers. The Aspirations Statement contained the topic of Ethical Management Practices, and it explained that the company needed to set and enforce clear, ethical standards in all areas of the corporation. In the late 1980s and early 1990s, Levi's Aspirations Statement guided the company through downsizing of U.S. factories, where it attempted to minimize the negative impacts of domestic factory closure on workers and communities by announcing closures far in advance, providing more severance than was typical in the apparel industry, extending health care benefits, and supporting job training programs for former employees.[2] When the company was accused of using prison labor for production in China, Levi Strauss & Co. was pressured to put its values to work again, this time in the international setting, where production was increasingly located.[3]

In this chapter we present a theoretical framework for understanding the first and subsequent steps apparel brands and retailers take in response to labor problems found in global factories producing their goods. Following that, we discuss the content and basis for codes of conduct in greater depth. The last portion of the chapter addresses the monitoring that is conducted to ensure compliance with codes of conduct, its strengths and shortcomings, and why monitoring has not provided the solutions hoped for by apparel brands and retailers.

⊙

The Path to Social Responsibility

Simon Zadek, Chief Executive of AccountAbility, proposes five steps in the path to greater social responsibility that reflect the often evolving responses of apparel brands and retailers to issues in factories producing their products (Table 6.1). These five steps, defensive, compliance, managerial, strategic, and civil, reflect the learning process that

Table 6.1. Five Stages in the Path to Social Responsibility

Stage	What Companies Do	Why
Defensive	Deny practices, outcomes, or responsibilities.	To defend against attacks to their reputation that in the short term could affect sales, recruitment, productivity, and the brand.
Compliance	Adopt a policy-based compliance approach as a cost of doing business.	To mitigate the erosion of economic value in the medium term because of ongoing reputation and litigation risk.
Managerial	Embed the societal issue in their core management processes.	To mitigate the erosion of economic value in the medium term and to achieve longer-term gains by integrating responsible business practices into their daily operations.
Strategic	Integrate the societal issue into their core business strategies.	To enhance economic value in the long-term and to gain first-mover advantage by aligning strategy and process innovations with the societal issue.
Civil	Promote broad industry participation in corporate responsibility.	To enhance long-term economic value by overcoming any first-mover disadvantages and to realize gains through collective action.

Based on Zadek, S. (2004). The path to corporate responsibility. *Harvard Business Review*, 82(12), 125–132.

companies experience as their organizations develop an orientation toward social responsibility and philosophy, goals, values, and activities that complement that orientation.[4]

The Defensive Stage

Apparel brands and retailers have often been unprepared when the media shows up at company headquarters to tell of a problem that has been found in a factory used to produce its apparel. When criticism such as this is unexpected, the company's initial response may be shaped by legal or communication experts who are focused on "damage control." Thus, in the defensive stage, the company's initial response typically involves denying the problem exists or denying that it should be held responsible for the problem. By denying responsibility for the problem, apparel brands and retailers hope to protect their reputations and reduce short-term damages to sales. In the 1990s, when many labor and workplace issues were graphically revealed in the paper and in news shows on television, a typical response of apparel brands and retailers was that because they did not own the factory, they should not be expected to uphold human rights conventions, fair labor practices, and basic health and safety for workers. Most apparel brands and retailers now realize the many risks associated with denying responsibility and have moved closer to social responsibility by entering into a second stage called compliance.

The Compliance Stage

Once the criticism threatens a company's reputation and litigation is a possibility, its management designs corporate policies to address the problem and enters the compliance stage. These new policies and practices maintain value for the company by demonstrating to stakeholders that the company is responding to the issue. They also reduce the chance of litigation and further erosion of brand image. In the mid- to late 1990s, representatives of NGOs, advocacy organizations, and labor unions heavily pushed for apparel brands and retailers to set base labor and environmental standards to which apparel brands and retailers would be held accountable. It was during this period that a wave of codes of conduct were created. However, apparel brands and retailers, along with the stakeholders pushing them toward greater responsibility, realized that without some sort of managerial systems to assure that the code of conduct was followed, the problems would not really be solved. Thus, some apparel brands and retailers expanded their commitment to social responsibility by moving to the managerial stage.

The Managerial Stage

In the managerial stage, managers assume responsibility for addressing the issue and are held accountable for solving the problem. New management systems are created to integrate social responsibility into the company's day-to-day practices. In the mid- to late 1990s, apparel brands and retailers leading the industry in social responsibility developed corporate divisions around the social responsibility function. They hired employees whose full-time jobs were to implement the monitoring programs needed to assure that suppliers complied with their codes of conduct. Others used their commitment to social responsibility as their core mission, developing their businesses around socially responsible practices and product development.

The Strategic Stage

As leading apparel brands and retailers implemented programs needed to assure compliance with their codes of conduct, they incorporated social responsibility work into their corporate strategy for long-term success. Instead of viewing socially responsible practices as a requirement, they started considering it an opportunity. Although we seldom hear that the firms leading efforts in social responsibility hope to profit by means of a "first-mover" advantage through their innovative practices, the leaders may have benefited in this way. For example, as part of their newly expanded strategies, some brands developed comprehensive reports to tell their stakeholders about the sorts of problems they were finding in their factories and how they were working to address them.

The Civil Stage

A final and especially valuable step in the path to social responsibility is encompassed by the civil stage, wherein apparel brands and retailers work together to make social responsibility practices the industry standard. By working together toward new industry standards, more firms benefit from long-term profitability, and the potential disadvantages of being a first-mover are reduced. As apparel brands and retailers leading social responsibility initiatives entered the civil stage, they joined multi-stakeholder initiatives, where they could work together and with their stakeholders for industry-wide social responsibility. Codes of conduct are especially useful in the earlier of Zadek's stages to guide a business's understanding and embracement of social responsibility. But even at the strategic and civil stages, codes are a useful tool.

◉

Codes of Conduct

During the 1990s, the primary means of addressing violations of labor rights was for apparel brands and retailers to adopt a code of conduct. Codes of conduct detail a company's standards for labor practices and working conditions, and sometimes the environment, in factories producing their products. Through their codes of conduct, brands and retailers pledge to prevent worker exploitation and abuse, and provide a healthy and safe workplace.[5]

Codes of Conduct in the 1990s

By the late 1980s, Levi Strauss & Co. employees had become concerned about working conditions in the factories producing their goods. The aim of the company's 1991 Global Sourcing and Operating Guidelines was to assure the workers who made its products were treated with dignity and respect and a safe, healthful environment.[6] That document included country assessment guidelines and the standards required of Levi's business partners. Excerpts from Levi's 1991 Global Sourcing and Operating Guidelines illustrate the dimensions of the company's early code of conduct or Terms of Engagement (Table 6.2).

Table 6.2. Levi Strauss Terms of Engagement from their Global Sourcing and Operating Guidelines of 1991

Code	Description
Environmental requirements	We will only do business with partners who share our commitment to the environment. (Note. We intend this standard to be consistent with the approved language of Levi Strauss & Co.'s Environmental Action Group.)
Ethical standards	We will seek to identify and utilize business partners who aspire as individuals and in the conduct of their business to a set of ethical standards not incompatible with our own.
Health and safety	We will only utilize business partners who provide workers with a safe and healthy work environment. Business partners who provide residential facilities for their workers must provide safe and healthy facilities.
Legal requirements	We expect our business partners to be law abiding as individuals and to comply with legal requirements relevant to the conduct of all their businesses.
Employment practices	We will only do business with partners whose workers are in all cases, present voluntarily, not put at risk of physical harm, fairly compensated, allowed the right of free association and not exploited in any way. In addition, the following specific guidelines will be followed:

(continued)

Table 6.2. Levi Strauss Terms of Engagement from their
Global Sourcing and Operating Guidelines of 1991 (*continued*)

Code	Description
Wages and benefits	We will only do business with partners who provide wages and benefits that comply with any applicable law or match the prevailing local manufacturing or finishing industry practices. We will also favor business partners who share our commitment to contribute to the betterment of community conditions.
Working hours	While permitting flexibility in scheduling, we will identify prevailing local work hours and seek business partners who do not exceed them except for appropriately compensated overtime. While we favor partners who utilize less than sixty-hour work weeks, we will not use contractors who, on a regularly scheduled basis, require in excess of a sixty-hour week. Employees should be allowed one day off in seven.
Child labor	Use of child labor is not permissible. "Child" is defined at less than 14 years of age or younger than the compulsory age to be in school. We will not utilize partners who use child labor in any of their facilities. We support the development of legitimate workplace apprenticeship programs for the educational benefit of younger people.
Prison labor/ forced labor	We will not knowingly utilize prison or forced labor in contracting or subcontracting relationships in the manufacture of our products. We will not knowingly utilize or purchase materials from a business partner utilizing prison or forced labor.
Discrimination	While we recognize and respect cultural differences, we believe that workers should be employed on the basis of their ability to do the job, rather than on the basis of personal characteristics or beliefs. We will favor business partners who share this value.
Disciplinary practices	We will not utilize business partners who use corporal punishment or other forms of mental or physical coercion.

SOURCE: Levi Strauss & Co.

You can see that Levi's first code of conduct, similar to the codes that many other apparel brands and retailers would adopt in the years that followed, provided broad guidelines with little operational detail. Standards regarding child labor were most precise, with Levi Strauss & Co. indicating that using workers under the age of 14 was not permissible. It required employees to have a day off every week and noted that freedom of association was expected. However, standards for working hours were less clear. The Levi code limited regularly scheduled work to a sixty-hour workweek, but exceptions were allowed with inclusion of statements such as "while permitting flexibility in scheduling" and "while we favor partners who utilize less than sixty-hour work weeks." Further, the Levi's code did not detail prohibited discriminatory practices, and it did not uphold the right of collective bargaining. As compared with current codes, even the Levi's code left a little to be desired, but for 1991 it was a strong first effort.

In 1999, a study analyzing codes of conduct adopted by 27 of the largest U.S. apparel brands and retailers on the U.S. Department of Labor's Trendsetter List identified five major issues covered in the codes:[7]

- Use of forced and underage labor
- Working conditions
- Employee rights
- Monitoring of supplier compliance
- Enforcement

But the analysis also concluded a similar lack of specificity in the codes similar to Levi's.

All codes prohibited the use of prisoners or indentured workers. Nearly all (n=20) codes prohibited child labor and explicitly defined the minimum allowed age of workers. The authors considered working conditions as hours worked per week, work schedules, overtime pay, and employee safety and physical facilities (Figure 6.1). Of the 27 codes, 13 referenced hours of work allowed per week as being whatever the legal limits were for the producing country. Only seven of the

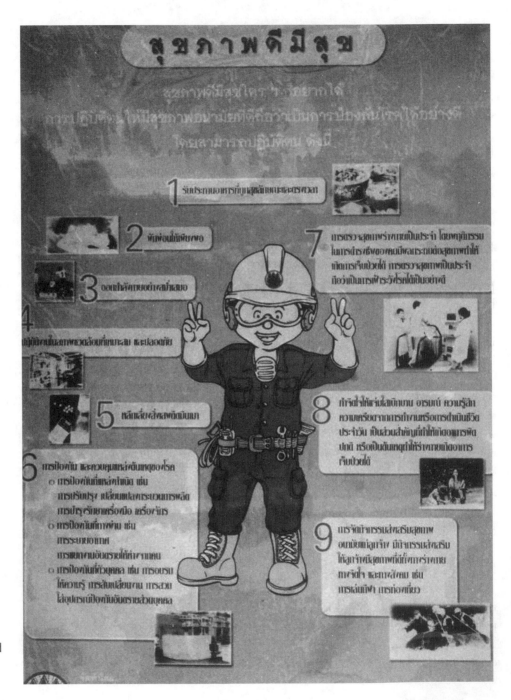

Figure 6.1

Many early codes of conduct focused on safety in the factory.

codes required workers to have one day off out of seven days. Most codes reviewed in the study did not detail expectations for physical facilities and safety requirements.

Most codes covered discrimination but did not offer specifics on discrimination related to hiring, promotion, or termination. Most did not discuss employee grievance systems, and only 6 of the 27 codes mentioned collective bargaining rights. All codes relied on a signed contractual agreement specifying that suppliers understood the provisions and were certifying they were in compliance. Most codes mentioned that the apparel brand or retailer might monitor facilities. Around two-thirds of the codes mentioned what the brands or retailers would do if noncompliance was found. These codes of conduct by themselves were not adequate for addressing the problems in apparel production (Figure 6.2).

As apparel brands and retailers gained more experience handling the problems they were finding in the workplace, and as vocal critics pointed out the shortcomings of their policies, they increased the precision and rigor and operational detail of their codes of conduct and monitored and enforced these strategies. For example, the Nordstrom code of conduct that was published in 2007 has more detail than the company's 1999 code (Table 6.3). Many new standards have

Figure 6.2
Young female workers benefit from collective bargaining.

Table 6.3. Excerpts from the 1999 and 2007 Nordstrom Codes of Conduct form provide examples of how codes have improved

Code Element	Nordstrom Standards and Business Practice Guidelines (1999)	Nordstrom Partnership Guidelines (2007)
Health and safety requirements	Nordstrom seeks partners who provide safe and healthy work environments for their workers, including adequate facilities and protections from exposure to hazardous conditions or materials.	Nordstrom seeks Partners who provide written standards for safe and healthy work environments and the prevention of accident and injury to the health of their workers, including adequate facilities and protections from exposure to hazardous conditions or materials. These provisions must include safe and healthy conditions for dormitories and residential facilities, and they must comply with local health and safety laws and standards.
Employment practices	Nordstrom firmly believes people are entitled to equal opportunity in employment. Although the company recognizes cultural differences exist, Nordstrom pursues business partners who do not discriminate and who demonstrate respect for the dignity of all people.	Nordstrom firmly believes people are entitled to equal opportunity in employment. Although the company recognizes cultural differences exist, Nordstrom will not pursue business relationships with Partners who discriminate in employment practices (including hiring, wages, benefits, assigned duties, advancement opportunities, discipline; termination or retirement on the basis of sex, race, color, religion, gender identity, age, sexual orientation, national origin, marital or maternity status, work or personal affiliations, political opinion or social or ethnic origin, or physical, mental or sensory disability).

Code Element	Nordstrom Standards and Business Practice Guidelines (1999)	Nordstrom Partnership Guidelines (2007)
Working wages, hours and over-time (now defined as two separate standards, (1) Wages and benefits and (2) Hours of work/overtime)	We expect our partners to offer wages, benefits and work conditions which are consistent with prevailing local industry standards. Nordstrom also expects them to comply with all applicable wage and hour laws, rules and regulations—including those related to overtime.	(1) Partners shall set wages, overtime pay and legally mandated benefits and allowances in compliance with all applicable laws. Workers shall be paid at least the minimum legal wage, or a wage that meets applicable local industry standards, whichever is greater. (2) While permitting flexibility in scheduling, we will identify local legal limits on work hours and seek Partners who do not exceed them except for appropriately compensated overtime. While we favor Partners who utilize less than 60 total hours per week, we will not use Partners who, on a regular basis, require in excess of 48 hours per week and 12 hours overtime per week, or as permitted by applicable law, whichever is lower. Employees must receive at least one uninterrupted, 24-hour rest period after every 6 consecutive days worked.
Prison or forced labor	Nordstrom will not conduct business with vendors who utilize prison, indentured or forced labor in the manufacture of its products.	Nordstrom will not conduct business with any Partner that uses involuntary labor of any kind; including prison labor, indentured labor, or forced labor. Overtime must be voluntary. Employees shall not be required to lodge "deposits" or identity papers upon commencing employment with the company or as a condition of employment.

SOURCE: Department of Labor (1999). Apparel industry and codes of conduct (pp. 167–168). Washington, DC: Author and http://about.nordstrom.com/aboutus/guidelines/default.asp.

been added, including ones focused on harassment and abuse, freedom of association, and subcontracting production. Further, almost all standards have specifically identified the business partners held to the code elements.

Leading codes of conduct are now based upon internationally agreed-upon human rights and environmental standards as expressed in the United Nations (UN) Declaration of Human Rights, the International Labour Organization (ILO) Declaration on Fundamental Principles and Rights at Work, as well as other ILO conventions, the Rio Declaration on Environment and Development, and the UN Convention Against Corruption and summarized in the UN Global Compact.

The ILO Declaration on Fundamental Principles and Rights at Work was adopted in 1998, and member states are expected to respect and promote its principles and rights, even if they have not ratified the relevant conventions. The declaration clearly expresses that these rights are universal, applying to all people in all states no matter their level of economic development. Eight "conventions" within the ILO document are especially important as a foundation for many apparel brands' and retailers' codes of conduct. The eight core conventions cover:

- Freedom of association and collective bargaining (Conventions C-87 and C-98)
- Elimination of forced and compulsory labor (C-29 and C105)
- Elimination of discrimination in respect of employment and occupation (C-100 and C-111)
- Abolition of child labor (C-138 and C-182)[8]

Table 6.4 details five of the critical labor conventions and connects each with the Phillips-Van Heusen code of conduct. As you can see, the company's code is clearly based on the ILO conventions. Apparel brands and retailers that do not address these core labor conventions in their codes of conduct have faced criticism from activist groups.

Freedom of association in itself is especially valuable for workers because joining a labor union puts them in contact with others who may be more educated about their rights and with whom they may seek

Table 6.4. Comparison of ILO Core Labor Conventions
and Phillips-Van Heusen Code Standards

International Labour Organization	Phillips-Van Heusen
Forced Labor Convention, 1930 (No. 29) This fundamental convention prohibits all forms of forced or compulsory labor, which is defined as "all work or service which is exacted from any person under the menace of any penalty and for which the said person has not offered himself voluntarily."	**Forced Labor** We will not be associated with any vendor who uses [any] form of mental or physical coercion. We will not do business with any vendor who utilizes forced labor whether in the form of prison labor, indentured labor, bonded labor or otherwise.
Discrimination (Employment and Occupation) Convention, 1958 (No. 111) This fundamental convention defines discrimination as any distinction, exclusion or preference made on the basis of race, color, sex, religion, political opinion, national extraction or social origin, which has the effect of nullifying or impairing equality of opportunity or treatment in employment or occupation. It requires ratifying states to declare and pursue a national policy designed to promote, by methods appropriate to national conditions and practice, equality of opportunity and treatment in respect of employment and occupation, with a view to eliminating any discrimination in these fields. This includes discrimination in relation to access to vocational training, access to employment and to particular occupations, and terms and conditions of employment.	**Nondiscrimination** We will not do business with any vendor who discriminates in employment, including hiring, salary, benefits, advancement, discipline, termination or retirement, on the basis of gender, race, religion, age, disability, sexual orientation, nationality, political opinion, or social or ethnic origin.

(continued)

Table 6.4. Comparison of ILO Core Labor Conventions
and Phillips-Van Heusen Code Standards (*continued*)

International Labour Organization	Phillips-Van Heusen
Minimum Age Convention, 1973 (No. 138) This fundamental convention sets the general minimum age for admission to employment or work at 15 years (13 for light work) and the minimum age for hazardous work at 18 (16 under certain strict conditions). It provides for the possibility of initially setting the general minimum age at 14 (12 for light work) where the economy and educational facilities are insufficiently developed.	**Child Labor** Employees of our vendors must be over the applicable minimum legal age requirement, or be at least 15 years old (or 14 years old where the law of the country of manufacture allows) or older than the age for completing compulsory education in the country of manufacture, whichever is greater. Vendors must observe all legal requirements for work of authorized minors, particularly those pertaining to hours of work, wages, minimum education and working conditions. We encourage vendors to support night classes and work-study programs.
Freedom of Association and Protection of the Right to Organize Convention, 1948 (No. 87) This fundamental convention sets forth the right for workers and employers to establish and join organizations of their own choosing without previous authorization. Workers' and employers' organizations shall organize freely and not be liable to be dissolved or suspended by administrative authority, and they shall have the right to establish and join federations and confederations, which may in turn affiliate with international organizations of workers and employers.	**Freedom of Association and Collective Bargaining** Employees should be free to join organizations of their own choice. Vendors shall recognize and respect the right of employees to freedom of association and collective bargaining. Employees should not be subjected to intimidation or harassment in the exercise of their right to join or to refrain from joining any organization.

Table 6.4. Comparison of ILO Core Labor Conventions
and Phillips-Van Heusen Code Standards (*continued*)

International Labour Organization	Phillips-Van Heusen
Right to Organize and Collective Bargaining Convention, 1949 (No. 98) This fundamental convention provides that workers shall enjoy adequate protection against acts of anti-union discrimination, including requirements that a worker not join a union or relinquish trade union membership for employment, or dismissal of a worker because of union membership or participation in union activities. Workers' and employers' organizations shall enjoy adequate protection against any acts of interference by each other, in particular the establishment of workers' organizations under the domination of employers or employers' organizations, or the support of workers' organizations by financial or other means, with the object of placing such organizations under the control of employers or employers' organizations. The convention also enshrines the right to collective bargaining.	(See previous page.)

SOURCE: Excerpts from www.ilo.org and www.pvh.com/CorpResp_WorldAction.html.

solutions. However, without the companion opportunity for representatives of the union to bargain collectively on behalf of the entire group of workers, each individual is left to his or her own resources when negotiating with management for pay and other benefits. Although this may seem like a minor difference, for a young woman of age 15 or 16 with little education and working for the first time, the opportunity to have someone more experienced with the laws and rights of workers bargain with factory management for appropriate wages and benefits can make a tremendous difference.

Many apparel brands and retailers include standards in their codes of conduct that go beyond the eight core labor conventions listed above, and they look to a variety of sources for guidance. For example, the ILO has a convention related to hours of work. Convention C1 was adopted in 1919 and sets the maximum workweek to be 48 hours—8 hours per day. The convention stipulates when it is appropriate to exceed this weekly total.[9]

To address proper wages, apparel brands and retailers often require remuneration at the minimum wage of the producing country. Alternatively, the codes sometimes specify paying a higher "prevailing" wage for the industry of a country. This makes sense because unless the prevailing industry wage is paid, the best workers will go elsewhere.

The practice of requiring minimum wages or prevailing wages has not satisfied all stakeholders. If you have ever tried to live on minimum-wage earnings, you can understand why. Some stakeholder groups demand payment of a living wage allowing workers to cover their basic needs. It is hard to disagree with the idea that workers should be paid enough to live on, and many apparel brands and retailers do not disagree. However, at the same time, many resist requiring a living wage standard in their codes of conduct. One reason is that it would be difficult if not impossible to calculate and enforce. Calculating a living wage must be done for each locale in which apparel is produced. A living wage for El Progreso, Honduras, would be very different from one for Ho Chi Minh City, Vietnam. There are also potential issues at the factory level because brands and retailers would be requiring the factory to share a greater amount of revenue with its workers. Payment of a living wage is also complicated by the fact that factories often serve multiple brands that may not be equally committed to paying a living wage. Finally, payment of a living wage may be one thing that brands and retailers have decided they cannot or will not do. Interestingly, Levi Strauss & Co. recently had to deal with this firsthand. Until 2007, the multi-stakeholder initiative it was associated with was the Europe-based Ethical Trading Initiative (ETI). The ETI code of conduct, along with that of another Europe-based multi-stakeholder initiative, the Fair Wear Foundation and the Worker Rights Consortium, indicates that a living wage should be paid. Levi Strauss & Co. did not believe this was something it had the capability of enforcing and therefore could not enforce. Thus, the brand was suspended from the ETI.[10] This example illustrates that every brand and retailer will ultimately decide what it can and cannot do with regard to social responsibility. Even leaders in social responsibility may not be able to adopt every requested social responsibility practice.

Adoption of Codes of Conduct in the Apparel Industry

Adopting a code of conduct has been a first step for many industry leaders attempting to become more socially responsible to workers making their products. But have these codes been adopted by all apparel brands and retailers? "Not likely" appears to be the answer to that question.

In 2007, researchers conducted an analysis of the Web sites of 119 U.S. apparel brands and retailers selected from the largest companies by volume of sales. Surprisingly, only about 27 percent published a code of conduct detailing their labor standards and required working conditions on their Web sites.[11] In addition, the researchers conducted a mail survey of the same 119 companies and received responses from only 13; the others were unwilling to share information about their practices, even though no company was to be named and the data from all respondents were to be pooled. Does the absence of a code of conduct on the company Web site or nonresponse to a survey mean that the apparel brand or retailer has not adopted a code? Not necessarily. We know from our involvement in the field that some companies do have codes of conduct but do not publish them. Yet at least some of the brands and retailers studied have probably not taken this basic step down the path to social responsibility.

⊙

Monitoring for Compliance

Even though codes of conduct have been adopted by many major apparel brands and retailers since the 1990s, another concern is that some may do little to enforce the codes beyond requiring suppliers to sign off in their contracts that the factories used were in compliance with the code.[12] These unenforced codes are termed "paper codes," and they have made little positive impact on the situations workers face in global factories producing apparel. Monitoring, sometimes referred to as social auditing, is the most commonly used way of determining whether a brand or retailer's supplier factories are in compliance with a code of conduct. Apparel brands and retailers that conduct monitoring against their codes of conduct have moved a step closer toward social responsibility at the managerial stage.

What Monitors Look For

When we reviewed the basic elements of codes of conduct, we pointed out how much more specific they had become over time. However, if you were to set out to monitor against those codes of conduct, you realize just how little guidance even present-day codes offer. You can't just walk into a factory, look around, and know whether the wages paid are appropriate, the hours worked are under the maximum allowable in the code, or the workers are harassed and abused. What does someone monitoring a factory actually do to determine whether the supplier is in compliance? What benchmarks are used to determine compliance? Examining benchmarks the Fair Labor Association (FLA) uses when monitoring for harassment and abuse reveals the depth that monitoring must reach in order to identify noncompliance (Box 6.1).

Whether conducted by the brand or retailer's own staff or by a hired organization, audits generally include document review, site inspection, and interviews with workers by which monitors check off whether a

Box 6.1. Details of Benchmarks the Fair Labor Association
Uses When Determining Whether a Factory Complies
with Its Harassment and Abuse Standard

The FLA Workplace Code of Conduct provision relating to harassment or abuse states: *"Every employee will be treated with respect and dignity. No employee will be subject to any physical, sexual, psychological or verbal harassment or abuse."*

The FLA Benchmarks for Harassment or Abuse are the following:
- Employers will utilize progressive discipline, e.g., escalating discipline using steps such as verbal warning, written warning, suspension, termination. Any exceptions to this rule, e.g., immediate termination for theft or assault, shall be in writing and clearly communicated to workers.
- Employers will not use physical discipline, including slaps, pushes or other forms of physical contact (or threats of physical discipline).
- Employers shall not offer preferential work assignments or other preferential treatment of any kind in actual or implied exchange for a sexual relationship, nor subject employees to prejudicial treatment of any kind in retaliation for refused sexual advances.
- Employers will utilize consistent written disciplinary practices that are applied fairly among all workers.
- Employers will provide training to managers and supervisors in appropriate disciplinary practices.
- Management will discipline (could include combinations of counseling, warnings, demotions, and termination) anyone (including managers or fellow workers) who engages in any physical, sexual, psychological or verbal harassment or abuse.
- Employers will maintain written records of disciplinary actions taken.
- Employers will prohibit screaming, threatening, or demeaning verbal language.
- Security practices will be gender-appropriate and non-intrusive.
- Access to food, water, toilets, medical care or health clinics or other basic necessities will not be used as either reward or punishment.
- Employers will not unreasonably restrain freedom of movement of workers, including movement in canteen, during breaks, using toilets, accessing water, or to access necessary medical attention.
- Employers will not use monetary fines and penalties for poor performance.

SOURCE: Fair Labor Association (2006). *Annual Public Report 2006* (pp. 29–30).

factory is in compliance with each benchmark.[13] The document review includes calculation of whether correct wages were paid or whether wages are owed to the workers. The monitors may also conduct factory surveillance, observing when the factory is open and when workers end their shifts.[14] As well as auditing suppliers that are already in contract with brands and retailers, many companies have audits conducted in advance of their contracting with a new factory to ensure that the supplier meets at least their minimum requirements (Box 6.2).

Box 6.2. What Happens in a Social Audit?

Social auditors will visit a supplier to check whether there is conformity with a labor standard laid out in the code of conduct they have been given. The objectives can include assessing the problems that exist in a factory or developing a corrective action or remediation plan.

A social audit typically includes three steps, sometimes referred to as the "circle of evidence" and takes anywhere from a few hours to a few days.

A **document review** is carried out to check wages and hours, bonuses, personnel management, the application of internal regulations, and collective bargaining agreements. Documents reviewed can include time cards, content receipts, union declarations, and personnel files. How useful a document review is depends first of all on how accurate these documents are.

A **site inspection**—also referred to as a physical inspection or factory walk-through—might reveal health and safety problems. Inspectors might look at emergency exits, fire extinguishers, bathrooms, alleys or passageways, ventilation, cleaning, safety equipment, and noise levels. A walkthrough might also reveal information on management-worker relations, for instance whether workers seem uncomfortable and stop talking when the line supervisor appears.

Interviews should be a key element of an audit. Interviews are usually held with workers, management, and in best practice cases, with local unions and/or NGOs. It is valuable for auditors to speak directly with workers about the conditions they work in. Auditors can use the interviews, which can also happen outside factory premises, to check if workers get paid the legal minimum wage and the legal overtime rate, whether management has prevented union activities, etc. (CCC, 2005, p. 23).

SOURCE: Clean Clothes Campaign (2005). *Looking for a quick fix: How weak social auditing is keeping workers in sweatshops*. Retrieved on 11/23/05 from www.cleanclothes.org.

Who Conducts the Monitoring?

Conducting factory monitoring for apparel brands and retailers has been a rapidly growing business over the last decade. The Clean Clothes Campaign estimates that at least 30,000 apparel factory audits are conducted annually, but notes that there is considerable variation in the quality of audits and the credibility of monitors.[15] Suppliers are often monitored by representatives of multiple brands and retailers. Factory management complains that the time spent with monitors interrupts production and diverts them from their primary responsibility of running the workplace. Suppliers are urging the apparel industry to arrive at a single set of standards, because small differences in requirements sometimes mean being in compliance for one brand but being out of compliance for another. The classic example is the location of the fire extinguisher or medical kit where one brand requires the equipment to be at a certain height and another brand requires the equipment to be installed 6 inches higher or lower so the factories move them depending upon which brand is auditing that day (Figure 6.3). Despite the large numbers of audits being conducted each year, large numbers of apparel factories have not been audited at all. For example, companies have focused on what is termed "first-tier" suppliers, ignoring the subcontract facilities and component suppliers used to make their products. Besides having a standard code used across the industry, retailers and brands could coordinate monitoring to reduce interruptions and increase efficiency, and to reach a larger number of factories.

Monitoring is classified in different ways depending on

Figure 6.3
Factory audits cover location of medical kits.

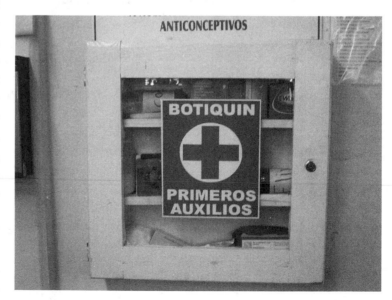

who conducts the audits. In the sections that follow, we discuss the various types of monitoring, including internal monitoring, external monitoring done by private organizations, and independent monitoring for verification.

Internal Monitoring

Internal monitoring is conducted by employees of the apparel brand or retailer, or by employees of a factory. An advantage of internal monitoring is that the individuals conducting the audits are more freely able to access information relevant to production without jeopardizing privileged information or trade secrets such as the design of the upcoming season's shoes or garments.[16] When monitoring was first initiated by companies, some used their quality control staff, who frequently visited the factories to check on production.[17] Other brands and retailers decided to hire their own compliance staff. When brands or retailers carry out the monitoring, it aids them in identifying the causes for noncompliance and creating and implementing corrective action plans.[18] Sometimes the problem is a factory-based issue, and other times it is an issue caused by the brand's or retailer's own policies and procedures.

Private External Monitoring

For apparel brands and retailers without the resources needed to inspect their own factories, third-party monitoring firms can be contracted to do so; this is called external monitoring. What type of firm is hired for factory monitoring?

There are generally four types of firms that engage in monitoring for hire:

- Global financial auditing firms (e.g., PricewaterhouseCoopers, Ernst & Young)
- Quality control firms (e.g., Intertek, Société Générale de Surveillance, or SGS)

- Specialized for-profit audit firms (e.g., CSCC—formerly known as Cal-Safety, A&L Group—also known as ALGI)
- Nonprofit organizations (often those based in the country or region they monitor)[19]

Global financial auditing firms were frequently used when monitoring was first initiated in the 1990s. The firms had an existing presence with offices around the world and employed local staff familiar with the language and culture in those regions.[20] The practice of using financial auditing firms for factory monitoring slowed, in part because of the conflicts of interest companies were having because they also provided other services to the brands and retailers hiring them.[21] PricewaterhouseCoopers decided to discontinue social auditing, and some of those who had been involved in monitoring for the company created their own company, known as Global Social Compliance.

Quality control firms had typically provided services to brands and retailers to ensure garments were produced with a specified quality, with appropriate labeling and packaging, and in compliance with other product-related criteria. As monitoring became increasingly important in the 1990s, these firms expanded into auditing for compliance with labor standards and working conditions.[22] Their knowledge about factories and expertise in production processes allow monitors to easily evaluate certain standards. For example, quality control firms can estimate whether factories have the capacity to produce all the contracted work or whether they are likely to have to subcontract or use home workers to complete orders.[23]

Entirely new firms offering these specific social audit services emerged over the last decade as well and include some located in production countries such as LIFT Standards, which was started in Bangladesh, T-Group Solutions in India, and others, such as CSCC and ALGI, which are located in the United States. These are all for-profit firms, which are sometimes distinguished from nonprofit organizations involved in monitoring because they may prioritize making a profit over finding and solving workplace problems.[24]

Nonprofit monitoring organizations include civil society organizations based in production regions, such as Groupo de Monitoreo Independiente de El Salvador (GMIES) and Commission for the Verification of Codes and Conduct (COVERCO) based in Guatemala. GMIES proved its credibility in monitoring factories with high-profile problems. GMIES was hired to monitor and work out corrective action plans for Gap's Mandarin International factory in 1996, where harassment and abuse, excessive working hours, and firing of workers attempting to organize a union had been found the previous year. Likewise, COVERCO was founded at least partly out of Liz Claiborne's request for an independent monitor.[25] Sometimes these civil society groups were originally formed to address certain conditions in their countries but have added the monitoring function as a profit-making service operation as more and more companies desired monitors with in-depth understanding of the issues in the region (Figure 6.4).

The large social auditing group Verité is classified as nonprofit, but some critics view its focus and operations as more similar to the private

Figure 6.4
Outside a factory in Guatemala.

firms because Verité's primary activity is conducting monitoring, and they are believed not to have close ties to the nonprofit grassroots organizations that work collaboratively with civil society in production regions.[26] However, Verité is involved at the grassroots level in China, where the organization has conducted training sessions for local NGOs to conduct audits. As well, Verité works collaboratively with Chinese NGOs and academics to run a mobile worker education program that has conducted training on labor rights and other topics with nearly 70,000 workers.[27] Further, when conducting a factory audit, Verité is known for spending up to two-thirds of its time on worker interviews, sometimes utilizing focus group discussions, which allows them to uncover and confirm compliance issues.[28]

Independent Monitoring for Verification

Independent monitoring is a type of external monitoring; however, it differs in that independent monitors have no direct relationship with the company, are not paid by the company, and usually provide some level of public reporting to verify what is found.[29] The monitors themselves may be private monitors or local civil society organizations from the area where production is located, such as those discussed in the previous section.

Teams of monitors having different skills and knowledge can be particularly effective in uncovering compliance breaches. Independent monitors are considered by many to be the most credible because they are usually independent from companies. Payment is typically handled by an intermediary, which reduces the possibility of conflict of interest that may occur when monitors want to please clients paying for their services.[30] Two multi-stakeholder initiatives, the Fair Labor Association and the Fair Wear Foundation, arrange and pay for unannounced audits to verify their member companies' efforts.

Both internal monitoring and independent verification are often necessary. As Roseann Casey explains, "Internal monitoring allows for the quality of relationships that is not possible with [independent] monitoring, including in-depth knowledge of issues and problems and a long-term commitment to solutions. . . . [Independent] monitoring will always have a degree of objectivity and legitimacy. The combination of the two will build stronger solutions."[31] The Web site analysis of 119 large apparel brands and retailers found 23 brands and retailers indicating that they required their factories to be monitored in some way. Of the 23, 18 reported they conducted both internal and independent external monitoring in their factories.[32]

Remediation of Problems

What happens when a factory is noncompliant with a brand or retailer's code of conduct? In the 1990s, many brands and retailers would "cut and run," immediately stopping production with factories that were found to be out of compliance. But firms quickly realized that they would be unlikely to find *any* completely compliant factories to which they could move production. In other words, there is no such thing as 100 percent compliance. Additionally, ending business with a factory could do more harm than good to the workers, who would potentially lose their jobs as the factory lost orders.[33] Many brands have concluded that it is better to effectively remediate the problems that are found than to stop production. They work with the factories to develop remediation or corrective action plans addressing problems they find.[34] Reports issued by the FLA indicate how problems found in factories are being addressed. Box 6.3 shows how a member company of the FLA dealt with a problem found regarding harassment and abuse in a factory in Bangladesh.

Remediation is most effective when the brands or retailers collaborate with workers and factory management to develop corrective actions. Casey explains that "if problems are not addressed the supplier is, in effect, defining the relationship as one of inherent risk and unacceptable terms of engagement."[35] To build a positive relationship with suppliers that defines compliance as a win-win opportunity, it is important that apparel brands and retailers take an active, collaborative role in defining, supporting, and verifying remediation with the

> **Box 6.3.** How an FLA Company Remediated
> a Problem of Harassment and Abuse
>
> A case in Bangladesh involved mainly verbal abuse by supervisors who tended to shout at workers when they did not meet their production goals, made mistakes, or had been absent from work. Based on interviews and discussions with supervisors and workers, FLA accredited monitors found that verbal abuse occurred when workers failed to meet production targets or produced product with several defects. Moreover, workers who took unauthorized leave were made to stand at the front of the sewing line for 30 minutes as punishment for not asking permission before taking off of work. In response to these issues, the FLA companies required the supervisors and management of the factory to attend a training program on the proper treatment of employees and progressive disciplinary actions and required the factory to revise its policies and procedures relating to discipline. With the help of a consultant, the factory established and posted its revised disciplinary policy and procedures, and training was provided to both management and workers. During a subsequent visit, worker interviews were conducted and no evidence of verbal abuse was identified.
>
> SOURCE: Fair Labor Association (2006). Annual public report 2006. Available from http://www.fairlabor.org/all/2006PublicReport.pdf.

suppliers' workers and factory management. Many brands and retailers now have a sort of "three-strike" policy whereby they will attempt to work with noncompliant suppliers, but if remediation efforts fail three times, they will stop using the suppliers.

◉

Positive Outcomes of Monitoring

A decade of monitoring factories for compliance with apparel brands' and retailers' codes of conduct has provided some important lessons. Monitoring has provided valuable baseline information about working conditions at the factory and supply chain levels and a basis for tracking progress over time. Monitoring is useful for screening whether potential suppliers meet the brands' and retailers' minimum standards.[36] Additionally, some factory conditions have improved as a result of monitoring and the remediation that followed. In particular, factories tend to be safer and healthier, with improvements in lighting and ventilation and sufficient and clean toilets.[37] The ETI has found more factories paying at least the home country's minimum wage and correct overtime rates, and reducing working hours.[38] The Clean Clothes Campaign does not agree that monitoring is helping improve working hours and wages but reports the presence of child and forced labor has declined.[39] Doug Cahn, former vice president of human rights for Reebok, explains that "[monitoring] isn't the game changer that we thought it would be 10 years ago. That's something that we've learned."[40]

◉

Shortcomings of Monitoring

Despite a considerable amount of time and money directed toward monitoring factories for compliance to a code of conduct, leading apparel brands and retailers recognize that monitoring has not provided the improvements in factory conditions that they had hoped for. A study conducted by Richard Locke, Fei Qin, and Alberto Brause using data from Nike's internal audits of apparel, footwear, and sports equipment (e.g., soccer balls) factories reveals these shortcomings. Mean scores on compliance for factories, based on a 100-point scale with 100 meaning the factory was 100 percent compliant with Nike's code of conduct, revealed that apparel factories were only 66 percent compliant and footwear factories were only 68 percent compliant. Additionally, there was considerable variability in individual factory scores, with at least one facility found to be only 20 percent compliant and another to be much closer to full compliance (90 percent). Over time, almost 80 percent of Nike's suppliers had stagnant or worsening compliance ratings. Locke et al.'s study found a regional effect to noncompliance, with Nike's factories in the Americas and the Europe, Middle East, and Africa (EMEA) regions having slightly higher rates of compliance than factories in North Asia (e.g., China and Vietnam) and South Asia (e.g., Indonesia and India). The study also found variability across factories within single countries.[41] Nike is one of the leaders in the social responsibility movement, with strong commitment to monitoring and remediation. This study underlines the importance of continuous improvement because 100 percent compliance is still far from being realized even in this leader's supplier factories.

A 2007 *BusinessWeek* article outlined the types of labor problems found in various apparel-producing countries around the world (Table 6.5).[42] In addition, from our experience, we know that treatment of migrant workers from Myanmar is a problem in Thailand, and Central America is noted for union busting and for discrimination in hiring. Although the specific problems vary somewhat in importance from country to country, it is obvious that there is still much work to be done in every location to ensure health and safety, human rights, and fair labor practices for apparel workers.

Table 6.5. Notable Labor Problems in Various Countries

Country	Problems
China	Occupational safety, wages and hours, and freedom of association are the most common problems in export manufacturing factories. Excess overtime and underpayment for regular hours and overtime are especially frequent. There are no independent trade unions, and attempts to form independent organizations are swiftly repressed. Health and safety violations also are high.
Brazil	The biggest labor problems are forced labor, unequal pay for women, and occupational safety. Women earn 54% to 67% of male counterparts.
India	India also rates poor in occupational safety, overtime, and fair pay in export factories. In 2004, 60% of factories audited by Verité violated minimum-wage rules, and 83% violated overtime rules. Machine, chemical, and fire safety problems were found in most factories audited. Up to 65 million work in slavery or bondage, most of them from the Dalit caste. Some 100 million children ages 5 to 14 work, according to one estimate, and at least 12.6 million work full time.

(continued)

Table 6.5. Notable Labor Problems in Various Countries (*continued*)

Country	Problems
Indonesia	Compliance is weakest regarding child labor, occupational safety, and work hours and wages. Enforcement of minimum-wage rules is poor in export manufacturing factories.
Mexico	A chief problem in export factories is freedom of association. About one-quarter of workers in the formal sector belong to unions. But forming an independent union is difficult—organizers often are fired and sometimes assaulted. Sweatshop conditions persist in many export assembly plants near the U.S. border and elsewhere in the country. Verité audits have detected high rates of discrimination based on pregnancy status.
Peru	While compliance with freedom of association, occupational safety, and forced labor rules is "moderate," Peru rates "poor" in compliance with wage and overtime standards. An estimated 21% of workers earn less than minimum wage, and violations are much greater among temporary workers, who make up a significant portion of the workforce. Mandatory overtime is common.
Philippines	Minimum-wage, overtime, and gender-discrimination offenses are common in export sectors. More than one-third of garment factories violate wage and work-hour rules, according to one study. Many employers avoid paying minimum wage by exploiting government exemptions for "apprentices" and companies employing less than 10 workers. An estimated 4 million children ages 5 to 17 work—more than half of them in hazardous conditions. Women average half the pay of men.
South Africa	Compliance is "moderate" in terms of freedom of association, but "poor" in child labor, occupational safety, and hours and wages.
Sri Lanka	Violations of health and safety, overtime, and wage rules are especially serious. Verité found safety violations in most factories audited in 2003 and 2004, including blocked exits, excessive noise, and lack of personal protection. Forced overtime, compulsory work on Sundays and holidays, and underpayment of wages are reportedly common.

Adapted from How China's labor conditions stack up against those of other low-cost nations. (2006, November 27). *BusinessWeek*, Online Extra.

Certain types of serious problems are especially difficult to identify with monitoring. Monitoring frequently misses problems in the hard-to-observe areas of freedom of association, working hours, abuse, and harassment.[43] Sometimes seemingly easy-to-identify problems are overlooked. For example, at the Hermosa apparel factory in El Salvador, monitors noted that factory management was documenting that money for various worker benefits was appropriately collected from worker pay. Unfortunately, monitors did not uncover that factory management was not submitting this collection to the government. The problem was not identified until the factory closed, and there was no money for severance or health care because financial difficulties had rendered the factory management unable to make the required payments to the government.[44]

◉

Effectiveness of Codes of Conduct and Monitoring

Why has monitoring against a code of conduct been so ineffective in improving labor standards and working conditions in apparel factories? The standards set in the codes of conduct are not the problem; rather, the interpretation and implementation of these is inconsistent. Various reports prepared by groups that analyze monitoring point to several broad reasons, including various aspects of the monitoring process, the quality of monitoring, fraudulent practices of factory management and others, and the limited involvement of workers and their lack of knowledge about their rights.

Monitoring Processes

The manner in which monitoring has been implemented has led to shortcomings in finding and remediating problems and have led to credibility problems. Brands and retailers spend a considerable amount of money on monitoring, whether paying their own staff or hiring a private monitoring firm. As a result, a large proportion of a labor compliance budget goes toward identifying problems, and a little is left to help factories in identifying ways to fix the problems. There is also needless duplication of monitoring and lack of standardization of codes. For example, monitoring conducted for one brand or retailer often duplicates monitoring being conducted for another brand that uses the same factory. It is not uncommon for brands and retailers using the same factory to develop conflicting plans to remediate problems.[45] When monitoring is done for a brand or retailer, the factory typically knows in advance the date on which the monitors will arrive. Consequently, the factory has an opportunity to "stage" the audit, preparing management and workers to say the "right" things and increasing the likelihood that management will hide problems.[46]

Most brands and retailers do not use independent monitoring to verify the conditions found; they rely solely on the monitoring they contract and pay for themselves. When a brand, retailer, or factory selects, contracts, and pays the monitor, there is a chance of conflict of interest. A monitor wishing to be rehired may be more lenient and provide a "pass" so as not to anger the factory management. Further, reports issued by a brand or retailer that are based on internal monitoring and voluntary codes are vulnerable to corporate manipulation.[47] The Clean Clothes Campaign explains the concerns with credibility that result from the lack of independent monitoring as follows:

> The very parties who already acknowledge responsibility for abusing and exploiting workers over the past years are also commissioning the vast majority of audits. . . . This is one of the reasons the more responsive brand name companies are unlikely to hold up an audit report as evidence to consumers that their supply chains are clean. And this is why merely having a factory audited or certified by one standard or another is not, on its own, going to protect workers, and it is not going to protect a sourcing company from the risk that exploitation and abuse will be uncovered at some stage of the supply chain.[48]

Quality of Monitoring

Beyond the way that monitors are hired and paid, the quality of the monitoring itself leaves much to be desired. The following quality issues are found with current monitoring practices:

- Monitoring is done too infrequently to determine what happens at the factory on a day-to-day basis.
- Too little time is spent at the factory during an audit—just a few hours or at most one or two days are allotted to the site visit. As a result, monitors are often unable to detect the large issues.[49]
- Monitors often do no advance work such as interviewing local NGOs and labor organizations that would better prepare them to identify problems prevalent in the area.
- Interviews with workers that are conducted at the factory—or even worse, in front of management—make it too easy for workers to be coached to say the right thing or intimidated from revealing the problems they face.
- Monitors conducting the interviews do not always explain whom they represent nor make any effort to establish rapport with the workers. These and the previously discussed interviewing practices make it unlikely that workers will share a true picture of their working conditions. The best interviewing is conducted off-site, includes confidential worker interviews, contains open-ended questioning, and involves all types of workers (contract, migrant, female).[50]
- Personal characteristics of the interviewer also matter. COVERCO has determined that the social class, gender, and age of the monitor are all critical to the success of the interview. For example, an older American man working in quality control for an apparel brand or retailer is unlikely to be able to establish rapport with a teenage girl working in a factory in El Salvador.
- The questions asked by monitors in the interviews can also be limiting. Questions need to cover the full range of relevant standards and elicit sufficient answers, not simply "yes" or "no."[51]

⊚ Monitors often receive inadequate training on labor laws, interviewing processes, and other essential tasks required for the audit. Quality control firms initially hired as external monitors had no prior expertise in worker rights.[52] Here is one person's account, which highlights the lack of training monitors receive:

> Halfway over the Pacific it dawns on me that I have no idea what my job is. It's October 15, 1998 and twelve hours ago, I was in the southern California offices of a [private] monitoring company that inspects factories for safety violations and human rights abuses throughout the world. I had been hired over the phone a few days before. My sole qualification for the job? I speak Chinese and have a friend already working for the company. I assumed there would be some sort of lengthy training process to teach me how to be a human rights inspector. There wasn't.[53]

⊚ Monitors generally do not investigate causes of problems. Therefore, any efforts to correct problems often do not provide long-term solutions and the problems resurface within a few months.[54]

Certain types of abuses are more difficult to identify than others. Generally, physical health and safety problems that can be easily observed are most likely to be found. But what would seem observable and clear-cut is not always the case. For example, a monitor may be shown a medical facility, but without spending considerable time on-site or following up in interviews, the monitor may not learn whether a doctor ever comes to the facility to treat workers.

The lack of skilled monitors becomes especially evident with the less easily observed problems. For example, discrimination and harassment are very difficult to identify. Young women can be embarrassed or afraid to share that they have been sexually harassed. The Clean Clothes Campaign describes a factory where nearly all of the women sewers were above the age of 45 or were unmarried. The auditor failed to recognize the suppliers' discriminatory hiring practices that avoided hiring anyone who might become pregnant and require maternity leave.

Do certain types of monitors do a better job than others? Interestingly, there is often inconsistency between brands' or retailers' own monitoring and that conducted for them by commercial firms. Third-party monitors often find *fewer* problems than the brands and retailers own compliance staff.[55] Nonprofit monitors representing civil society are often better trained about the issues and do a more thorough job monitoring than those from private firms that have added on the activity for expanded profits, especially when the nonprofit employs local expertise.[56] COVERCO describes the ideal monitor as "a labor lawyer-accountant-sociologist-investigative reporter-health and safety specialist under thirty." Because all these attributes are unlikely to be found in one person, some monitors put together teams to provide the needed expertise.[57]

Fraudulent Practices of Factory Management

Fraudulent practices severely limit the ability of monitors to identify problems. Factory management have been found to falsify documents, coach workers or stage audits, bribe workers and monitors, and engage in other practices to make it appear that the factory is in compliance with a brand's or retailer's code of conduct when in fact it is not. Double bookkeeping of payroll documents and work hours is prevalent. Coaching workers prepares them to tell the story that the factory management wants to share with the monitor, not the true factory practices. Workers are sometimes offered concert tickets or other bribes, or put in fear that they will lose their jobs if they do not "correctly" answer monitors' questions. Ironically, staging audits and coaching may be educating workers of their rights. For example, workers in a dyeing and bleaching factory in India learned the importance of wearing personal protective devices when factory management required them to put on goggles and gloves when auditors visited.[58]

With the majority of audits preannounced, it is especially easy for factory management to stage the audit. Prior to the audit, the factory is cleaned, the bathrooms are stocked with soap and towels, and first-aid boxes unlocked. Supervisors are briefed on how workers should answer questions (no overtime or Sunday work) and the image they should present, and quotas for the day are set low and attainable. When the monitors arrive, a certain song or message will be broadcast over the factory loudspeakers whereupon all illegal and underage workers immediately leave through a back exit, workers don personal protective devices such as earplugs or masks that they otherwise do not like to wear, and supervisors unlock exit doors.[59] Another staging approach is to maintain a model factory with good compliance for monitors to inspect but then to subcontract the bulk of work to other, unmonitored factories.

The Clean Clothes Campaign describes "counter-compliance," especially in China, as "a sophisticated art."[60] The efforts to use fraud to pass audits reached a new level in 2006 when it was uncovered that a new business had sprung up in China. For a few hundred dollars and a weekend of their time, factory management can attend workshops offered by former auditors who teach them how to pass an audit without really making any changes in business practice.[61] Here is the English translation of a memo that was distributed to management in a Chinese factory before a scheduled audit. "First notify underage, full-time workers and workers without identification to leave the manufacturing workshop through the back door. Order them not to loiter near the dormitory area."[62]

Workers' Limited Knowledge of Their Rights

The processes and quality of monitoring against codes of conduct would not be so limiting if workers were more involved in the process and were educated about their rights. With monitoring, workers are not provided copies of the audit report to verify accuracy, nor are they engaged in developing solutions to the problems. The prevalence of young workers in their first jobs means that workers often have little knowledge about their rights.[63] Having informed workers in the factory who are unafraid and willing to exercise their rights would provide the best possible way to ensure that codes of conduct are followed because it would provide round-the-clock monitoring of factory practices.

Brands and retailers have made various attempts to inform workers of their rights under their codes of conduct. The typical initial tactic was to post the code on the wall of the factory in the home country language, but this is not enough to make certain that workers understand their rights and can defend them (Figure 6.5). More innovative brands and retailers have produced comic books or created games that

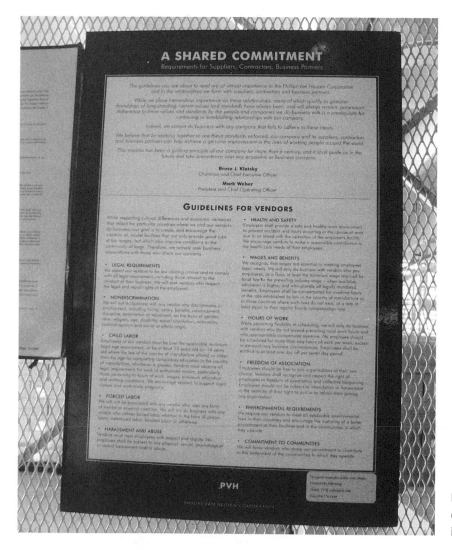

Figure 6.5
Code of conduct posted
in a factory.

teach workers their rights, and the Better Factories program conducted by the Cambodian government and the ILO produced a soap opera on worker rights. Where possible, actual training workshops focused on worker rights have been conducted for management and workers.

◉

The Challenge That Lies Ahead

Adopting codes of conduct and implementing monitoring procedures is sometimes viewed as the first-generation solutions to poor labor standards and working conditions in apparel factories. But although monitoring has led to some improvements in factories, many conditions have not improved. As lamented by the Clean Clothes Campaign, "In spite of the tens of thousands of audits which are taking place year upon year, the patterns of exploitation and abuse of workers is continuing. Given the amount of resources and thinking devoted to tackling the difficulties faced by workers in supply chains over the last decade and a half, the lack of progress to date is scandalous."[64]

The inability to solve problems in the factories with monitoring and subsequent corrective action plans exists because the quality of monitoring is not especially good, collaborative remediation plans are not always developed or verified, factory managers have not taken ownership of the problems in their factories and cheat to obtain good audits, and workers lack knowledge of their rights and seldom have a say in workplace conditions. Given this situation, what role should codes of conduct and monitoring play in future efforts to improve labor standards and working conditions in apparel factories?

Even though there are problems with monitoring, experts agree that it will continue to be a necessary part of labor compliance programs because it provides important information. Monitoring practices will need to be improved so that the data provided from audits are consistent and of high quality and proposed remediation plans are verified.[65] Continuous improvement should be the goal that is reached by collaboration, support from the brands for remediation, and ownership of the problems and solutions by the factory.

It would also be helpful if more apparel brands and retailers became involved with the drive toward greater social responsibility. Over the last decade, codes and compliance programs have matured, and good practices and leaders have emerged; these advances provide an important foundation for other companies to follow. As Casey explains, "Progress will only happen once a critical mass of participation is achieved."[66] There are still many apparel businesses to engage and plenty of work to be done to provide workers with safe and fair workplaces.

Chapter 7

How Manufacturers and Retailers Organize for Social Responsibility: Internally, Collaboratively, and Strategically

◉

Starting his commute to the office at company headquarters, Tom is thinking of the busy day that lies ahead of him. As head of labor compliance for a multinational apparel brand, he is in charge of a multimillion-dollar budget and a team based around the world. Tom's daily work is widely varied. Regional staff members are responsible for the routine factory inspections but consult with Tom when creating corrective action plans to solve problems found in the factories. Today he is reviewing the latest factory monitoring reports from South Asia to determine whether there is an indication of an increasing child labor problem. Because another leading brand, which has a compliance program similar to Tom's, experienced a widely publicized incident when children were discovered working at a contractor's factory a few weeks earlier in Pakistan, he is especially alert to the possibility that this child labor episode was not an isolated incident. Tom wishes the activists would reduce the attention currently paid to his and the other brands that are leading the apparel industry's efforts in social responsibility. He believes there would be greater progress in social responsibility in the apparel industry if the activists compared the factories where his company's products are being sewn with some of the factories that he sees being used by the brands and retailers that are investing little in compliance.

Tom also leads the company's efforts to manage especially sensitive labor issues that arise, such as the one he has been working closely on with an NGO in Honduras and the compliance head of another brand regarding a sudden factory closing. Factory management slipped away during the night without paying workers their final week's wages and severance. He also negotiates with the vice president for sourcing when the business wants to use a factory that has not been preauthorized for compliance with the code of conduct or that has been ignoring corrective action plans to resolve a compliance issue. In fact, today Tom must manage just this sort of conflict. He just learned that one of the designers has added a new style into the line at the last minute, and she wants to get it into the stores as soon as possible. The problem is that sourcing wants to use a factory that just two months ago his firm banned for use for one year because of its failure to carry out training for supervisors about harassment. The supervisors had been observed shouting at workers and preventing them from taking toilet breaks in hopes that they would meet daily production quotas. Tom is pretty strict with the compromises he is willing to make on substandard factories because using them could quickly erode the improvements his department has seen among factories that satisfy their corrective action plans.

Pulling into his parking spot, Tom remembers that he needs to get copies of the documents to read for next week's meeting of the multi-stakeholder organization to which his company belongs. He's on the board of directors of that group and has been heavily involved in creating the policies and practices the organization uses in pursuit of improved labor standards and working conditions and expanded industry membership in the organization. There are some difficult decisions pending for the organization, so he will need to give considerable thought to the ramifications of various choices the board might make. He'll review the board materials on the way home from his trip to Indonesia, where he is meeting with representatives of a labor union that claims a supplier has fired union members without due cause. Whew! He has a lot to do before tonight's 8:30 flight. He would think twice about enduring the long hours and stress of this job if it he weren't so confident that his efforts to obtain compliance with the business's code of conduct were making small improvements in the lives of workers every day. Hopefully the future will bring a more consistent industry effort that involves all brands and retailers in the pursuit of social responsibility in the apparel industry.

◉

Organizing Business for Social Responsibility

In Chapter 6, we examined the five stages of organizational learning that businesses proceed through as they advance toward greater social responsibility—defensive, compliance, managerial, strategic, and civil.[1] In this chapter, we describe and analyze the labor compliance departments apparel brands and retailers develop at the managerial stage. We also explore two ways that businesses take social responsibility to the strategic level. The first involves public reporting and transparency about issues of social responsibility, and the second concerns incorporating labor compliance into sourcing decisions.

The first four stages of organizational learning—defensive, compliance, managerial, and strategic—all encompass activities undertaken by individual businesses. The fifth and final stage, the civil stage, moves away from individual business activity to collective actions among collaborating businesses and stakeholders. We discuss two types of collaborative initiatives for greater social responsibility—multi-stakeholder and business initiatives. We end the chapter with a discussion of the responsibilities of business toward social responsibility and the important concepts of power, responsibility, and accountability.

⊙

Labor Compliance Departments

Our in-depth examination of the adoption of codes of conduct and the monitoring of factories for compliance against the codes indicated the inadequacy of these strategies in protecting workers in global apparel supply chains. Organizational structures within individual business provide one way for businesses to more effectively address and improve in socially responsible practices. Over the past decade, some businesses have developed a department or division charged with code implementation, monitoring, and remediation of problems identified. In addition, the departments take responsibility for strengthening a culture of social responsibility within company headquarters. Depending on the company, these can be called labor compliance, human rights, or social responsibility departments and can incorporate efforts toward environmental stewardship as well. The development of these departments is not surprising. If compliance with a code of conduct is required of suppliers, someone has to arrange for data collection, analyze the data that is gathered, and make decisions about the continued use of factories that fail to comply. Additionally, someone needs to ensure that social responsibility efforts are integrated into all aspects of the business to support a triple bottom line philosophy.

Let's take a closer look at the departments that brands and retailers leading in social responsibility have developed—where they are placed in the organization and reporting lines. We analyze two programmatic approaches—centralized and decentralized—and the benefits and drawbacks of each approach. Finally, we consider the reluctance or failure of some businesses to take on the responsibility and cost of a labor compliance program.

Structure of Programs

A research project conducted by Ivana Mamic, an employee of the International Labour Organization (ILO), in the early 2000s investigated management systems and processes that apparel, sports footwear, and retail businesses were using to implement codes of conduct. The research involved interviews with representatives from 22 multinational corporations and 74 supplier factories in various locations around the world.[2] Findings from a survey and Web site analysis of large U.S.-based apparel brands and retailers conducted by Marsha Dickson and Kevin Kovaleski provide additional information about the structure of labor compliance programs in the industry.[3] We couple conclusions from these two research studies with our own experiences and knowledge working with professionals in labor compliance in our analysis of the organization of social responsibility in business.

Business Size

There is not a one-size-fits-all approach to labor compliance; however, the size of a business influences how its compliance programs are structured. Compliance can be handled by one person in a company, or there can be 100 or more people whose jobs are dedicated primarily to labor compliance. Large businesses (in terms of volume of sales and variety of products sold) tend to have labor compliance departments that are structured differently from those found in small businesses. As compared with small businesses, large businesses are able to deploy greater financial resources for labor compliance, and they are more likely to hire personnel whose entire responsibilities focus on labor compliance.[4]

Although in some respects it would seem that lower-volume businesses can better manage labor compliance, this is not necessarily the case. Small businesses often still require a large number of suppliers to produce the variety of products they sell, and it is often necessary for staff to split their time and focus among various responsibilities such as quality control and labor compliance.

Responsibilities

Responsibilities of the labor compliance team may or may not include internal monitoring of factories by the firm's employees. Staff members arrange for pre-audits of factories under consideration for sourcing and arrange for occasional audits of factories in the supply base that they rely on for production. Whether or not they conduct the monitoring themselves, the staff members receive data from audits and either independently or with the assistance of their monitors design action plans for correcting the problems. In best practices, labor compliance information on factories is communicated to sourcing departments so that compliance performance is taken into consideration in the selection of suppliers. Additionally, the compliance team conducts an ongoing dialogue with stakeholders about a wide range of topics, such as meeting with labor union representatives, workers, and activist groups. The more inclusive the stakeholder engagement process, the more effective the program for management of the code of conduct.[5]

Compliance departments are also responsible for fostering a culture of social responsibility within the company, ensuring that company personnel from all functional areas understand their role in social responsibility. Apparel brands and retailers vary on how well they have addressed these responsibilities. Members of the compliance department must also understand the core business of the company and recognize high-risk situations that could potentially harm the business. Finally, executives in these departments take responsibility for developing the next generation of social responsibility experts, both at headquarters and in offices they maintain around the world.

Reporting Channels

Apparel brands and retailers have structured their labor compliance departments in various business ways. Some departments are freestanding and report directly to the chairman, chief executive officer, or chief administrative officer. In other cases labor compliance is not a department, but rather a program positioned within another department, such as quality control, manufacturing, human resources, or legal. Reporting is sometimes channeled through a senior vice president or vice presidents of operations or ethics.[6] Figure 7.1 depicts the Puma

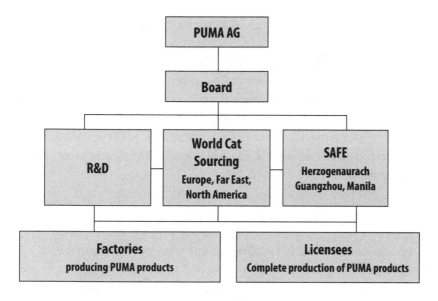

Figure 7.1
Puma organizational structure.

organizational structure. That company's labor compliance department is known as Social Accountability and Fundamental Environmental Standards (SAFE). In Puma's case, the department reports directly to the board of directors.

Reporting to the CEO or chairman may indicate the department's activities are highly supported by the business, but this reporting structure is not a requirement for a strong compliance program. Most important is whether the head of the labor compliance department or program has the ability to influence other executives. Doug Cahn, who headed Reebok's human rights program from 1991 to 2006, reported to various people during his tenure, including the CEO and legal counsel. He believes that the reporting channel mattered less than his being empowered to make decisions and having those decisions supported by top management. To uphold the integrity of the labor compliance program, the decision of the compliance executive concerning whether to use a factory for production should only in exceptional cases be overridden by sourcing or another division of the business.[7]

Centralized versus Decentralized Approaches

There are two primary approaches for a labor compliance program. One is to have the program situated at a central location such as at the business headquarters. The other is to decentralize the program with field staff positioned in key producing regions. The approach taken by a brand or retailer tends to be related to the size of the company's supply base and available budget for labor compliance—some companies have mixed structures.

A Centralized Approach

A centralized approach to labor compliance provides flexibility. Because monitoring tends to be outsourced to external firms, it can easily be targeted to regions and countries with the greatest need and greatest levels of production. A centralized approach is more likely when the base of suppliers is fairly small and/or budgets for labor compliance are small.[8] For example, Patagonia, which has annual revenues of around $1.5 billion, has a small team of headquarters-based staff whose jobs focus on labor compliance. The brand relies on external monitors to audit its 239 factories for compliance to the code of conduct.[9]

Decentralized Compliance Programs

Alternatively, decentralized programs are more common among businesses with large supply bases and larger budgets designated for labor compliance. Brands and retailers taking a decentralized approach to labor compliance position teams of professionals in key producing areas around the world. This corporate staff conducts internal monitoring and works with suppliers on corrective action plans. These decentralized teams are also responsible for engaging with local trade unions and civil society groups in their regions.[10] In contrast to Patagonia, Nike, which has more than ten times the revenue of Patagonia, employs over 75 compliance staff, only 10 of whom are based at headquarters in Beaverton, Oregon.[11]

Figure 7.2 depicts a generic organizational map for a brand or retailer with a decentralized approach to labor compliance. In the depicted organization, an overall director oversees directors for the Americas, Asia, and a region that includes Europe, the Middle East, and Africa. Each regional director then further assigns responsibility by key production areas, and the number of personnel for each area reflects the volume of suppliers there. This generic organization is similar to the structure of the social and environmental affairs program in the adidas Group. The brand has an overall director and directors in the same three regions outlined in the generic map.

Figure 7.3 provides a detailed organizational map for the adidas Group's Social and Environmental Affairs (SEA) department in Asia. It shows how a decentralized labor compliance program is organized at the regional level. The Director for SEA Asia is based in Hong Kong.

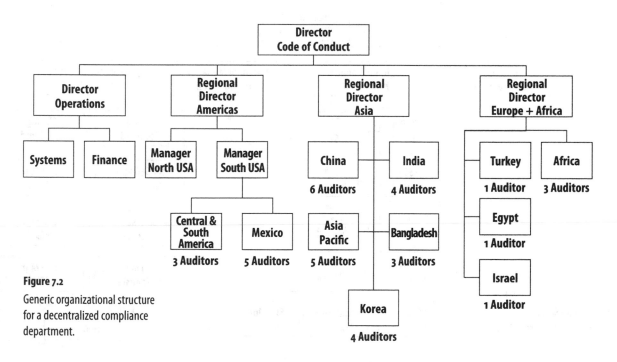

Figure 7.2

Generic organizational structure for a decentralized compliance department.

There are regional managers for North and South Asia. The North Asia division has staff based in Guangzhou, Shanghai, and Fouzhou, China, as well as Taiwan, Japan, and Korea. The South Asia group has field staff in Thailand, Indonesia, Ho Chi Minh City in Vietnam, and India. The SEA program addresses both labor and environmental concerns in the factories they use in the region. The adidas Group's SEA department has a total staff of 35 employees, indicating the importance of Asia to the business based on this large number of positions in that region. The Americas and Europe, Middle East, and Africa divisions each have smaller teams of compliance personnel.[12] What might some of the benefits and costs of a decentralized compliance program be?

Taking a decentralized approach to labor compliance and placing field staff in key producing regions of the world can require much more investment in salaried personnel than a centralized approach,[13] though this is not always the case. Annual budgets for labor compliance activities

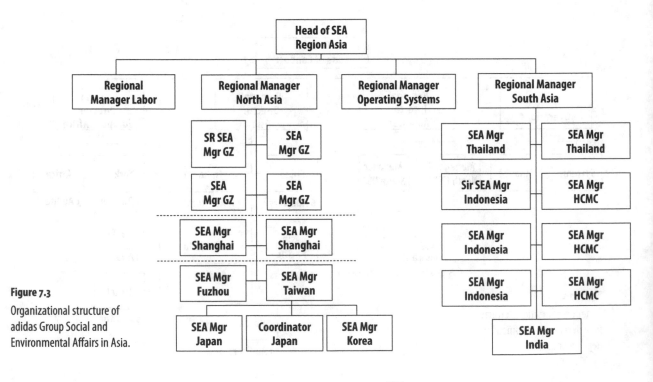

Figure 7.3

Organizational structure of adidas Group Social and Environmental Affairs in Asia.

vary widely. For example, some businesses with smaller labor compliance programs spend only $120,000 annually, whereas larger labor compliance departments have annual budgets that exceed $8.5 million.[14]

Having large numbers of compliance staff based around the world can make communications among team members tricky when regular conference calls and meetings are required between regional team members. The decentralized approach also requires significant training investments to ensure that the field staff has a suitable level of professional competency. Field staff must be trained to monitor factories and find solutions to problems found during the audit.[15]

An important benefit from a decentralized compliance program is that field staff members are more likely to have the needed language and knowledge of culture and local laws than someone who flies in from New York City or California or even Hong Kong to handle a compliance issue. Because they are available in the region, field personnel are able to form supportive relationships with factory management as they develop corrective actions and implement training for workers. The factory managers for key vendors are usually accustomed to working with the brand's or retailer's field staff and have established good rapport. By being in the field, decentralized staff will more frequently engage with local stakeholders, and these relationships may inform them about pending issues before the issues manifest themselves in the brand's or retailer's factories. Mamic reports that "field personnel are an integral component for any proper functioning of a [multinational corporation's code of conduct] implementation programme."[16]

◉

Socially Responsible Practices beyond Monitoring

As well as adopting codes of conduct and monitoring programs and creating departments to manage this work, apparel brands and retailers may pursue other activities to enhance social responsibility. In this section we discuss public reporting and transparency and using compliance in sourcing decisions.

Public Reporting and Transparency

One indication that brands or retailers have reached the strategic stage of organizational learning is the public reporting of problems found in the factories making their goods and how they were managed. Transparency of actions is an important way that apparel brands and retailers demonstrate they are taking charge of social responsibility. Without transparency, there is no opportunity to examine the quality of an auditor's methods, and the weaknesses of auditing are hidden from the public.[17] An analysis of company Web sites found that only 8 of 119 large apparel brands and retailers published results of their code implementation efforts.[18] In preparing these reports, the few apparel brands and retailers doing so often followed the guidelines for public reporting on social responsibility provided by the Global Reporting Initiative (GRI).

The GRI was started in 1997 as a joint initiative between an environmentally focused program of the United Nations and a U.S. NGO. The GRI guidelines cover economic, environmental, and social dimensions of the reporting company's activities, products, and services. Besides developing a general set of guidelines for use by all businesses, the GRI has also developed sector supplements with specific guidelines for some industries, including a set of guidelines for the apparel and footwear sector. The GRI guidelines are available for businesses to adopt voluntarily, and the specific guidelines can be implemented in an incremental fashion or all at once.

The content of the guidelines has been selected to reflect the most relevant and useful information for stakeholders, including NGOs, labor unions, consumers, and investors. Besides containing specific guidelines for measurement and reporting on economic, environmental, and social dimensions in the apparel industry, the Apparel and Footwear Sector Supplement also includes sections on "business integration" and "codes of conduct." There are a total of 50 items in the Apparel and Footwear Sector Supplement, which provide guidance to companies on what stakeholders want to know about their labor and environmental programs.[19] Many large apparel businesses fall far short of being transparent as defined by the GRI.[20] Commenting on the importance of public reporting, Freeman states that:

the most effective corporate responsibility and sustainability communications and reporting offer stakeholders a series of snapshots of a company's commitment and performance as works in progress. This kind of approach is consistent with the evolving spirit of corporate responsibility as a continuing process, one that values a willingness to tackle tough long-term challenges over satisfaction with positive short-term results.[21]

Incorporating Labor Compliance into Sourcing Decisions

Beyond public reporting, applying labor compliance data to sourcing decisions would make social responsibility a strategic aspect of the business. Some brands and retailers have devised ways to grade or rate their suppliers' compliance to their codes of conduct. Nike uses a grading system that breaks out two categories of information, one on compliance with the code of conduct's environmental, safety, and health standards (ESH) and another focused on factory management practices. The components of the ESH rating are ones Nike considers to be the greatest environmental, safety, and health risks, including chemical management, worker protection, fire/emergency action, and health, as well as the ability of the factory to address these problems. The management component includes age verification, employee training, forced labor, freedom of association, harassment and abuse, hours of work, nondiscrimination, women's rights, and others. Nike's grading system recognizes that environmental, safety, and health issues are easier to identify and solve than labor management issues—Nike expects factories to be fully compliant in ESH areas but may have isolated management issues and still receive an A rating (see Table 7.1). The management rating expectations reflect the difficulties in both identifying and correcting problems with discrimination, freedom of association, and others. Compared with A factories, those receiving a B grade are mostly compliant in ESH and may have unresolved issues on their corrective action plans for past violations. Factories rated C or below have many more violations.[22]

Table 7.1. Nike System of Grading Suppliers' Labor Compliance

Firm Degree of Compliance	Details of Compliance
A ⊙ Fully compliant ⊙ Demonstrates best practice. ⊙ Considered a leader.	⊙ Isolated violations of management standards found, but none considered serious or critical. ⊙ No more than five minor issues outstanding on the Master Action Plan (MAP*).
B ⊙ Mostly compliant ⊙ Minor system failures are found. ⊙ Factory is making progress.	⊙ Isolated violations of management standards found, but none considered serious or critical. ⊙ More than five minor issues on the MAP, but none serious or critical.
C ⊙ Non-compliant ⊙ Serious system failures. ⊙ Factory is making no progress.	⊙ Factory does not provide basic terms of employment (contracts, documented training on terms, equal pay, discriminatory employment screening). ⊙ More than 10 percent of employees work between 60 and 72 hours each week. ⊙ More than 10 percent of employees exceed annual legal limits. ⊙ More than 10 percent of employees work seven or more consecutive days without a break. ⊙ Factory violates local migrant labor laws. ⊙ Non-income-related benefits fall short of legal provisions. ⊙ Some evidence of verbal or psychological harassment or abuse. ⊙ One or more serious issues on MAP, but none considered critical.
D ⊙ Non-compliant ⊙ Demonstrates general disregard for Nike Codes and Standards. ⊙ Unwilling or unable to drive important change. ⊙ Deliberately misleads auditors. ⊙ Audit shows critical systemic and repeated problems.	⊙ Management refuses or continues to demonstrate unwillingness to comply with Nike Standards. ⊙ Management provides false information (statements, documents or demonstrates coaching). ⊙ Factory fails to provide verifiable timekeeping system to accurately record work hours. ⊙ Factory fails to pay legally mandated minimum wage.

Table 7.1. Nike System of Grading Suppliers' Labor Compliance (*continued*)

Firm Degree of Compliance	Details of Compliance
	⊙ More than 10 percent of employees work more than 72 hours each week.
	⊙ More than 10 percent of employees exceed daily work hour limits.
	⊙ More than 10 percent of employees work 14 or more consecutive days without a break.
	⊙ Factory requires pregnancy testing as condition of employment.
	⊙ Factory uses workers under the minimum legal age.
	⊙ Factory uses bonded, indentured, or prison labor.
	⊙ Factory uses force to compel illegal work hours.
	⊙ Audit finds confirmed evidence of physical or sexual abuse.
	⊙ Factory management denies access to authorized compliance inspectors.
	⊙ Factory denies freedom of association for workers, including demotion or dismissal of workers seeking to exercise their rights.
	⊙ Factory provides no benefits tied to security (workers' compensation, medical coverage, social security, retirement funds).
	⊙ Factory outsources to unauthorized facilities or issues homework to employees.

*The MAP Nike refers to regards the status of the factory's remediation of problems.
SOURCE: www.nikebiz.com/responsibility/.

When choosing factories for production, sourcing specialists typically consider the various products factories are capable of making, production capacity, the ability to complete an order on time with few defective products, and the cost for the factory to make the products, among others.[23] Communicating the results of monitoring across the company or its functional areas is a step to integrating factory compliance in sourcing, buying, and product development decisions.[24] The balanced scorecard provides a tool for simultaneously considering a supplier's compliance record with product quality, reliable delivery, costs, or other factors important to the brand or retailer. The scorecard incorporates all key criteria under consideration into one easy-to-view graphic that provides a snapshot of progress being made in each area.

Nike incorporates quality, on-time delivery and planning, percent of shoes built with lean production systems, labor compliance ratings, on-time seasonal product readiness, and cost in its scorecard (Figure 7.4). Excellent suppliers are those that score highly on each criterion.

Although grading suppliers' performance on labor compliance and integrating that into the sourcing decision is a good way for apparel brands and retailers to improve their social responsibility, few businesses are fully incorporating this strategy. The need for commercial market success is strong, and factories that can deliver the required

Figure 7.4

Sample balanced scorecard used by Nike.

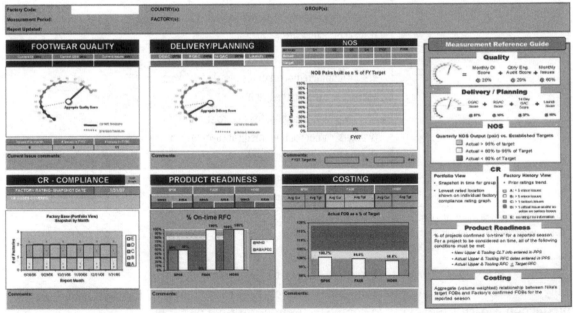

(NOTE: This scorecard is for illustrative purposes only and does not reflect current scores. These targets are owned and driven by a cross-sectional team of performance influencers inside the company. Compliance is now a part of this integrated team, supporting business improvements as part of its mandate is a significant shift in focus, expertise, and energy.)

goods are not always ones with strong compliance records. Some brands and retailers are developing long-term partnerships with compliant suppliers that also meet the brands' standards in other key criteria, but these alliances benefit only a small number of each brand's suppliers.[25] Brands and retailers have reported dropping suppliers with continued poor performance or unwillingness to work on improvements in compliance. For example, in 2006, Gap dropped 23 factories from its approved-for-use list and Wal-Mart banned 187 factories from producing for the business for one year after they had been rated "high risk" for two years in a row.[26] Some apparel brands and retailers conduct pre-audits of factories they are considering as suppliers, trying to avoid placing orders with factories that are considered feasibly unable to reach the brand's or retailer's standards.

◉

Collective Efforts for Labor Compliance and Social Responsibility

During the civil stage of social responsibility, businesses shift from individual to collective action. Efforts are made not only to improve social responsibility in a particular business but to improve it in the industry as a whole. The focus of these efforts is to make social responsibility the norm—a general expectation of all businesses.[27] These collective initiatives can significantly improve socially responsible practices in the industry through sharing of opportunities, challenges, and approaches. The determination and success of one company can influence others to work toward the same goals for greater social responsibility.[28]

There are two types of collective initiatives in which apparel brands and retailers have been involved. The first is the multi-stakeholder initiative (MSI). MSIs often include members of civil society or nongovernmental organizations, labor unions, businesses, and other stakeholder groups and are governed by multiple stakeholders. The second type of collective action is governed primarily by representatives of business and industry.

Multi-Stakeholder Initiatives for Labor Compliance and Social Responsibility

Multi-stakeholder initiatives for improving labor standards and working conditions bring together a variety of stakeholders, most frequently companies, trade unions, and NGOs, that work together to improve conditions. MSIs were initiated in the mid-1990s by stakeholders representing business, labor, and advocacy organizations who were concerned with how apparel was produced.[29] Businesses, many of which had already adopted codes of conduct, realized they could make more significant improvements by cooperating with their stakeholders who had expertise in labor and international development issues.[30] As Dan Henkle of Gap explains, "Anything we do on our own can be magnified by working with others."[31]

As well as developing codes of conduct that their members are expected to follow and that are more comprehensive and more consistent with ILO conventions than the early codes set by companies, MSIs develop processes and procedures on how to implement a code and monitor and verify compliance with the code. MSIs also often engage in experimental pilot projects focused on improving social responsibility. There are many systemic issues that individual companies cannot solve on their own, such as ones that are found across entire countries or regions and where there is little or no government intervention.[32] Discrimination is an example of a systemic issue in many countries.

MSIs are valuable because they allow brands and retailers to learn from each other and also act as a sort of peer pressure for others to get on the path to social responsibility. Many consider the work of MSIs essential to widespread improvement in social responsibility and see their collaborative efforts as the only way to systematically improve the quality of monitoring.[33]

There are five prominent and respected MSIs working on labor issues in the apparel industry: the Ethical Trading Initiative, Fair Labor Association, Fair Wear Foundation, Social Accountability International, and Worker Rights Consortium.[34] We will evaluate each MSI through discussion of the following topics, some that are used by activist stakeholders in determining organization credibility and relevance:

- How each group was formed and its relevant history
- What roles civil society plays in governance and decision making, including whether labor unions are involved
- Whether the code of conduct adheres to international labor conventions and includes a living wage requirement
- What the MSI does and its accomplishments
- What the MSI requires of members
- Who the members are and why they might choose to join the particular MSI
- Whether the policies and activities of the MSI are transparent, with information made available to the public
- How the MSI is evaluated by stakeholders
- What new initiatives are sponsored by the MSI

Ethical Trading Initiative

The Ethical Trading Initiative (ETI), based in the United Kingdom, was formed in 1998 because companies were receiving pressure from consumers to ensure that food and clothing be made under decent working conditions. Labor unions and NGOs had a role in the ETI from its inception. They were involved in development of ETI's code of conduct, called the Base Code, and an initial set of Principles of Implementation. The nine-member board is equally represented by companies, labor unions, and NGOs. The Base Code adheres to ILO conventions, and it requires workers be paid a living wage.

ETI describes itself as a learning organization rather than a code enforcement group. ETI does not field monitors to audit whether the suppliers of member companies comply with the ETI Base Code; rather, it conducts pilot projects and convenes working groups looking at various aspects of code implementation. Learning is shared through forums and publications made available on its Web site. Current projects associated with the apparel industry include a Purchasing

Practices project focused on how a company's purchasing or buying practices affect working conditions and a Sri Lanka Garment Industry project that is aimed at improving monitoring. A new initiative addresses health and safety in China by helping suppliers understand the benefits of involving workers in health and safety committees.

Accomplishments of the ETI have been documented with an impact assessment conducted by the Institute of Development Studies. Findings from the study show that many workers are benefitting from code implementation but that changes evolve slowly and certain workers remain in vulnerable positions. The 2005/2006 annual report indicates that 9,614 supplier factories were inspected by the corporate members or their hired monitors in those two years.[35]

Member companies are required to submit an annual report to the ETI secretariat outlining the practices of its suppliers, specifically demonstrating their progress on code implementation and meeting the code standards over time. However, the ETI does *not* require member companies to report this information publicly and the 2005/2006 annual report limited statements on individual companies to just a sentence or two each.[36] Company members also participate in ETI activities and ETI retains the right to suspend members if a company is failing to demonstrate its commitment.

Corporate members include Gap, Marks & Spencer, Next Retail, the Pentland Group, Inditex, and other British and European brands and retailers. Roseann Casey, a Harvard scholar who has researched labor compliance initiatives, explains why a company might join the ETI: "For those with a desire to do more in-depth analysis and pilot projects, and to increase exposure to the European market, ETI may be the best forum for engagement."[37] ETI has been lauded for its success in gaining corporate members, but this is credited in part to the MSI being a learning organization rather than a code enforcement body that requires changes in members' business operations.[38] As described by *Guardian* reporter Bibi Van der Zee:

> The ETI lives and dies by its admirable "base code". . . . But one of the biggest problems is that, although any companies signing up to the ETI must

sign up to the base code, they are not committing themselves to living by these principles, only to working towards them. There is a big difference.[39]

ETI asks member companies to continuously improve their social responsibility practices to be in compliance with the code but maintains no system of verifying whether actual improvements are made.

Fair Labor Association

In 1996, President Clinton and Secretary of Labor Reich asked key apparel brands, trade unions, and various NGOs to work together to solve the labor issues that were so prevalent in the industry. The Apparel Industry Partnership (AIP) had three objectives: (1) to develop a code of conduct that could be used across the industry, (2) to create an organization to monitor compliance against the code, and (3) to develop a mechanism to identify to consumers garments that were made under fair and safe working conditions. The first two objectives were especially important to NGO and labor union representatives who pushed the AIP to take a rigorous approach to both the code and its implementation. The mechanism for consumers was envisioned as a hangtag that said "No Sweat."

By 1998 the AIP had completed two of its objectives and most of the companies and board members involved continued their commitment under the new organization—the FLA—that would implement the monitoring procedures.[40] The FLA is headquartered in Washington, DC, and has a European office in Geneva, Switzerland. Regional managers in South Asia; East Asia; Europe, Middle East, and Africa; and the Americas coordinate the FLA's work in their respective regions. The FLA's code of conduct, called the Workplace Code of Conduct, is based on ILO conventions and requires that workers be paid at least the minimum wage or the prevailing industry wage in a country if it is higher. The code and monitoring plan were negotiated among companies and representatives of labor unions and NGOs.

The FLA is governed by a board of directors with equal representation from its three major stakeholder groups: companies, colleges and universities, and NGOs. Colleges and universities sought to join the FLA, however, for assistance in ensuring the factories producing their logo goods were socially responsible. As well as being involved at the board level, advocacy and labor rights organizations play an important role for the FLA at the grassroots level, where they consult with FLA regional coordinators and with FLA companies producing in their area on issues affecting workers in the region.[41] Labor unions were initially involved in the work of the AIP, but in the heated debates involved with forming the code of conduct and devising monitoring procedures, labor union representatives resigned from the board.[42] Representatives of UNITE had a range of concerns, many that have since been resolved, but a major issue that remains regards the wage requirements set in the code of conduct. As reported by UNITE, "[The code] takes no meaningful step toward a living wage."[43]

FLA member companies are required to implement an internal program to monitor compliance within all of their factories; the number of factories internally or externally monitored by each company varies because of their different supply chains, but many members monitor hundreds of factories each year. The companies may choose to hire external monitors to conduct their monitoring or may field their own teams of monitors, depending on resources available within the business. The FLA also requires companies to educate workers on the code of conduct standards and to engage with local stakeholders. Member companies are given a two- to three-year window to put these requirements into place. At the end of the implementation period, the organization reviews the labor compliance programs and accredits those that have been satisfactorily implemented. Accreditation of a brand's or retailer's labor compliance program does not mean that all factories are compliant with the FLA Workplace Code of Conduct, but rather that the member company is making the necessary steps to ensure improvements are made.[44]

An important role of the FLA is to verify compliance of member companies' suppliers with the FLA Workplace Code of Conduct. The organization accredits independent monitors that audit a sample of member companies' factories. The FLA chooses and hires the monitors rather than the member companies, thus monitoring is independent and provides a layer of protection from potential conflict of interest between the monitor and the brand or retailer compared to when monitoring is conducted internally by the company or hired by them.[45] Over 629 independent external audits of factories had been performed by the FLA by the end of 2006, and in 2007, 147 audits were conducted.[46] The FLA works with member brands and retailers as they remediate violations and the FLA verifies remediation with follow-up inspections.[47]

As well as its core monitoring program, the FLA has a procedure called the Third Party Complaint, whereby individuals or organizations (third parties) can report confidentially to the FLA a violation of its code at factories producing goods for a member company. Once it receives a third-party complaint, FLA staff review, investigate, and take steps to involve the brand or retailer, the factory, and local civil society organizations in resolving the complaint. When a third-party complaint is resolved, reports are published by the FLA, detailing the problems and how they were corrected.[48]

The FLA is known for its transparency. The FLA publishes information on its Web site about affiliated companies' compliance programs and progress toward compliance with the FLA code. Detailed reports from each FLA audit describe problems found and how they have been or are being corrected, though not the name of the factory that was monitored. The public reporting requirement prevents some apparel brands and retailers from joining the FLA because of fears about how their customers and shareholders will react to reports of problems found in factories producing their goods. Yet research analyzing the media coverage of these reports indicates that this fear may be an overreaction. Although news articles about the FLA reports have often included a line or two about the brands' problems at its factories, the greater portion of the coverage focuses on the successes of the FLA program in improving labor practices.[49]

The FLA also conducts projects that involve participating companies in finding ways to strengthen compliance with the FLA Code of Conduct. For example, as a result of the FLA's growing knowledge that monitoring is only a partial answer to improving labor practices, it is implementing a new approach called FLA 3.0 that focuses on building the capacity of factory management to sustain social responsibility for the long term.[50]

Because of the requirements it places on member companies, the FLA is referred to as a "brand accountability" model. In other words, the organization views the brand as having key responsibility for ensuring the rights of workers in factories making its products. Member brands and retailers are held accountable for implementing labor compliance programs. The brands and retailers are responsible for the conditions found in the workplaces making their products rather than passing responsibility to factories.[51]

Affiliated companies are categorized based on their revenue and on their business model. The category referred to as participating company members includes large, well-known brands and retailers such as the adidas Group (which also owns Reebok), Nike, Puma, Nordstrom, Liz Claiborne, Eddie Bauer, Phillips-Van Heusen, and Patagonia, among others. The number of participating companies is relatively small at 24. However, in 2006 the impact of their work in social responsibility reached an estimated 3.8 million workers.[52] These firms serve as models and strive to lead the rest of the industry toward more socially responsible practices.

A new membership category is for suppliers making the commitment to implement the same standards as participating companies—they tend to be suppliers of well-known brands and retailers, many of whom are FLA participating companies. The FLA currently has 11 supplier members based in Hong Kong, China, Pakistan, Thailand, Bolivia, Korea, and Sri Lanka.

Another membership category includes over 200 member colleges and universities. Each of these institutions requires its licensed suppliers to join. The nearly 2,000 licensees of FLA colleges and universities must implement the FLA Code of Conduct in factories producing their licensed apparel and other goods.[53] Casey reports that "for those looking for proven monitoring and compliance methodology and a road tested remediation process, FLA offers great value."[54]

The FLA has received considerable criticism, especially from United Students against Sweatshops (USAS), which, during 2006, maintained an FLA Watch Web site designed as a watchdog for what the organization claimed was "ineffective monitoring." The FLA has also been criticized for not requiring a living wage be paid to workers[55] and for having no labor union representatives on its board of directors.[56] However, activist criticism regarding lack of union representation has been somewhat "weakened due to [the FLA's] mediation in union conflicts in supplier factories of member companies."[57]

The FLA has also been widely praised. Its first public report of working conditions in factories of member companies issued in 2002 was groundbreaking in the social responsibility movement.[58] Further, the FLA has been praised for quickly responding to third-party complaints and for developing solutions that have positively affected workers.[59] It is implementing strategies that involve factories in developing solutions, giving them ownership of the process and the improvements. Ultimately, Casey describes the FLA as "a 'tremendous tool' that provide[s] structure, systems, processes, and credibility."[60]

Fair Wear Foundation

The Netherlands-based Fair Wear Foundation (FWF) was founded in 1999 in response to Dutch consumer campaigns about working conditions in apparel factories, and the need to independently verify companies' code implementation. Its members include a garment retailers' association, Dutch trade unions, and NGOs, and representatives of these member categories plus suppliers sit on its governing board.

The FWF Code of Labor Practices aligns with ILO conventions and requires payment of a living wage. Similar to the FLA, the FWF conducts independent external audits to verify compliance of company members with its code of conduct. The scope of FWF's work is smaller than that of the FLA—according to its annual report, a total of 32 audits were performed in 2006. The FWF works with local stakeholders in producing countries to develop background reports on workers' issues, monitor working conditions, create plans for corrective action, and educate workers about their rights. The FWF also has a system by which workers can make complaints about violations of the code of conduct in member companies' factories.

Requirements of member companies are to develop management systems for tracking and monitoring suppliers and remediate identified problems. In addition, member companies annually report their progress to the FWF.[61] However, the only information about member companies that is included in the FWF annual reports is their countries of production. The FWF's approximately 29 member companies are primarily small or medium-sized firms, many of which specialize in workwear. Recently, the MSI has expanded the membership of fashion brands, including the Netherlands-based brand Mexx.

The early domination of small, workwear companies as members was unique among MSIs but put the FWF at a disadvantage in enforcing compliance. Large and powerful brand-name companies can be more successful in requiring suppliers to improve compliance. Small and medium-sized companies generally have limited resources to devote to compliance work and lack leverage with suppliers because their orders are small.[62] The group's strengths lie in its extensive collaboration with NGOs, unions, workers, and others in the field, which ensures greater local ownership of the process and greater likelihood of sustained compliance with the code. The FWF is also lauded for its ability to field qualified monitoring teams, which typically include an accountant, health and safety expert, and a professional with strong interviewing skills.[63]

Social Accountability International

Social Accountability International (SAI) was founded in 1997 by the Council on Economic Priorities, a research institution focused on corporate responsibility. The organization is based in New York City. SAI has both a board of directors and an advisory board. In 2007, the board of directors was composed of two SAI staff, one advisory board member, an NGO head, and two financial experts. The board of directors evaluates the performance of SAI and its management. The SAI advisory board in 2007 included 26 members, over half affiliated with business, with the remainder representing NGOs, labor unions, and other stakeholders. The advisory board provides expert advice regarding the SA8000 policies and procedures and serves on review panels that accredit monitors.

SAI certifies that supplier factories are in compliance with its code, called the SA8000 standard. The SA8000 stipulates that workers be paid enough to meet the basic needs of workers and their families, or a living wage. A manufacturer wishing to be certified hires an accredited monitoring organization to check that its factory working conditions and management systems comply with SA8000. If there is a certain level of compliance, the certificate is granted by the monitor, and the supplier can use that to assure buyers of their social responsibility.[64]

Unlike the FLA and FWF, which require apparel brands and retailers to take responsibility for labor compliance, SAI takes a "factory accountability" approach to social responsibility. In other words, the organization views the factory as having key responsibility for ensuring the rights of workers.[65] As of June 2007, 216 apparel factories, 95 textile factories, and 36 footwear factories were among the 1,373 SA8000-certified factories serving a wide range of industries in 64 countries. Of the 216 certified apparel factories, the largest number was in India (82). Another 45 certified factories were in China, and 17 were in Thailand. The only certified factory in the Americas was one in Peru.

In addition to certifying factories, a few years ago SAI added a corporate program aimed at providing knowledge and tools needed to implement social responsibility policies and procedures. The corporate program places no requirements on member companies, which include Cutter & Buck and Eileen Fisher in the United States, Charles Voegele of Switzerland, Otto Versand of Germany, and others.[66]

SA8000 provides suppliers and corporate members with standardized tools for good labor management that are useful for suppliers taking greater ownership of compliance. As explained by Casey, "For those looking for a program that can fill a management systems gap, SA8000 is an excellent choice."[67] SAI relies heavily on specialized for-profit auditing firms that have been criticized for not having adequate training and background for monitoring compliance with a code of labor standards. These firms are hired and paid by the factory desiring certification. Because the monitors make decisions on whether the factory should be certified, this creates a potential conflict of interest and diminishes SAI's effectiveness.[68] In fact, some certified factories have been found to have major noncompliances. For example, in 2006 five factories in India obtained SA8000 certification despite reports by the Clean Clothes Campaign that there were labor rights violations. After a formal complaint was filed with SAI, the MSI investigated and confirmed that certification was not justified and would be suspended.[69] This type of incident leads some critics to question the whole concept of factory certification.[70] SAI is also criticized for its lack of transparency. The list of certified factories is made public, but the results of audits and criteria for certification are not.[71]

Worker Rights Consortium

The Worker Rights Consortium (WRC) was founded in 2000 to assist colleges and universities in enforcing codes of conduct for the production of licensed logo products. The WRC was founded because USAS members believed the FLA's code and monitoring procedures, which many colleges and universities were following, were not stringent enough.[72] The organization is not structured exactly like the other MSIs, but because it pursues similar goals and activities to some of the others, we are discussing the WRC here.

The WRC is headquartered in Washington, DC, and has field staff based in Hong Kong, Thailand, and India. The governing board of the WRC is composed of representatives from colleges and universities; labor and human rights experts from academe, civil society, and labor unions; and members of USAS. The Model Code of Conduct references ILO conventions and requires workers be paid a living wage.

Rather than monitor a portion of the factories producing goods for their affiliates, the WRC relies on complaints, spot checks, and worker interviews to identify factories with labor rights problems. Once a situation is brought to the WRC's attention, it gathers additional information from documents, worker interviews, local NGOs, and others and makes a visit to the factory. The investigators report their findings to colleges and universities and the general public and then work with the involved schools, brands, factories, and relevant stakeholders to correct the problems found.[73] A total of 21 reports were listed on the WRC's Web site in 2007, representing the organization's work since inception. The WRC investigations have resulted in some improvements to working conditions,[74] and some of these successes resulted from collaborations between the WRC and the FLA. For example, the WRC and FLA worked in cooperation with their member colleges and universities, and the FLA's member companies, to develop solutions at the BJ&B factory in the Dominican Republic and the New Era factory in Derby, New York.[75]

A total of 172 colleges and universities were affiliated with the WRC as of summer 2007,[76] many of which also belonged to the FLA. Some schools join the WRC because of protests conducted by their student members of USAS.[77] WRC members are expected to include their code of conduct in contracts with licensees and hold them accountable to those standards in the production of apparel for the schools. Universities are also expected to leverage the licensees to correct problems found in their factories.[78] When problems in factories are found, WRC relies on its ability to activate USAS to pressure colleges and universities, and thus their licensees, to comply with the code of conduct.

The WRC has been praised for investigating problems quickly and posting detailed information about the problem and its remediation on the organization's Web site.[79] Additionally, the WRC does not use commercial monitors, and it partners with local stakeholders in its work. The major limitation to the WRC's factory investigation is the scale of operation, which requires a large amount of its resources to be used on individual cases, with no system to directly benefit other factories.[80] The WRC's exclusive focus on university-licensed products, which is a small proportion of total apparel produced annually, also limits the scope of its impacts;[81] however, it is exploring expanding its work to include assessment of factories providing goods for public school districts, cities, and state governments.

Business Initiatives to Improve Labor Standards and Working Conditions

Another type of collective action for greater social responsibility is through collaborative business initiatives. Regarding labor compliance, business initiatives and MSIs are viewed differently by stakeholders. Business initiatives are groups that are controlled by business and are therefore sometimes viewed suspiciously. Many NGO and labor union stakeholders do not consider business initiatives to be credible, believing it is not possible for industry to improve the working conditions and labor standards previously accepted as good enough. In fact, groups like USAS argue that in order to ensure workers' rights, businesses should not be involved in deciding the standards to which they are held accountable.

In this section we briefly examine four business initiatives related to apparel. Included are descriptions of Business for Social Responsibility, the Business Social Compliance Initiative, the Global Social Compliance Programme, and the Worldwide Responsible Accredited Production Program.

Business for Social Responsibility

Founded in 1992, Business for Social Responsibility (BSR) is a non-profit, multisector business association providing tools and strategies to apparel brands and retailers as well as other businesses to address issues such as business ethics, environment, human rights, and workplace conditions. BSR is headquartered in San Francisco but also has offices in Paris and China.[82] BSR differs from the other initiatives we discuss in this section in that it does not have a code of conduct.

BSR's mission is to help companies achieve business success while demonstrating ethical values and respect for people, communities, and the environment. The organization conducts research on emerging issues, provides consulting services to companies wishing to strengthen their social responsibility initiatives, and hosts meetings of members and stakeholders.[83] The organization's Web site provides reports published by BSR and other stakeholder groups with which it collaborates.

BSR engages with civil society organizations, thus serving as an intermediary between those groups and business. Doing so ensures that companies gain a variety of viewpoints that help them formulate better decisions and actions. BSR also provides avenues for business to collaborate and exchange ideas with one another. Resources available through its Web site, some for members only, include labor laws for more than 60 countries, reports that introduce more than 50 social responsibility issues, and featured and in-depth reports and publications on a variety of social responsibility topics.

BSR has 250 member companies, including many large apparel brands and retailers, and it offers them advisory services, research, and meetings.[84] The organization has not received the extensive criticism of the other business initiatives, probably because it has never adopted its own code of conduct nor made claims of trying to enforce one.

Business Social Compliance Initiative

The Business Social Compliance Initiative (BSCI) was established in 2004 by the Foreign Trade Association of importing retailers in Europe and is based in Brussels. The BSCI Supervisory Council consists of three persons representing regular members, which include companies and industry associations. The Supervisory Council officially represents the BSCI to government and other institutions. The organization reports that it has a Stakeholder Board of up to 12 members, proportionately representing labor unions, NGOs, suppliers and import and export business associations, government, international organizations, and BSCI members. No names are listed on its Web site, and the exact responsibilities of the board are not stated.[85]

When the BSCI initially created its code of conduct, the Clean Clothes Campaign viewed its standards as weak and not conforming to ILO conventions, especially with regard to the right to freedom of association and collective bargaining.[86] Recently, with the help of SAI, the group has refined its code of conduct to more closely conform to internationally recognized labor standards. It does not require workers be paid a living wage.

The goal of BSCI is to monitor member companies' suppliers against a common code. The audit is preceded by a factory self-assessment and is announced in advance. BSCI does not provide independent verification of monitoring; rather, member companies hire their own monitors who are accredited by SAI.

In its work with BSCI, SAI has also urged the organization to be more transparent about its activities. This has led the group to comment on its Web site about the involvement of NGOs at the local level, where production occurs, and to issue a public report with some summary findings from its monitoring.

Member companies currently number around 80 European retailers from Sweden, Switzerland, the Netherlands, Germany, and other countries. They are asked to have some of their suppliers audited every year, to include the BSCI code in contracts with suppliers, and to communicate publicly that they are involved with the BSCI.[87]

Stakeholder groups have reported weaknesses with the BSCI, such as its sole reliance on monitoring to ensure workers' rights and problems with the monitoring process. BSCI does not have projects to improve practices, a grievance system for workers, or explicit requirements of member companies.[88] The Clean Clothes Campaign contends that BSCI stakeholders are marginalized because they are invited to participate in a "weak advisory council."[89]

Global Social Compliance Programme

The Global Social Compliance Programme (GSCP) is a part of the International Committee of Food Retail Chains (CIES), which represents food retail chains. The GSCP was started in 2006 in order to harmonize efforts businesses were making to improve labor conditions in their supply chains for a variety of products, including apparel. It is headquartered in Paris and is governed by an executive board that manages the program. An advisory board that includes experts from NGOs, labor unions, and other groups provides opinions and perspectives to inform the program. Neither the advisory nor executive boards' memberships are reported on the GSCP Web site.

The goal of the GSCP is for members to collaborate and integrate innovative best practices through consultations with NGOs, academic, and intergovernmental organizations. The GSCP aims to reduce "wasteful auditing" by making data from audits useful to all member companies. The GSCP also aims to build a knowledge base and communications between the similar companies. A GSCP code of conduct was being developed in 2007.

GSCP members include a collection of big-box retailers, many of which are based in Europe, including Metro, Carrefour, Migros, and Tesco, but also U.S.-based Wal-Mart. Joining the GSCP requires that members commit to the principles and objectives of the GSCP and share knowledge and best practices with one another.[90]

The GSCP is pursuing an important goal. Multiple audits against varying codes of conduct create difficulties for factory management both in resources needed to work with monitors and conflicting requirements.[91] However, many NGOs and activists were dismayed that another organization was forming and reinventing the wheel, so to speak, rather than building on the knowledge of the older and now experienced MSIs. In response to the emergence of business initiatives such as the BSCI and the GSCP, the Clean Clothes Campaign reported that:

> At a point in time when there is so much energy to improve the lives of workers in supply chains, others are missing the chance to help build a sustainable model of code compliance. Instead, they risk supporting a model that fools consumers and achieves only limited risk management. It is particularly striking that this is happening . . . when so many companies learned their lessons on this issue three or four years [earlier].[92]

Time will tell whether the GSCP effectively reduces duplicate auditing or whether a Joint Initiative on Corporate Accountability and Workers Rights (JO-IN) being pursued by the five MSIs discussed earlier in this chapter and the Clean Clothes Campaign is a better answer to this problem. The JO-IN project aims to create more effective and collaborative multi-stakeholder approaches to code implementation.[93]

Worldwide Responsible Accredited Production

The Worldwide Responsible Accredited Production (WRAP) business initiative was established in 1998 by the American Apparel and Footwear Association and became independent from the industry association in 2000. Until mid-2007 the initiative was known as the Worldwide Responsible Apparel Production program and is based in Washington, DC. WRAP requires that the majority of its board of directors must "be from other walks of life. Certain representatives of the industries in question bring a needed perspective to the Board, because the purpose of WRAP is to make progress in the workplaces of their industries."[94] The charter detailing the organization's operation and the board's responsibilities is not made public, so it is unclear what control, if any, is given to nonindustry representatives.

WRAP's goal is to certify factories around the world that have fair and safe working conditions in compliance with its Worldwide Responsible Apparel Production Principles. The WRAP Principles do not reference ILO conventions and do not require a living wage.[95] The WRAP Principles have been criticized for excessive hours of work allowed weekly in certified factories in some countries; the code requires the factory not exceed the legal limitations in their locale.[96]

Like SAI, WRAP operates under a factory accountability model.[97] Factories wanting to be certified by WRAP undergo a three-step process. First, the factories self-assess against the WRAP Principles. Next, they hire a monitor accredited by WRAP to perform an audit. Depending on the outcome of the audit, WRAP either requires the factory to correct specific procedures and submit to additional monitoring or recommends to the board of directors that the factory be certified. A new certification process implemented in 2006 distinguishes companies as A-level, B-level, or C-level depending on the extent of their noncompliance with the code of conduct. WRAP allows certified factories wishing to disclose their names to the public to do so on the organization's Web site.[98] WRAP reports that it has certified 775 factories in over 85 countries.[99]

Although the processes WRAP reports using may seem reasonable, many stakeholder groups have intensely criticized the organization. For example, labor unions and NGOs argue that WRAP was set up by industry to prevent factories from having to submit to external monitoring. The organization is further criticized because there is no public disclosure of information, audits are prearranged and rely heavily on private monitoring firms, and monitors are not required to consult with local civil society organizations. As well, there is no formal system for complaints when problems are found in certified factories.[100] WRAP lacks transparency because it does not disclose the results of its audits or the minimum criteria required for a factory to be certified. Casey describes the value of WRAP as follows: "WRAP has a more narrow focus, but offers a forum for participation for companies who may not be ready for the level of engagement required in other initiatives."[101]

Business Initiatives to Improve the Environment

A number of organizations focused on environmental concerns in apparel production and sourcing have developed out of efforts by individual companies and industry organizations. Business initiatives focusing on the environment seem to be viewed more positively than those focused on labor compliance—probably because the industry has been more proactive than reactive in addressing environmental issues. We describe the following business initiatives for environmental stewardship: 1% For the Planet, GreenBlue, Organic Exchange, and the Organic Trade Association.

1% For the Planet

1% For the Planet (1% FTP) is a nonprofit organization initiated by Yvon Chouinard, founder and owner of outdoor apparel company Patagonia, and Craig Mathews, owner of Blue Ribbon Flies in West Yellowstone, Montana. Its goal is to expand the difference an individual or company can make to preserve and restore the natural environment through collaboration and a consolidation of efforts. Chouinard and Mathews started the nonprofit in November 2001 when 21 businesses pledged to contribute 1 percent of their annual sales to domestic and international grassroots groups working toward a better environment in their local communities. But, as its Web site states, it goes beyond philanthropy. "It is about activism within the private sector, and about being a part of a groundswell of change to become part of the solution as a member of the private sector."[102]

In 2006, almost 500 members from over 42 states and 22 countries contributed 1 percent of their annual revenues, a total of approximately $6 million. Member businesses range from clothing and consumer products to engineering, financial services, and music and Web design businesses. Members can choose which groups to donate in-kind or cash to each year, documenting their annual revenues in return for membership and the use of the 1% FTP logo.

Recipient organizations support a diverse range of activities from education, research, and advocacy to wildlife rehabilitation, conservation, and action campaigns. The groups are categorized into four focus areas that address the environmental crisis: air quality and climate change; forest and wildlife protection; oceans, watershed, and wetlands; and ecotourism.

GreenBlue

GreenBlue is another business initiative focused on environmental concerns. GreenBlue describes itself as "a nonprofit institute that stimulates the creative redesign of industry by focusing the expertise of professional communities to create practical solutions, resources, and opportunities for implementing sustainability."[103] Its focus is on the way transforming design can lead to fundamental change in the economic and social approach to business. In the organization's own words, "GreenBlue uses design as a leverage point for effective action."

GreenBlue was established in 2002 as a nonprofit institute committed to the social and environmental goals of its private-sector founder, McDonough Braungart Design Chemistry (MBDC). It offers a number of online educational resources and serves as an organizing agency to engage business, research, and civil society participants in its projects, which are designed to develop and provide resources toward sustainability. Its focus is on design as informed by ecological principles and the cradle-to-cradle design framework developed by MBDC. Cradle-to-cradle design follows the example that nature has given us, both in approach and processes. Design is viewed as a system with materials that are safe and can be reused and processes that continue the cycle from birth to death and rebirth, that is, cradle to cradle.[104]

The benchmarks for GreenBlue's success are the quality and usefulness of the products it develops as well as the number of participants it engages during the process. Educational resources such as online materials and videos are posted on the Web site for general promotion and application of GreenBlue's general vision—that design and environmental sustainability can prosper in coexistence. The institute's projects are organized for stakeholder participation and use through either membership or subscription.

Organic Exchange

The Organic Exchange is a nonprofit organization with a mission to expand organic agriculture. It has "a specific focus on increasing the production and use of organically grown fibers such as cotton." Its long-term goal is to expand "the amount of certified organic land farmed for fiber production by 50% per year." It recognizes the importance of both developing organic production and increasing the demand for organic fiber among apparel, home furnishings, and personal care brands and retailers.

The Organic Exchange has more than 50 member companies, including producers, brands, and retailers that use organic fibers in their products. It provides its members with a number of resources related to organic agriculture production and using organic products. The organization has held conferences several times each year since 2003 in the United States and international locations, sited to highlight local organic agriculture ventures. The conference agenda offers sessions on how to become a business that embraces organic products and analysis of the major challenges to the organic industry, and offers tours of working organic agriculture fields. Its Web site provides information about organic production as well as a "matching" service between organic fiber and fabric producer and apparel brands and retailers. The site also connects consumers with brands that offer organic apparel, home furnishings, and personal care products and links consumers directly to the brand's Web site for easy purchase.[105]

Organic Trade Association

The Organic Trade Association (OTA) is a membership trade association supporting, representing, and informing producers, consumers, NGOs, and government policies about organic food and fiber products. One of its committees developed the North American Organic Fiber Standards in April 2002, a voluntary standard that is compatible with the Global Organic Textile Standards and the U.S. Department of Agriculture (USDA) organic standards but with more details. The standard focuses on fiber handling, processing, and labeling procedures for organic fibers such as cotton and wool.

The USDA initiated its National Organic Program and organic label in the early 1990s. Both OTA and USDA first focused on organic food production, processing, and handling but have now turned to organic fibers as well. The organic fiber standards from USDA and others differ from organic food standards by attempting to bring organic principles to traditional fiber handling and processing approaches while making the standards achievable. For example, textile processing and coloring have traditionally used a variety of chemical compounds. The standards identify the most environmentally sound and work toward reducing rather than eliminating their use.[106]

◉

The Challenge That Lies Ahead

This chapter has reviewed business efforts to improve social responsibility that include developing a department responsible for implementing the labor code of conduct, publicly reporting information about that work to stakeholders, and using labor compliance information in sourcing decisions. The chapter also evaluated collective efforts businesses can make to improve social responsibility through MSIs and business initiatives.

The efforts of individual businesses and multi-stakeholder initiatives would be much more effective if more apparel brands and retailers carried out company activities for social responsibility in more transparent ways and participated with multiple stakeholders to find sustainable solutions.

The departments we describe that deal with labor compliance represent only a handful of mostly large apparel brands and retailers that have made information about their efforts public or have participated in research; they are not the norm in the apparel industry. A content analysis of the Web sites of 119 large apparel brands and retailers found that only 28 percent published a code of conduct regarding labor standards. Even fewer provided evidence that they were attempting to implement the code. Only 14 percent included information indicating they had either a department or personnel within their firm whose responsibility included labor compliance.[107]

What will it take to get all apparel brands and retailers to develop and share their strategies to advance social responsibility? As explained by the Clean Clothes Campaign:

> If they are serious, companies must invest in compliance. Different sources have indicated that apart from the more responsive companies who have made some investments in this area, the reality is quite the opposite—companies are tending to try to spend less and less on social compliance, both by engaging with less stringent auditing programmes, and by transferring the cost of compliance with standards to their suppliers.[108]

Adequate investment requires having in-house staff charged with compliance responsibilities. Without a management system supporting social responsibility, apparel brands and retailers are unlikely to know whether their codes of conduct are being followed and how the workers producing their garments are treated.[109]

We describe a number of MSIs and business initiatives aimed at increasing social responsibility. Participation in the five MSIs included here—the ETI, FLA, FWF, SAI, and WRC—is a respected way to enhance social responsibility, but even MSIs differ substantially in approach and mission and should be differentiated based on their requirements of members and the transparency with which they share their work with the public.

Few apparel brands and retailers have affiliated with any of the MSIs. Expanding on the limited participation, Casey explains that:

> The number of brands and companies actively engaged in multi-stakeholder partnerships is very small. Dusty Kidd of Nike estimates that the combined total revenue of the brands actively involved in multi-stakeholder initiatives makes up only 10% of the total for the apparel and footwear industries. For those involved, collaboration is very strong, and is redefining compliance practices, but significant change won't happen until more players take part. The circle must expand.[110]

With the exception of BSR, which provides member companies with valuable resources and guidance, participation with one of the business initiatives for improved labor compliance (BSCI, GSCP, or WRAP) is currently viewed by stakeholders as less likely to improve socially responsible practices than the MSIs, which have credible monitoring and continuous improvement strategies.

Some large apparel brands and retailers have made significant strides on their own and in collaboration with multiple stakeholders in improving the situation of workers making their products. Progress is also being made to ensure that apparel production and sourcing does not negatively affect the environment. Yet the work described in this chapter cannot be viewed as the final solution to unfair labor practices, human rights abuses, and health and safety violations. The FLA has found an average of 17 noncompliances for every audit the organization conducted in 2006. These are factories producing for apparel brands and retailers that are some of the most respected for their social responsibility. Brands and retailers affiliated with the FLA and other MSIs work for continuous improvement in factories they use for production. The fact that unfair labor standards and poor working conditions continue to be found attests to the continued work needed in this area. Greater progress might be made when a larger number of apparel brands and retailers, including both small and large companies, and factory management from around the world, join efforts for social responsibility.

Power, Responsibility, and Accountability

In the past 15 or 20 years, apparel brands and retailers have undergone large-scale mergers and acquisitions to increase competitiveness through economies of scale. As a result, many brands and retailers have significant power in the global supply chain. This power translates to the ability to dictate prices or to make other demands on suppliers, such as their compliance with codes of conduct.[111] Likewise, consolidation of supply chains is creating fewer and much larger suppliers that themselves are gaining considerable power, especially over the workers they employ. With this power comes responsibility.

In his book *Slaves to Fashion*, sociologist Robert Ross discusses the important concepts of responsibility and accountability. He explains that "we are morally accountable for that for which we are empirically responsible. We are not held to account for the weather, but we are accountable for that part of our behavior about which we may reasonably presume to have some discretion."[112] These concepts—power, responsibility, and accountability—help us understand why it is necessary for all apparel brands and retailers to ensure that workers making their products are treated fairly and work in safe conditions. An apparel brand or retailer that makes an order with a supplier is surely responsible for what happens with that order. Given the business had the choice to make the order, it must be held accountable for how its production affects the workers who make its products and the environment. How can apparel brands and retailers that avoid responsibility and accountability expect business success? One way to evaluate these

risks of avoidance is to consider the stages of organizational learning—defensive, compliance, managerial, strategic, and civil—alongside
Zadek's descriptions of the stages of issue maturity. When combined,
these two scales provide an effective tool.[113]

Civil Learning Tool

The stages of issue maturity in social responsibility include latent,
emerging, consolidating, and institutionalized. A latent issue is one for
which awareness is primarily limited to the activist community, there
is limited hard evidence indicating the issue exists, and it is generally
ignored by the business community. At the emerging stage of issue
maturity, there is growing media and political awareness of the issues
and an emerging body of evidence that supports their existence. At this
stage of issue maturity, leading businesses begin to explore ways to address the problem. At the consolidating stage of issue maturity, a set
of business practices for addressing the issue have emerged, including
voluntary initiatives that businesses can join for guidance to solve specific problems. At the consolidating stage of issue maturity, there is also
litigation associated with the issues and increasing belief that legislation
is needed to prevent future problems and to institutionalize the issues.
At this point, work that solves problems of labor standards and working
conditions in factories becomes a part of everyday business excellence,
and laws may support businesses in this effort. In the first decade of the
twenty-first century, issues associated with labor standards and working conditions in the apparel industry, and related environmental issues,
have reached the consolidating stage of issue maturity, and more work
is needed to reach the institutionalizing stage.

Now let's look at the stage of organizational learning an apparel
brand or retailer is at in relation to issue maturity with the civil learning
tool depicted in Figure 7.5. If the issues affecting workers in factories
are at the consolidating level, then a business not yet at the managerial
level is in what Zadek refers to as the "risky red zone." Likewise, if
the environmental sustainability of production and transportation in

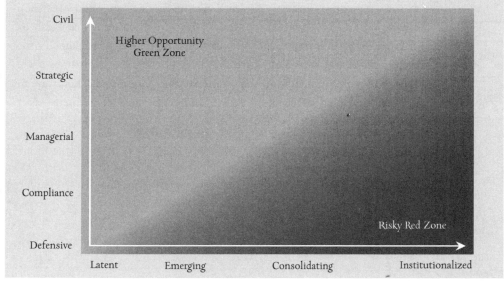

Figure 7.5
Zadek's Civil Learning Tool.

the apparel industry's supply chain is at the consolidating level, then a business not yet at the managerial level is in the risk area. The risky red zone represents a gap between societal expectations and company practice on an issue. Businesses in this zone are not meeting the normative requirements of society for social responsibility.

Businesses in this zone run the risk of societal backlash in a variety of ways. For example, shareholders may decide to divest, moving their funds to more responsible brands and retailers. Consumers may choose to purchase clothing and footwear from brands that demonstrate more responsible actions and policies. Activist organizations may choose to launch a campaign or file a lawsuit against the business, resulting in negative media coverage and financial loss.

Enlightened apparel brands and retailers will work to move their businesses toward the higher-opportunity green zone, where they can assure the public that they are taking appropriate steps toward social responsibility, or even position their companies as leaders in social responsibility. As explained by Bennett Freeman, a communications specialist who has held several political appointments,

No one company or industry can curb climate change, [and] end sweatshop labor . . . but every company, especially large multinationals, can lead by example in its industry and contribute solutions to these problems in the communities and countries where they operate. Leading companies make innovative commitments and deliver measurable progress, and find ways to communicate that progress, even if it is imperfect and incomplete—as it almost always will be.[114]

Chapter 8

Strategies for
Environmental Responsibility

⊙

Emily works as a sourcing manager for a U.S. apparel business that designs, sources, and markets a branded line of women's, men's, and children's wear. She has recently read about a number of apparel firms that have begun using environmentally friendly materials for their products and proposed to her firm's management team that they consider an eco-friendly approach to their materials sourcing. All agreed, but they gave Emily the responsibility to conduct research about environmental issues and strategies and then to report back to the team. Emily wondered where she should begin.

The first thing she did was to identify a number of apparel firms that consider environmental issues in their business and that she had heard about in the media and through business contacts. Knowing that this was not a complete list, she still decided that researching the environmental policies and activities of these businesses was a good place to start.

Emily noted that none of these companies produced clothing exactly like her company, but she decided this was okay. She could identify the issues, the possible approaches, the opportunities and challenges regardless of size, product type, and business organization. Emily conducted Internet research on each company, using *social responsibility* and *environmental initiatives* as search terms when necessary. Then she read published information and interviewed contacts who worked in the selected companies.

What a surprise Emily had. She had outlined the problem to her management colleagues as choosing environmentally responsible materials for their products. But the problem was addressed by most of these companies much more broadly. She had heard that organic cotton is an eco-friendly fiber because it uses lower amounts of insecticides and herbicides than traditionally grown cotton, and this was confirmed. She also found that hemp is considered eco-friendly, as its fibers are grown naturally rather than produced from petroleum products.

But Emily realized that the origin of materials was just the first environmental impact in the life cycle of a garment or shoe. Some companies considered six distinct parts of a product's life cycle in determining its environmental friendliness: product design, materials selection, production and sourcing (fiber, textiles, apparel), distribution (packaging and transportation), product care or maintenance, and end-of-use management.[1] What started as a materials selection problem for Emily had now grown into a life cycle analysis that touched every functional area of her company and its entire supply chain.

Emily continued her research by checking out the social responsibility links on the businesses' Web sites. She found that many of these businesses had developed codes of conduct that included environmental principles and goals as well as human rights, health and safety, and fair labor practices. The environmental principles were often adapted from the UN Global Compact principles as follows:

- Precautionary approach to environmental challenges
- Promotion of greater environmental responsibility
- Environmentally friendly product development and diffusion[2]

These principles address not only the recognition of environmental issues involved with choices of materials, production processes, and transportation but also a proactive approach to future materials' development, production processes, and logistics activities, for example, to reduce the use of fuel for transportation.

The Web sites also included reports of other activities by the selected businesses that were initiated from the corporate headquarters and related in some way to environmental responsibility, such as "green" buildings, environmentally sound procurement and recycling processes, community involvement activities, and philanthropy projects related to the environment.

Finally, Emily found that the apparel industry was not a leader in this movement, and the employees she spoke with who were passionate about the importance of environmental responsibility expressed some frustration. They had to fight for every small change that would lower the impact of product development or energy use in their companies. However, she discovered several businesses that incorporated environmental stewardship or sustainability into their mission statements, building strategic value into the foundation of the businesses. Environmental responsibility was at the core of these businesses by design rather than as an afterthought. Sustainable environmental practices were in place to realize the goals of the policy for the long run, rather than for one season or several years.

Emily organized the information she gathered about each business into a matrix based on approaches to environmental responsibility in Table 8.1. The columns describe the four categories of strategies that she identified from her research, and the rows indicate the types of actions her sample of businesses conduct within each strategy. Emily noted that there were a variety of ways for businesses to address environmental responsibility and that only one business had activities in all four categories. She figured that businesses could incrementally develop their environmental responsibility program rather than adopt all strategies at once. Now Emily was ready to analyze the information more thoroughly, using these categories in order to develop her proposal to the company's management team.

Table 8.1. Matrix of Environmentally Responsible Business Strategies

Business	Code of Conduct	Life Cycle Analysis	Corporate Strategies	Strategic Environmental
A	Code and external monitoring along with social responsibility		—Reduced and recyclable packaging program —Corporate contributions to 1% for the environment	
B	Code and external monitoring along with social responsibility		Recycling program at headquarters and for waste in apparel production	
C	—Code monitoring based on ISO 14001 —Member of multi-stakeholder organization for environmental initiatives	LCA of 10% of existing styles		
D			Sponsors fundraiser for statewide environmental organization	
E		LCA of independent eco-friendly apparel line		Value proposition and mission to promote eco-friendly apparel materials
F	Code and continuous improvement guidelines for ER	LCA of 50% of styles and all new styles, approval based on ratings	—Member of Organic Exchange and 1% for Environment —Headquarters built "green" and in LEEDS certification process	—Value proposition and mission focuses on environmental sustainability and continuous improvement —Functional areas and employee performance evaluation based on environmental principles —Organizational and product evaluation includes environmental criteria

◉

Background: Environmental Responsibility

Throughout the twentieth century in the United States and other industrialized countries, national and regional environmental regulations have been developed and strengthened to address the impact of businesses and consumers on the environment. Toxic emissions into water from manufacturing plants and sewage from municipalities and farming operations were blamed for killing fish, wildlife, and plants. Toxic emissions into the air were found to adversely affect both humans and the ecosystem, causing lung and other diseases and killing forests hundreds of miles away with acid rainfall. As waste removal and disposal practices grew in dimension, safer processes and waste reduction methods were developed and implemented at every level of the waste stream. Regulation of business, government, and consumer practices was instituted both nationally and regionally in such policies as the EPA's Clean Air Act of 1990 and its amendments and water quality legislation starting in the 1960s. These early approaches to environmental stewardship set base standards that businesses and communities were required to meet, and other industrialized countries did the same. Unfortunately, these base standards were often set so low that negative environmental impacts were still great. In addition, environmental standards were and are usually country-specific and developing countries were less able to set even these base standards and to enforce them.

With Rachel Carson's 1962 book, *Silent Spring*, and a growing awareness of the precious and precarious balance of the natural world, a variety of nongovernmental organizations and activists emerged. These organizations called for greater action and higher expectations to save the environment from the long-term impacts of our everyday living. They view the environment as a precious resource for our children, with open land, healthy streams and lakes, and clean air. The Sierra Club, the National Wildlife Federation, and others promoted actions from public policy to citizen reforms that highlighted the need for constant vigilance of our natural resources for long-term health.

There were debates about how much logging should be allowed in the Northwest, and the term "tree huggers" was coined to describe environmental activists. Dams and power plants were held responsible for the decreasing numbers of migrating salmon from ocean to spawning grounds, and tuna fishing nets were blamed for catching and discarding many other fish and lowering the fish populations in our oceans. The safety of pesticides and herbicides in farming was questioned, and organic farming was adopted by a growing number of farmers of both food and fiber.

The 1987 *Our Common Future* report from the UN World Commission on Environment and Development called for countries to come together in the search for a path to sustainable development,[3] and its definition of sustainable development is often quoted: "Sustainable development is development that meets the needs of the present without compromising the ability of future generations to meet their own needs." Also referred to as the *Brundtland Report* for the chair of the commission, Norwegian Prime Minister Gro Brundtland, the report set a purpose and built international enthusiasm to call for the Earth Summit in 1992 in Rio de Janeiro, where 27 principles for sustainable development were proposed in the Rio Declaration (short for the Rio Declaration on Environment and Development).[4]

In 1997 the United Nations Framework Convention on Climate Change produced the next international discussion and report on the environment in the Kyoto Protocol.[5] Its provisions focus on limiting or reducing greenhouse gas emissions, specifically these six: carbon dioxide, methane, nitrous oxide, hydrofluorocarbons, perfluorocarbons, and sulphur hexafluoride. Approximately 175 parties have ratified the protocol, and of those, 36 countries and the European Economic Community (EEC), are bound to individual targets that will in total lower greenhouse gas emissions by at least 5 percent from 1990 levels during the commitment period of 2008-2012. The United States is the only developed country in the world that has not ratified the treaty.

These three reports have shaped the environmental agenda in international political arenas since they were published. Other important activities have also advanced the awareness of the environment and the importance of its stewardship. For example, the 2007 Nobel Peace Prize was shared by former Vice President Gore for his book, slide-show, and movie, *An Inconvenient Truth*, and the scientists working as the Intergovernmental Panel on Climate Change (IPCC) for their efforts to build up and disseminate greater knowledge about man-made climate change, and to lay the foundations for the measures that are needed to counteract such change.[6]

Here are some statistics presented in recent publications relating to environmental issues associated with the apparel industry. These statistics point to areas where environmentally responsible activities could be initiated.

⊚ "[The] total environmental cost is $3.79 per conventionally grown cotton T-shirt and $3.45 per organic cotton T-shirt. For both shirts, the stage with the greatest environmental impact is consumer care [more than growing, processing, distribution and transportation], accounting for 71% and 78% of costs, respectively."[7]

⊚ "25% of the annual worldwide insecticide use and 10% of the annual worldwide pesticide use are applied to conventionally grown cotton, even though cotton fields occupy less than 3% of the world's farmland."[8]

⊚ "Corporations extract resources and manufacture them into saleable products, leaving 11.4 billion tons of hazardous waste behind every year."[9]

⊚ "The average American throws away about 68 pounds of clothing and textiles per year, and while a few communities have textile re-cycling programs, about 85% of this waste goes to landfills today, where it occupies about 4% of landfill space."[10]

Recent publications also attest to environmentally responsible innovations in the apparel industry:

⊚ "Cotton items are commonly washed at 70° C whereas synthetics are washed at 40° C . . . [B]y substituting 'synthetic' fibers for 'cotton,' there is considerable potential to reduce impact associated with consumer care."[11]

● "[We] considered more than 8,000 chemicals [for finishing, dyeing, and processing] used in the textile industry and eliminated 7,962. The fabric was created using only thirty-eight chemicals [free of mutagens, carcinogens, heavy metals, endocrine disrupters, persistent toxic substances, and bio-accumulative substances]."[12]

● "For every 150 virgin polyester jackets that we replaced with post consumer recycled (PCR) polyester, we saved 42 gallons of oil and prevented a half-ton of toxic air emissions."[13]

As the environmental responsibility movement has matured, businesses have developed strategies and looked for standards to help them organize and continuously improve their environmental records. The four strategies of environmentally responsible business that Emily outlined can provide a framework for our analysis. Let's consider each strategy in more depth and illustrate with examples of apparel businesses that embrace them.

◉

Codes of Conduct and Monitoring for Compliance

Codes of conduct developed by businesses are the foundation of a system of monitoring for environmental compliance throughout the production process, from raw materials through fiber growing or development from polymers, dyeing and finishing, and garment production. Unlike labor-related codes of conduct that are almost universally based on International Labour Organization (ILO) conventions, environmental codes vary in the basis of their foundation. For example, national laws and regulations often set minimum standards for impacts on the environment and therefore vary dramatically by production location. Monitoring for environmental codes is sometimes conducted at the same time as monitoring for human rights and health and safety practices or quality assurance. Indicators that can alert an apparel brand or retailer to environmental performance are poor quality, poor construction, and bad coloration.

Codes relating to the environment can be based on the UN Global Compact Principles, but more guidance from planning through implementation and evaluation is provided by ISO 14001, an international environmental management standard.[14] The International Organization for Standardization, usually referred to as ISO, is a nongovernmental organization headquartered in Geneva, Switzerland, that oversees a network of national standard institutes in about 157 countries. Many of its members work for their national governments or are mandated by their governments in an effort to bring some international structure to standards for business application. Besides the ISO 14001, another generic management standard is ISO 9001 for quality management.

The foundation of ISO 14001 is two principles: "to minimize harmful effects on the environment caused by [business activities] and to achieve continual improvement of [a business's] environmental performance."

More specifically, ISO lists five life cycle assessment (LCA) categories to be used with products including apparel and textiles that a business should consider as part of its environmental management:

- Safety for public health and environment
- Renewable energy and energy efficiency
- Material that is bio-based or recycled
- Company-based systems in place, for instance, LCA and social responsibility codes and monitoring
- Reclamation, sustainable reuse, and end-of-use management

ISO 14001 guides a business through the process of planning, implementing, and evaluating its environmental program, beginning by considering every aspect of the business and designing a plan that matches the business's mission, organization, and products. Businesses can be certified as ISO 14001 compliant through ISO as the last step of the process. ISO 14001 certification is an indicator of business commitment to environmentally responsible practices, although certification is awarded to businesses for documenting their practices rather than for meeting any particular standards set by ISO or planning for improvement.

Regardless of whether a business establishes its own code of conduct or follows ISO 14001 or another set of environmental standards, the objective is continuous improvement. All codes should be reconsidered and revised at reasonable time intervals so that they reflect the changes in society and business spheres and continue to promote environmental responsibility.

◉

Life Cycle Assessment

Life cycle assessments consider the entire life cycle of apparel and textiles, from raw materials through consumer use and disposal. These stages include the production cycles of textiles and apparel, consumer use, and end-of-use product management through landfill disposal, incineration, reuse, recycling, or redesign. Most envision the ideal LCA as a closed circle, using unwanted materials or garments to make the next generation of products; or as McDonough and Braungart express it, waste is used as the raw material or food for the next products, so waste = food.[15] LCA can reveal the root causes of environmental costs, such as energy use or toxic chemicals, as well as indicate the place in the life cycle like design or consumer use to denote specific apparel and textile considerations, such as use of organic cotton or laundering preference. LCA helps to analyze the problem of environmental sustainability in the apparel industry and to propose some solutions.[16] Figure 8.1 presents the five stages in the life cycle of an apparel product that has been applied in a variety of research.[17]

The objective of LCA is to evaluate the environmental impacts in each of the stages for any given product's life cycle. Businesses can use this information in deciding whether to make, redesign, or reject a product design plan. Consumers can use this information to inform their buying decisions. Public policy experts can use this information in formulating policies and providing evidence in their support.

The five life cycle assessment stages defined by the Sustainable Textile Standard developed by GreenBlue, a nonprofit educational and

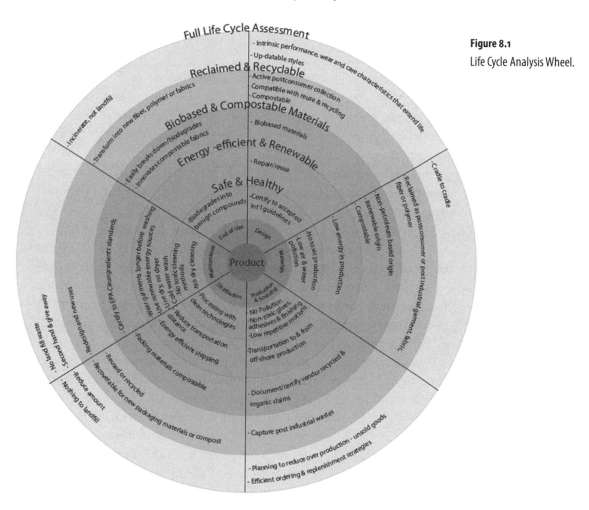

Figure 8.1
Life Cycle Analysis Wheel.

research organization promoting the reinvention of design, and others[18] were adapted to help us identify and evaluate actions specific to certain products and businesses. The circles surrounding the product life cycle stages in Figure 8.1 represent each of a sustainable standard's categories: safe and healthful; energy-efficient and renewable; bio-based and compostable; materials reclaimed and recycled; and overall life cycle assessment and socially responsible practices, including human rights and fair labor practices. We'll use this matrix to organize our discussion about life cycle assessment.

Product Design

Product design begins with setting criteria based on functional and psychological consumer needs, aesthetics, business niche, cost, and other requirements. Certain limitations are set based on a business's mission and value proposition or its competitive advantage. These are givens without which the business cannot compete. Increasingly, environmentally responsible (and socially responsible) criteria are being identified and incorporated at this stage of an apparel item's life cycle for easy inclusion.

For example, designers can decide to choose only materials that (1) are bio-based, from recyclable materials, or can be recycled, (2) are not processed or finished with toxic chemicals, (3) are safe for humans during production or use, as no toxins are produced, (4) have intrinsic characteristics that extend product life, minimize care requirements, or ease of disposal (e.g., durability, no-wash, and other performance characteristics), and (5) have end-of-use plans such as recycling or reuse.[19]

Beyond materials choice, designers can select garment features (e.g., fabric, lining, zippers, and snaps) that are (1) similar in fiber content to ease care and disposal processes,[20] (2) updatable through classic style, modularity, or modifications, (3) reusable in another format, such as a sweater that can be raveled and re-knit for other clothing and home furnishings such as hats, gloves, or afghans, and (4) "super satisfying" in aesthetic, physical, social, and psychological functions so that consumers will wear garments many times and for extensive life spans—that is, years rather than weeks or months.[21] In a fashion culture, these design choices are particularly noteworthy. They address the fleeting nature of fashion, excess consumption of clothing, poor quality for a throwaway society, and conscientious end-of-use options that have the potential to transform the way we think about and act toward our clothing, from buying more and more to environmental sustainability.

Involving designers in the quest for environmental sustainability through product design at the very initiation of the design process and making it part of the evaluative criteria for production decisions place environmental responsibility at the foundation of the product assessment rather than an afterthought. This is an example of values-led business that seeks to make a difference as well as a profit, of making a difference by design. [22]

Materials Selection

Materials selection is probably the most recognized step in environmental responsibility. Much attention has been paid to the origin, production processes, and life cycle of textile fibers and fabrics. Indeed, the sustainable textile standards proposed by ISO, GreenBlue, and other NGOs focus on this stage in the apparel and footwear life cycle. Another organization, EPEA (Environmental Protection Encouragement Agency), and its principal, Dr. Michael Braungart, have created the Intelligent Products System,[23] which provides a three-part rating system to evaluate dyes and other chemicals used in developing, processing, and finishing textile products. These three types of products/processes are consumable, service, and unmarketable. Consumables are those textiles that are actually compostable and can go back to the ground. These are often bio-based and have not been treated with toxins. In other words, they are produced using sustainable practices. Organic cotton and wool fibers are perhaps the most well known and available compostables.[24] During the entire growing and production process, including cutting and sewing, organic fiber or fabric must be segregated from fiber grown and processed with any nonorganic practices. Organic cotton and wool have recently been adopted by large firms, such as Patagonia (100 percent organic cotton in all sportswear since 1996) and Nike (pledged to have all cotton items include a minimum of 5 percent organic cotton by 2010), and small firms as one added value to their products. Table 8.2 describes these fibers considered to be friendly to the environment as well as innovative eco-friendly fibers discussed below.

A variety of innovative fibers for apparel have been or are being developed as environmentally responsible, based on inputs, processing, care requirements, recycling and reuse options, and end-of-use

Table 8.2. Natural, Organic, and Innovative Eco-Friendly Fibers for Apparel

Name or Brand	Characteristics	Producer or Apparel User
Organic Wool	No pesticides on grazing lands, all organic feed, regulated antibiotic use, limited number of sheep per acre	Vermont Organic Fibers
Ingeo™	Made from polylactide acid (PLA) polymers, often using corn as raw material	NatureWorks LLC, Cargill and Teijin
Climatex® Lifecycle™	Biodegradable and compostable upholstery fabric	Rohner Textil AG and Environmental Protection Encouragement Agency (EPEA)
Trigema	Fully compostable T-shirt	Trigema and Environmental Agency (EPEA)
ECO CIRCLE	Post-consumer recycled polyester from Capilene and Polar fleece	Teijin and Patagonia

management. Examples of these fibers include Ingeo™, a polymer made by Natureworks LLC from corn, a 100 percent renewable source;[25] compostable upholstery fabric (Climatex Lifecycle)[26] and T-shirts (Trigema)[27] made from materials and with processing that allow products to be returned to the earth as mulch; and ECO CIRCLE, a closed-loop recycling processing pioneered by Japanese fiber processor Teijin where polyester material can be chemically recycled back to the polymer state and re-formed into "new" fibers from that state.[28] A number of apparel brands, such as Patagonia, Nike, and Timberland, purchase ECO CIRCLE polyester for use in some of their products.

Other examples of selection and use of recycled fibers and fabrics as environmentally responsible approaches include the following:

- Recycled soda pop bottles being turned into Polartec® fleece by Malden Mills and others[29]
- Used T-shirts recut and embellished into high-priced ready-to-wear shirts, skirts, and dresses by Alabama Chanin (Figure 8.2)[30]
- Secondhand garments being recycled into new designs and sold by retailers such as Urban Outfitters' Urban Renewal collection and What Comes Around Goes Around to reflect a chicness to recycling. Carol Young coined the term "undesigned" to describe this approach, and it has been widely adopted in the industry [31]

McDonough and Braungart were pioneers in consideration of nontoxic chemicals and dyes in textile production and processing for use in the interiors of buildings. Their book, *Cradle to Cradle*, has become a classic in the environmental responsibility movement for its vision and set of principles, its illustration of the possibilities of design through materials selection, and the composition of the book itself from polypropylene film that reflects its sustainability message. [32]

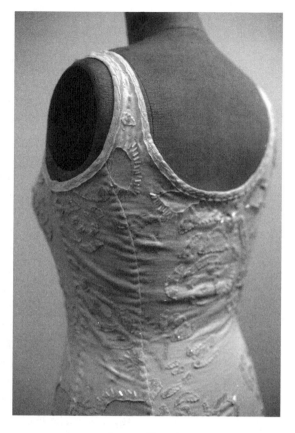

Figure 8.2
Alabama Chanin apparel from recycled T-shirts.

Production and Sourcing

Production and sourcing can also reduce environmental impacts through selection of fiber, spinning, cutting, sewing, and finishing processes such as water-based adhesives for shoes and nontoxic laundering and fading processes for jeans. Evaluating the health and safety practices during the textile fiber and spinning processes and garment cutting and sewing processes is an important step in assuring environmental standards that can include designers, production supervisors, and even workers. The assessment should consider the health and safety of the workers from exposure to toxic emissions in air or water as well as the impact of repetitive motions and production noise. Levi Strauss has been a leader in addressing harmful water emissions in dye houses and laundering facilities, a major concern in the finishing of denim and denim products, developing Global Emissions Guidelines in 2005 that are available to others on its Web site. In addition, Levi Strauss and Nike have led the industry by developing a Restricted Substance List to ensure health and safety for workers and consumers of its products.[33] Social issues related to human rights and fair labor practices can be evaluated at the same time. The trend to use codes of conduct to establish and monitor socially and environmentally responsible practices in factories is one approach to compliance that encourages continuous improvement. Being informed of alternative production processes that support environmental responsibility, such as nontoxic dyes and colorants and water-based adhesives, helps designers, buyers, and production managers to make eco-friendly decisions.

Production planning is another part of the production process that can incorporate environmental responsibility. In the United States and some other industrialized countries, there is currently a mismatch between the quantity and types of clothing that are being produced and those that are being purchased in the marketplace. More product is being produced than sold, and yet some consumers are dissatisfied with the choices. This mismatch points to a systemic problem in the way businesses decide on the apparel styles and the quantity produced to meet their customers' needs and buying habits. Three practices that explain part of this mismatch are (1) the forecasting process used by most businesses, (2) the system of ordering, and (3) the globalization of production that takes it offshore rather than local.

The forecasting process determines how many of what color and style to produce and where. Some businesses base this decision on expected orders, others on what clients have already ordered. The problem is that to get the product to market, the product often has to be made 3, 6, or even 12 months in advance of the product's arrival in retail stores. It is very hard to predict so far in advance what clothing and footwear the consumer will want and what will sell well, and fashion makes a point of routine change in silhouettes. A variety of strategies have been implemented to address this problem, such as (1) just-in-time manufacturing or quick response, wherein product is made closer to the time it is needed, using consumer demand data to inform the production plan, (2) use of both regional and offshore production factories—regional to produce faster, smaller, more fashionable orders and reorders, and offshore to produce larger, basic styles that are sure to sell in high quantities, and (3) replenishment programs whereby buyer and producer work together using point-of-sale consumer data to plan orders and systematic reorders and are able to add extra or cancel orders when necessary.[34] The objective in all of these strategies is to reduce production of unwanted product that will move into the waste stream as secondhand clothing or wiping cloths, converted to new products, or incinerated.[35] If fewer clothing products are produced, the amount of clothing flowing into a waste stream will be reduced.

Innovative retail approaches also address the production mismatch. Nau's small square footage for its retail stores is possible because it inventories just one item in each size and color in each store. Consumers try on and order in the store and then receive their product purchases directly from a central distribution facility servicing all Nau's retailer stores, a more efficient model for controlling inventory and minimizing unsold product. Retailer Zara is admired for its efficient and profitable fashion replenishment cycle that adds new product styles every two weeks and encourages consumers to frequently return. Unfortunately, although this "fast fashion" may reduce unsold inventory by limiting production of any one style, it also promotes overconsumption by increasing the number of store visits by each consumer.

Distribution

Distribution includes both transportation and packaging considerations that affect the environment. Environmentally sound choices can be made about efficient energy use, choice of materials, and added flow to the waste stream.

Transportation costs that are incurred as garments are moved from the apparel factory to the distribution center and then to the retail store are obvious. We notice the large trucks emblazoned with apparel business names on the highway or delivering at retail stores and immediately think, "Ah yes, these are the transportation costs in the apparel supply chain." But there are also environmental considerations of transportation during the acquisition of fiber, yarn, fabric, or other raw materials. Materials are shipped to dyeing and finishing factories and then to a variety of sewing factories—often offshore—where garments will be made. Garments are then shipped to distribution centers and finally to the retail store to be sold to consumers. For mail-order and Web-based businesses, transportation costs are similar but products go directly to the consumer from distribution centers or, in best practices, from the factory. Energy use in the entire apparel supply chain must be considered.

The most effective transportation energy reduction strategy is, of course, to reduce the distance materials and garments travel. Apparel businesses can consolidate their supplier networks to more efficiently manage multiple production locations and use the most energy-efficient shipping method, even when it is not the lowest cost. Seeking regional or same-hemisphere production factories to reduce the miles of travel each item of clothing takes is another option.

The amount and composition of packaging are both environmental concerns. Environmentally responsible businesses question each piece of packaging at each point in the production, distribution, and sales processes. No packaging is the most effective waste management strategy, so the questions should begin with: "Do we need packaging to ship finished products to distribution centers and stores? To present products to the consumer? To ship multiple items home to the consumer?"

Packaging that is necessary should be tested for optimization—that is, how can we use as little as possible?

Choice of materials is the other packaging consideration, and one NGO, the Sustainable Packaging Coalition,[36] has developed the following best-practice standards when packaging is necessary:

- Provides safety and health for individuals and communities through life cycle and in end-of-use scenarios
- Uses renewable energy through life cycle
- Maximizes use of renewable or recycled materials
- Manufactured using clean technologies and production processes
- Designed to optimize materials and energy
- Recoverable for use in biological or industrial cradle-to-cradle cycles.

Notice the similarity of these principles to the textile sustainability standards in Figure 8.1.

The final distribution opportunity is informing and educating the consumer through labeling. Progress has been slow in this part of environmental responsibility in part because of the difficulty of adding item-specific information to so many styles that continuously change and in part because of the lack of consumer demand for such labeling. But there are some exemplary models for environmental impact labeling. Timberland instituted *Our Footprint* labels on its footwear boxes made from 100 percent recycled post-consumer waste fiber in 2006. [37] Figure 8.3 illustrates the information provided about the environmental impacts by energy costs, community impacts by its use of fair labor practices and volunteer hours, and social impacts by indicating the factory name and location. Timberland's commitment to community actions for environmental and social responsibility is well known, and its labeling innovations are one more example.

Product Maintenance

Several studies have argued that consumer product care uses more energy than all other parts of a clothing item's life cycle. Specifically, a

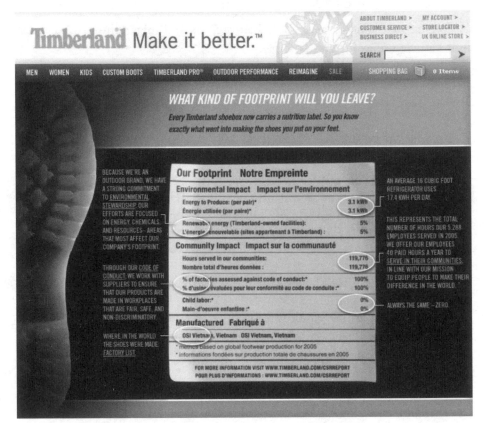

Figure 8.3

Timberland label gives environmental impact information to consumers.

Franklin Associates study[38] found that 85 percent of life cycle energy for a polyester blouse was used in the consumer care phase, compared to 14 percent during production and 1 percent for disposal. It went on to show that energy requirements were lowered to only 36 percent of the whole by washing the garment in cold water and line drying it. Similar results were found for a cotton T-shirt in the Well Dressed report from University of Cambridge Institute of Manufacturing.[39] The recommendations for reducing energy costs in garment care can be taken a step further to wearing the blouse and other clothing longer between washings.[40]

The important conclusion is that the consumer care and use stage of an apparel product's life cycle can have a significant effect on a

product's life cycle environmental impact. Designers can help by selecting materials and garment construction methods that allow the
most energy-efficient care requirements, such as cold- or warm-water
wash and line drying. Avoidance of materials and garment designs that
require dry cleaning methods that use toxic chemicals, laundry deter-
gents with phosphorus or other environmentally unsound surfactants,
and tumble drying is also eco-friendly. We shouldn't let consumers off
the hook either. They have responsibilities but need more information
than is usually easily available. Hang tags and marketing campaigns
can inform the consumer about the high energy and environmental
costs of specific clothing care options. Eco-friendly consumer action
is the ultimate solution to environmental responsibility at this stage in
the product life cycle.

Katie Dombek-Keith developed a clothing care calculator based on
published sources (Figure 8.4 and Box 8.1).[41] It is one example of an
educational tool using Excel that calculates a consumer's energy outputs in clothing care based on a set of questions about wearing and
laundering behaviors. It is one method to help consumers realize the
impacts of their everyday activities and their relation to the broad picture of environmental issues such as global warming and clean water.

End-of-Use Management

There is general agreement that end-of-use management is a significant issue that should be addressed at the time of a product's design.
Apparel and textile products contribute 4 million tons to U.S. landfills annually, or 4.5 percent of the total waste stream entering landfills, despite the availability of alternative disposal methods for textiles
such as used-clothing markets, conversion to new products, and wiping cloths.[42] Although sources advise that disposal by incineration is
a more environmentally sound practice than diversion to the landfill,
there are alternative approaches that can be built into the design process or created through recycling and reuse waste stream systems. For
example, the carpet industry, particularly Shaw Industries, has been a

Figure 8.4

Calculator for energy use in clothing care.

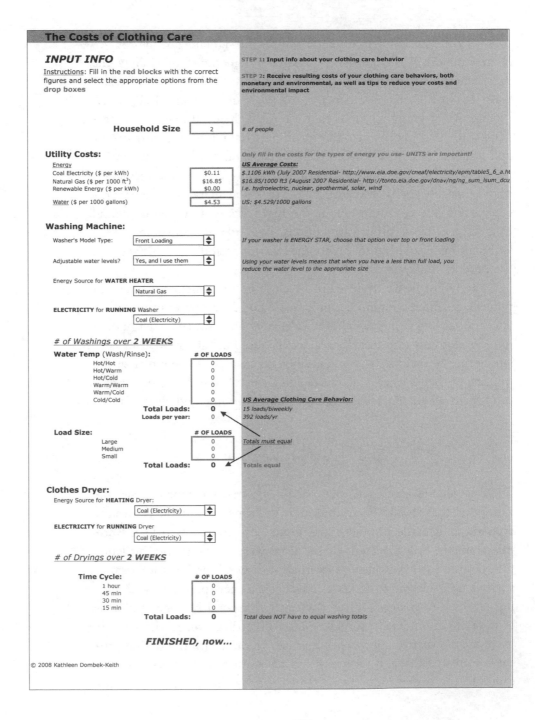

The Costs of Clothing Care

INPUT INFO

<u>Instructions</u>: Fill in the red blocks with the correct figures and select the appropriate options from the drop boxes

STEP 1: Input info about your clothing care behavior

STEP 2: Receive resulting costs of your clothing care behaviors, both monetary and environmental, as well as tips to reduce your costs and environmental impact

Household Size | 2 | # of people

Utility Costs:

Only fill in the costs for the types of energy you use- UNITS are important!

US Average Costs:

Energy	
Coal Electricity ($ per kWh)	$0.11
Natural Gas ($ per 1000 ft³)	$16.85
Renewable Energy ($ per kWh)	$0.00

$.1106 kWh (July 2007 Residential- http://www.eia.doe.gov/cneaf/electricity/epm/table5_6_a.ht
$16.85/1000 ft3 (August 2007 Residential- http://tonto.eia.doe.gov/dnav/ng/ng_sum_lsum_dcu
i.e. hydroelectric, nuclear, solar, wind

Water ($ per 1000 gallons) | $4.53 | US: $4.529/1000 gallons

Washing Machine:

| Washer's Model Type: | Front Loading | If your washer is ENERGY STAR, choose that option over top or front loading |
| Adjustable water levels? | Yes, and I use them | Using your water levels means that when you have a less than full load, you reduce the water level to the appropriate size |

Energy Source for **WATER HEATER**
Natural Gas

ELECTRICITY for **RUNNING** Washer
Coal (Electricity)

# of Washings over 2 WEEKS

Water Temp (Wash/Rinse):	# OF LOADS
Hot/Hot	0
Hot/Warm	0
Hot/Cold	0
Warm/Warm	0
Warm/Cold	0
Cold/Cold	0
Total Loads:	**0**
Loads per year:	0

US Average Clothing Care Behavior:
15 loads/biweekly
392 loads/yr

Load Size:	# OF LOADS
Large	0
Medium	0
Small	0
Total Loads:	**0**

Totals must equal

Totals equal

Clothes Dryer:

Energy Source for **HEATING** Dryer:
Coal (Electricity)

ELECTRICITY for **RUNNING** Dryer
Coal (Electricity)

# of Dryings over 2 WEEKS

Time Cycle:	# OF LOADS
1 hour	0
45 min	0
30 min	0
15 min	0
Total Loads:	**0**

Total does NOT have to equal washing totals

FINISHED, now...

© 2008 Kathleen Dombek-Keith

Box 8.1. Clothing Care Calculator

Katie Dombek-Keith's Clothing Care Calculator is an interactive tool that can help consumers evaluate their clothing care practices for energy use and alternative methods. The calculator asks for the number of people in the household; average household utility rates; types of washing machine and dryer; and usual use patterns for cleaning clothing by water temperature, load size, and number of loads per month. Results of calculations present average household energy and water costs, environmental cost by water and electricity use, and carbon dioxide emissions. Hints for changing behaviors and reducing environmental costs are suggested, as the clothing care calculator was designed to encourage consumers to rethink and adjust down their impacts on the environment from clothing care.

leader in end-of-use management by not only using recycled materials but building carpet recycling into its sales process. The approach integrates a take-back service into carpet purchases whereby consumers return worn-out or unwanted carpet to the carpet manufacturer for recycling, shifting the end-of-use process from landfill to reuse. [43]

Secondhand and Vintage Clothing

The secondhand and vintage market for used clothing is certainly one valuable reuse alternative. It has consistently been popular with young people because of its low cost and its value in building personal identities that symbolize unique character and sometimes rebellion toward the mainstream fashion system. At the turn of the twenty-first century, secondhand and vintage clothing provided a market alternative that all ages were accessing. Some businesses like What Comes Around Goes Around in New York City built their business model on a combination of recycling and reuse strategies, including retail sales of vintage and cheaper, less iconic secondhand clothing, as well as a wholesale business selling redesigned used clothing to major retail stores. The success of these businesses depends on developing collection strategies for used clothing, selecting garments that will sell, creating methods to redesign or modify used clothing, and identifying markets for excess inventory and waste.

Modular and Seamless Knitted Clothing

Modular clothing that transforms from one use to another has been introduced in the outerwear market, extending the number and extent of lifetime wearing. For example, hiking pants are available that have zip-off pant legs to protect hikers from cold and brush in their full length but also convert to shorts when the day gets hotter or the hike more demanding. Jackets and shirts with removable sleeves are another example of modular clothing that serves multiple purposes. There is also potential in modularity to extend the life span of a garment through style changes that adapt to current fashion or wearing situation. Dombek-Keith designed a line of suits that can attach multiple components to the base jacket and skirt pieces to change suits from casual to business and from one silhouette to another (Figure 8.5).[44]

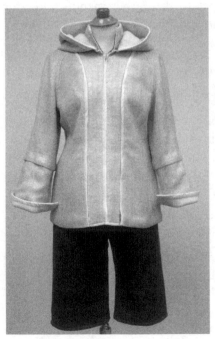 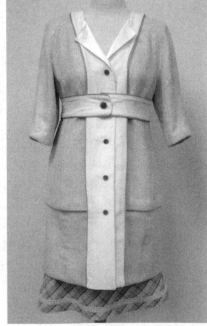

Figure 8.5
Modular designs to extend clothing wear.

Issey Miyake designed his A-Poc conceptual collection in 2000 that consisted of knit garments that consumers could cut according to their preferences for silhouette, length, and sleeve designs.[45] It is an example of involving the consumer in the design process to increase connection to and personal meaning for the garment through ownership and personalization. It also demonstrates how one garment can change, by design, through its life span.

Seamless knitting develops a completed apparel product during the knitting process. Fit, silhouette, and surface texture are designed and accomplished all in one process with this revolutionary seamless knitting technology. It also eliminates production waste.

The Five Lives Life Cycle

Chen and Lewis developed a life cycle system that follows a piece of cloth through five lives (Figure 8.6).[46] Notice that the cloth has three incarnations as a garment, first as a piece of fabric draped on the body, second as a cut-and-sewn garment, third as a recut-and-resewn

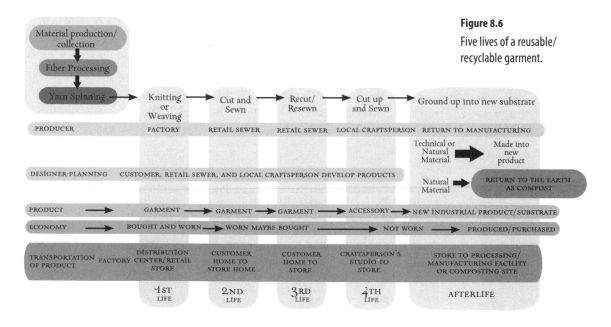

Figure 8.6

Five lives of a reusable/recyclable garment.

garment; then a fourth life as an accessory; and finally a life as a new product made from recycled fiber or compostable waste.

Cradle-to-Cradle Fibers

Most revolutionary is the work of several fiber companies in combination with apparel businesses to develop "cradle-to-cradle" fibers—that is, fibers that can be recycled right down to the fiber or polymer state and start over again at the same level of quality. Teijin, a Japanese fiber manufacturer, has worked with Patagonia to develop the ECO CIRCLE fiber-processing system and with Cargill in a joint venture, NatureWorks LLC, that produces and markets biopolymers derived from 100 percent renewable resources.[47] The environmental concept behind ECO CIRCLE is a process that recycles Patagonia's Capilene fibers back to its polymer state so that new fibers can be produced from the recycled Capilene garments returned by customers. The waste stream is reduced by providing an alternative to throwing old garments into a landfill. Natureworks and Ingeo brands represent the first family of commercially available low-carbon-footprint polymers derived from 100 percent renewable resources with cost and performance that compete with petroleum-based packaging materials and fibers.[48] Natureworks' objective is twofold: to use bio-based raw materials and to develop materials that can be returned to the soil; most well-known is its Ingeo fiber that uses corn in its polymer production. These revolutionary approaches to end-of-life management illustrate the potential of applying cradle-to-cradle concepts by design.

Quantitative Analyses of Environmental Impacts

Several life cycle assessments have been conducted by independent organizations and apparel businesses to evaluate energy use and environmental impact of individual apparel garments. An LCA was conducted by Franklin Associates in 1993 to compare the amount of energy used during the manufacture of a polyester blouse with the energy used during the consumer and disposal stages and has been used as the foundation for other life cycle analyses.[49] One of the most important findings was that consumer use, washing and drying over the blouse's lifetime, comprises two-thirds of the energy used, while disposal used about one quarter the energy and the manufacturing process even less. This suggests that consumers are indeed part of the problem and must be part of the solution. Other examples that have been published compare environmental impacts for T-shirts made from conventional or organic cotton,[50] showing that the biggest differences in environmental impact are at the growing stage, with pesticide use and soil erosion big contributors. These are examples of life cycle assessment used with a specific product. This process is now being used by some apparel businesses as part of their environmental responsibility activities. The output from the process have real potential as information tools for consumers as they compare available products based on environmental impacts such as energy use, resource protection, and distribution costs.

◉

Corporate Strategies for Environmental Responsibility

Strategies that are centrally planned offer a third approach to environmental responsibility for businesses. These can focus on (1) business operations such as facilities planning, procurement, and operations such as energy use and recycling programs or on (2) community involvement of the business through volunteer efforts and philanthropy.

Facilities, Procurement, and Operations

A number of firms have redesigned their corporate headquarters in recent years to include environmentally sound materials and energy-efficient strategies. Ford Motor Company and Patagonia are two that have received media notice. The Leadership in Energy and Environmental Design (LEED) certification system provides a method for designing and implementing "green" building strategies and furnishes guidelines, recommendations, and a certification process to rate buildings for compliance.[51]

The LEED process can be used in part to steer smaller steps toward environmentally sound facilities as well. Selecting interior materials with low VOCs (volatile organic compounds emitted as gases), nontoxic building materials, ENERGY STAR rated fixtures and appliances, natural lighting approaches, and air filtering systems all help to reduce health and safety issues for employees and reduce overall energy use.

Implementing work hours and all-corporation vacation times to coincide with very cold or very hot times of the year can substantially reduce energy costs. Other structural approaches to reduced energy use and enhanced employee quality of life are opportunities for further progress toward environmental sustainability.

Community Involvement

A number of businesses contribute to their local communities, some with initiatives related to environmental responsibility. One exemplary model is Timberland, a footwear and apparel company that has received numerous awards for its environmental and community involvement activities.[52] It engages its employees in community service through its Timberland Serve programs, for example, contributing over 55,000 employee volunteer hours through its Path of Service program in 2004. Employees active in Path of Service are also eligible for a fully paid ten-day science service expedition led by the Earthwatch Institute. Timberland's community grants program offers cash and in-kind product grants to community organizations, often related to community building and environmental stewardship. Its mission statement clearly articulates the company's commitment to communities that are "actively engaged with the ecosystem and that work to increase the understanding of environmental sustainability; primarily those organizations whose innovative practices support the exploration and development of alternative energy resources." The Evelina's Gift recycling program is named for an employee who quietly started laundering and mending returns for donation to others. Her project was institutionalized in semiannual workdays when employee volunteers prepare returned products for a secondhand giving program.

Philanthropy

A number of multi-stakeholder and business-led initiatives collaboratively promote environmental responsibility through planned giving, such as 1% For the Planet and the Organic Exchange. These are examples of philanthropy that advance a business's environmental responsibility program as well as give back to society through planned giving. All philanthropic giving is important to help those who are less fortunate and should be valued. Some businesses focus their philanthropy on environmental stewardship, which is important to the environmental responsibility movement.

◉

Strategic Environmental Approach

Harvard Business School Professor Michael Porter is a leading authority on competitive strategy and international competitiveness. Porter recommends that businesses should analyze what they do well, where they have an advantage either over their competitors or as an industry leader, and then strategically build their position using this knowledge and these advantages. He argues that sustaining a strategic position goes beyond operational efficiency—such as productivity of employees, efficient use of resources, and cost-effective logistics—that operational efficiency is a given and something that every business should be good at, not a competitive advantage.[53]

Patagonia provides a good example of a business using environmentally responsible activities to its competitive advantage. Patagonia is an outerwear apparel company that produces technical products for the active outdoors person as well as sportswear for a broader target market. Yvon Choinard, its founder, wrote *Let My People Go Surfing*, a book outlining Patagonia's philosophy and its unique position based on its environmental sustainability approach to all of its activities, such as:

- Buying and even developing materials that promote environmental stewardship, recycling, and reuse, such as organic cotton, fleece made of recycled soda bottles, and ECO CIRCLE fiber that can be reused at the fiber level
- Using its promotional materials, catalog, and Web site to promote care of the environment
- Giving its employees paid time to work with community environmental activist groups[54]

Patagonia attracts employees who embrace its mission and approach, and its management integrates environmentally responsible principles into all activities. In other words, Patagonia follows Porter's advice for sustainable competitive advantage as it uses environmental responsibility to create its unique competitive position with activities tailored to environmental responsibility that can be sustained.

Porter and Kramer divide social responsibility including environmental responsibility into three categories: generic social issues, value chain social impacts, and social dimensions of competitive context. They argue that businesses should recognize these categories and the actions that address them as three different levels of socially responsible activities.[55]

Generic Social Issues

A generic social issue may not have any relationship to a business's operations or supply chain nor affect its competitiveness. Examples would be Nike's partnership with Lance Armstrong using the LiveStrong bracelets to fight cancer and the Red campaign founded by Bono and Bobby Shriver that organizes retail and other business campaigns to contribute part of sales of specially designed "RED" products to the Global Fund to fight AIDS in Africa.

Value Chain Social Impacts and Dimensions of Competitiveness

A company's ordinary business operations that affect individuals or communities somewhere along its supply chain are considered value chain social impacts. In other words, the operations make good business sense and result in societal gains. Porter and Kramer's last category, social dimensions, affects the company's underlying competitiveness in locations where it operates. These categories offer opportunities for using strategic approaches to connect competitiveness with socially responsible activities. The compliance to fair labor and human rights practices in offshore production can positively affect the workers and their community as well as a business's value chain operations. The adoption of water-based glues and nontoxic dyes provides health and safety for workers as well as efficient business operations and is another example of value chain social impacts.

The final category transforms the social issues of labor and the environment into a competitive advantage through proaction and hard work in collaboration with key stakeholders. For example, Maggie's Organics and Project Alabama have done this with their development of good production jobs in places where few jobs are available and using environmentally responsible fabrics. Maggie's Organics helped Nicaraguan women develop their own sewing cooperative and placed a majority of Maggie's product orders through the co-op, realizing its social mission and also its environmental mission by using only organic cotton in its products.[56] Project Alabama produced its sought-after, one-of-a-kind products from predominantly recycled T-shirts in rural Alabama by featuring the sewing and crafts traditions and skills of local employees. The business, now reincarnated as Alabama Chanin, demonstrates an environmental and social consciousness as its mission and business value proposition.[57]

◉

The Challenge That Lies Ahead

Emily's explorations, described at the beginning of this chapter, identified one of the main challenges that lie ahead for dramatic gains in environmentally responsible business practices—recognizing its breadth. Emily thought that the question was whether or not to add environmentally friendly materials to her company's apparel line and that this question encompassed the extent of environmental responsibility. Through research she concluded that it was a given that environmentally responsible practices should be adopted, but the important question was how and to what level. She found both baseline and incremental approaches that her company could take to embrace environmental responsibility and continuous improvement toward it.

Using the matrix of environmental responsibility strategies, Emily designed four proposals to present to the management team based on the four categories of business strategies. Her first proposal was to develop a code of conduct and methods for evaluating the company's selection of raw materials, production process, and distribution. The second was to develop life cycle assessments for their best-selling products to investigate the impact on the environment of their materials selection, processing, energy use, and consumer care requirements. Based on the results, recommendations would be made to embrace or alter the choices of materials, processing, distribution, and care requirements to increase environmental responsibility, and LCA would become an ongoing part of the production development and selection process. The third was to evaluate the corporate headquarters' environmental impact through investigating building and operations, procurement, and recycling programs and propose a program of continuous improvement. The final proposal was to consider the company's mission and value proposition to consider whether the environmental responsibility should or could be at its foundation. Emily did not view these proposals to be conflicting. She thought that any or all could be accepted and implemented either immediately or phased in. She was advocating incremental change and continuous improvement toward environmental responsibility in a form that her company could accept and work toward over the next few years.

~

Chapter 9

~

The Future of Social Responsibility in the Apparel Industry

⊙

Sara sat down at her desk in her New York City office after return-ing from the latest trip to Hong Kong. While in Hong Kong she had organized a successful stakeholder collaboration involving the apparel brand for which she is vice president of sourcing, one of the foremost trading companies, with a network of over 200 contractor factories and raw material firms, several NGOs, and the Chinese government. She has been in this business since graduating from college with degrees in apparel design and management in 1996, before the phase-out of the Multifibre Agreement (MFA) and during the development of responses to the call for social responsibility in the apparel industry by labor and environmental groups, NGOs, the media, and consumer groups.

Sara reflected on her latest trip and the advances she's seen in industry approaches to social responsibility in the second decade of the twenty-first century. She remembered the numerous newspaper and magazine articles in the 1990s about U.S. brands and retailers being accused of unfair labor practices such as child labor, unpaid wages and overtime, health and safety violations, and toxic chemical use in textile and apparel processing and production. The initial responses to these accusations were first denial, then development of codes of conduct and monitoring systems to measure compliance. Sara pondered about how far the industry has come in social responsibility today.

On this trip she visited the Taevan Apparel Group, which serves apparel brands and retailers around the world, and talked to a number of workers. The workers said they enjoyed their work at the factory. The company provides them with a good salary and benefits, such as a company preschool for their youngest children and enough money for education for older children at the local academy. In addition, there are in-house educational programs on both work-related and self-improvement topics such as patternmaking, cutting, and marker making, and English language, financial management, and child development. Sara realizes that at one time she would have had to worry that the workers had been coached to say all these nice things—boy, have times changed. The company also pays for classes workers want to take in the community as well as encouraging employees to volunteer their time with community organizations to help others. There is a record of worker advancement within the factory system to supervisors, managers, and labor union representatives and a strong camaraderie among the workers and management. Management and workers work collaboratively, identifying and solving problems together. Workers attend internal and external training programs the factory management offers all employees in all aspects of social responsibility such as labor laws, workers' rights, environmental regulations, and health and safety as well as management resources and strategies. Some workers have left the company to start their own small businesses in designing and sewing clothes, and some of these now have contracts with the Taevan Apparel Group.

Many of the contract factories in the Taevan Apparel Group open their doors for tours for local schoolchildren, the local community, and tourists to show how apparel is made. Fair Factory labels are applied to all of the group's apparel to indicate the strong health and safety measures, fair labor practices, and environmental standards its factories have in place. These labels were the result of a broad-based consumer campaign in the United States and several countries in Europe for clear labeling procedures that indicate socially responsible practices were used in producing the clothing. The campaign was even success-ful in getting governments around the world to support their ideas for the Fair Factory label, and policy was created that put almost all the factories, brands, and retailers that exploited workers out of business. In fact, an international school was created through collaboration among governments of apparel-producing countries, where factory managers were trained on policies and practices supporting social responsibility. The school built several branches around the world, and some manag-ers even took the courses through the Internet.

Sara considered the Taevan Apparel Group a good example of an international apparel business that has built social responsibility into the mission of its company. Although it has a formal code of conduct with benchmarks related to social responsibility toward which each factory and management team strives, the team of inspectors from an intergovernmental organization that audits the factories every year to make sure they comply with the international code of conduct is basi-cally unnecessary because the management of both the Taevan Ap-parel Group and her brand are so committed to these practices. For example, Sara's brand formed a special team on social responsibility that crossed the functional divisions of design, buying and sourcing, and production that has operated since 2010. The team developed a set of strategies to evaluate internal product development and purchas-ing practices for their alignment with social responsibility goals. Before production, each product is evaluated for its impact on a factory's abil-ity to meet fair labor, health, and safety practices as well as its impact on the environment. Products that do not meet a certain rating are modified to increase their level of social responsibility before going into production.

Sara smiled to herself. Her job has become so much easier in the past twenty years. Intergovernmental agreements on apparel trade that include standards of social responsibility have increased, as has business transparency regarding social responsibility practices, making it easier for businesses choosing supplier partners, and for consumers purchasing apparel that is sweat-free and environmentally friendly. Consumers are well informed and demand socially responsible actions from the apparel industry. There have been some innovative fiber and apparel developments that increase the life span of clothing through multiple functions and care requirements, reducing the end-of-life waste going to landfills and overall impact on the environment. Most of all, the workers in the factories around the world are treated fairly, empowered through information and advancement and earning a living wage. Sara is encouraged by these positive changes.

There have certainly been improvements in working conditions and labor standards, and approaches to environmental responsibility, but more can be done to advance socially responsible practices. This chapter explores the shifting contexts surrounding the apparel industry that affect socially responsible practices and identifies new problems as well as potential solutions to social responsibility issues. We end with a proposal for the future, when socially responsible practices become institutionalized in the way business is conducted every day.

◉

Shifting Contexts Affecting Social Responsibility

A wide range of situations influence the ability to implement socially responsible practices and develop sustainable solutions to societal and environmental problems. In this section we address how changes resulting from the phaseout of quotas under the MFA, development of preferential trade agreements such as CAFTA-DR, and changing understanding of and expectations for environmental sustainability are influencing social responsibility. External environments affecting social responsibility are constantly shifting, and the future will bring additional challenges that shape the ways businesses approach social responsibility.

Social Responsibility after the MFA Phaseout

The phaseout of quantitative restrictions that had been in place under the MFA created new challenges in social responsibility for the apparel industry. Trade restrictions under the MFA had pushed apparel production to many new countries and resulted in the creation of an apparel industry in some countries where no real competitive advantage was offered—only available quota. The availability of quota provided guaranteed access to the lucrative U.S. and E.U. markets, but with the dissolution of the quota system, many were expected to find it more difficult to compete with the economies of scale and variety of products offered by such countries as India and China, even with sometimes lower wages (Box 9.1).[1] Although global competition already fueled social responsibility issues, the final phaseout of MFA restrictions in 2005 was expected to intensify that competition.

Decisions on which countries to source from no longer revolve around availability of quota; rather they are based on industrial development of the industry, education and cost of the workforce, domestic availability of fabrics and other component parts, political stability, and other factors.[2] Countries that already had competitive industries were ones filling their quotas, and these countries were expected to gain even more production, because they would no longer be limited in amounts that could be exported. For example, India's educated workforce and special technique for embellishing garments; China's large production capacity and sizeable, low-wage labor force;[3] and Vietnam's and Cambodia's integration into regional supply chains through membership in ASEAN[4] and even lower wages made them likely winners. On the losing side of freer trade are countries such as Madagascar, Mauritius, and Sri Lanka.[5]

A serious social responsibility issue resulting from freer trade is that apparel brands and retailers are shifting and consolidating production to the most competitive countries, and suppliers in less competitive countries are being forced to close—in fact, entire industries appear likely to collapse in some countries (Box 9.2). These changes are affecting millions of workers and hundreds of thousands of businesses

Box 9.1. China—The Big Winner from Quota Phaseout

The big winner from the phaseout of Multifibre Arrangement (MFA) quotas was anticipated to be China. As with many developing economies, several decades ago the Chinese government identified the apparel industry as important for fueling economic growth. In the 1970s China's government began subsidizing the industry by building factories, creating export processing zones, and developing the necessary infrastructure while keeping wages low. Although wages in such countries as India, Sri Lanka, and Pakistan are lower than those in China, China has built up such competitive advantages as short lead times, efficient logistics, an experienced and skilled workforce, reliable infrastructure, and a strong capital investment record. Also, China's apparel industry has incorporated lean manufacturing and low prices, coupled with reliable quality and new technology, and has proximity to Hong Kong and Taiwan, where important full-package suppliers are located.[1] China has vertically integrated textiles with apparel and other inputs that enhance sourcing capabilities. Finally, China's large and increasingly wealthy consumer market is attractive to apparel brands and retailers considering locating retail stores there.

Figure 9.1
Cargo ship being unloaded at the Los Angeles port.

In spite of temporary trade restrictions imposed upon China that extended quotas until 2008, exports to the United States from China increased dramatically as the Agreement on Textiles and Clothing (ATC) ended; China's total apparel and textile exports to the United States in 2006 were valued at over $27 billion and accounted for 33.3 percent of total U.S. apparel and textile imports. This one-third share of the U.S. market compared with China's 17.5 percent share in 2004 and 25.1 percent share in 2005. China's exports were on the rise in 2007 as well.[2] The Port of Los Angeles has moved to daily double shifts to accommodate increasing shipments from Asia (Figure 9.1). Data concerning the Chinese apparel industry are staggering, with an estimated employment of 19 million and production of up to 25 percent of the world's apparel.[3]

[1]Allwood, J. M., Laursen, S. E., de Rodriquez, C. M., & Bocken, N. M. P. (2006). *Well dressed? The present and future sustainability of clothing and textiles in the United Kingdom*. Cambridge: University of Cambridge Institute for Manufacturing.

[2]Office of Textiles and Apparel, U.S. Department of Commerce. Major shippers report. Retrieved February 2006 and December 2007 from http://otexa.ita.doc.gov/MSRCTRY.htm.

[3]Allwood, Laursen, de Rodriquez, & Bocken (2006).

Box 9.2. On Bangladesh

The working conditions in Bangladesh are often dismal. Similar to the conditions in other export processing zones, wages of workers producing apparel in Bangladesh are legally set below the country's standard manufacturing wage. Workers are willing to work for such a low wage because of their low level of living and the relatively low skill level required for employment. This low labor cost plays an important part in the competitive advantage Bangladesh has over its competitors in the apparel industry. According to research from a variety of sources, apparel industry employees in Bangladesh work 14 to 16 hours per day, may wait for a significant amount of time—sometimes two months—for their pay, are prevented from joining a union, and work in facilities with low safety standards.[1] Demonstrations and protests by workers have forced the industry to promise workers such benefits as paid days off, union participation, and better pay. Companies in Bangladesh realize that they may be risking losing markets in the United States and the European Union if they do not comply with international labor standards.

[1]Doumbia-Henry, C., & Gravel, E., (2006). Free trade agreements and labour rights: Recent developments. *International Labor Review*, 145(3), 185–206.

in both developed and developing countries.[6] The number of countries where global suppliers of textiles and apparel were located after the phaseout of the MFA was expected to decrease from 160 countries to between 115 to 120 countries.[7]

Social Responsibility Problems from Globally Shifting Production

The significant production shifts we are seeing as a result of the MFA phaseout can diminish the attempts by apparel brands and retailers to be socially responsible. Questions like the following arise:

- Are companies responsible for continued sourcing in countries whose economies are heavily invested in apparel production for export?
- If companies leave a country, potentially causing factories to close, how do they ensure the closure is carried out in a responsible manner?
- What are the ramifications for social responsibility of moving vast amounts of production to China, where freedom of association is illegal and where many in the industry have avoided labor compliance?

Proposed Solutions to MFA Phaseout Problems

Recognizing the increased likelihood of factory closures due to shifting production, the Fair Labor Association (FLA) in 2004 adopted a resolution setting standards for expected business behavior resulting from the elimination of quotas.

Having discussed the implications of the elimination of quotas; and

Noting with concern the attempts by some governments to remain competitive by de-regulating and lowering labor standards,

The FLA Board:

Urges FLA Companies to adopt guidelines to ensure they fulfill their commitment to manage shifts in sourcing in a manner consistent with the FLA Charter, Code and national law; and

Encourages all Companies to support the work of the MFA [Forum] and other multi-stakeholder initiatives addressing the consequences of quota elimination.[8]

In 2005, the FLA adopted guidelines for "responsible closure" of factories, detailing the responsibilities of buyers in ensuring that suppliers producing for them are adequately prepared to treat workers fairly and with dignity in the event of layoffs or closure.[9] The FLA's experiences from remediating problems associated with factory closures previously producing for its participating companies provide some valuable lessons, including the need for factories to maintain written policies on equal opportunity and treatment during layoffs and for the brand or retailer to ensure the factory is following all domestic laws on contributions to unemployment benefits.[10]

The MFA Forum is another group working on issues related to the phaseout of quotas—it was established as the final phaseout of the MFA trade restrictions loomed in 2005 and consists of brands and retailers, NGOs, and trade unions. The group was interested in investigating what might be done to retain apparel production in some countries that had benefited from quota restrictions under the MFA, or to diminish the negative impacts if production was moved. The MFA Forum's work resulted in the development of *A Collaborative Framework for Guiding Post-MFA Actions,* which outlines responsibilities of various stakeholders in the post-MFA period. The MFA Forum has developed country-level projects relating to the collaborative framework in Bangladesh and Lesotho, where serious challenges were being faced in maintaining competitiveness and decent labor standards.[11]

Addressing the precedents set when companies move production from countries that might have relatively good records of labor compliance or higher rates of unionization to countries where factories have limited records in dealing with codes of conduct, low rates of unionization, and limited compliance with the standards is very important to the social responsibility movement. Should a key supplier be expected to collaborate with apparel brands and retailers in support of social responsibility efforts? For example, many Chinese factories have avoided these expectations, instead choosing to falsify records and stage their factories to pass audits without truly embracing the core labor conventions that underlie apparel brands', retailers', and MSIs' codes of conduct. On the other hand, can apparel brands and retailers be expected to continue production where it does not make good business sense? Countries that developed an apparel industry under the MFA often lack necessary human resources, infrastructure, and value-added skills to work in partnership with brands and retailers in developing high-quality merchandise that meets the needs of consumers. Should apparel sourcing be driven by altruism?

Central America–Dominican Republic–United States Free Trade Agreement (CAFTA-DR)

Of the many free trade agreements signed by the United States, one of the most recent is that designed to create a free trade zone among Costa Rica, the Dominican Republic (DR), El Salvador, Guatemala, Honduras, Nicaragua, and the United States. CAFTA-DR provides enhanced economic opportunities for workers, manufacturers, consumers, farmers, and service providers[12] in the participating countries by eliminating trade barriers such as tariffs (Figure 9.2).

CAFTA-DR promotes social responsibility by requiring participating countries to enforce labor laws, advancing social responsibility in breadth of participation and effectiveness of approach. The agreement also specifies a framework for "labor capacity building" that, along with the predicted economic benefits from the free trade zone, will have the greatest impact on improving working conditions in the region.[13] In addition, the United States has invested $20 million to address priorities concerning social responsibility that are modernizing the judicial system for labor issues, strengthening labor law enforcement, reducing discrimination against women, building collaborations for establishing an effective monitoring program, and supporting a parallel agreement for environmental cooperation.[14] The CAFTA-DR agreement advances the role of public policy in improving social responsibility in the apparel industry.

Global Warming, the Energy Crisis, and Environmental Sustainability

With the 2007 Nobel Peace Prize shared by former U.S. vice president Al Gore and an intergovernmental panel of scientists all working on global warming, efforts have turned from *whether* we have global warming to actions that can address the problem. The term *sustainability* has been applied to the environment to describe an approach whereby we leave the planet as close as possible to how it was when we arrived, with respect to

Figure 9.2
Worker hand-stitching shoes in a factory in the Dominican Republic.

ecological balance, natural habitats, and climate. Nonrenewable energy sources are already at crisis levels, with various predictions about how much oil and natural gas are left to be discovered for our use. Research and development on renewable energy sources such as solar, wind, and biofuels are promising, and the transformation toward these sources is progressing. The apparel industry, as well as every other industry, must be engaged in the discussions about and innovative approaches to sustaining our environment through responsible energy and resource use. The International Labour Organization (ILO) recognizes the challenge and connects the environment and social responsibility in its statement: "Societies that pursue the goal of decent work for all are best equipped for meeting the challenge of using natural resources in a sustainable way."[15]

The involvement of the apparel industry in these dialogues and search for solutions has taken a different form than its activities addressing fair labor practices, where it is one of the dominant industry sectors involved in promoting human rights at work. The environmental responsibility dialogue is broader and less focused on specific industry sectors. The apparel industry is just one of many industries that, along with governments and individuals, are struggling to identify ways to be proactive. The dialogue itself is already in the public policy arena, with the Kyoto Protocol, emission standards for automobiles, and public debates about where wind farms can be located, among others. Several broad-based approaches have been to (1) reduce energy use and environmentally unfriendly activities, (2) find alternative energy sources, and (3) identify innovative new products and processes. Coalitions with cross-industry, government, NGO, and consumer membership will be the groups to watch for direction and major initiatives related to environmental sustainability.

Yet we can cite a variety of approaches that apparel businesses have taken to lessen their impact on the environment. Some have adopted organic and other fibers to make their products more environmentally friendly. Some have integrated environmental standards into their codes of conduct along with fair labor practices, human rights, and health and safety, and discontinued contracting with factories that are unwilling to work toward compliance. Others have evaluated their energy use or carbon footprint and reconfigured transportation costs for production and distribution by using regional manufacturing facilities closer to the ultimate distribution points. Still others have audited their company headquarters and modified it to make the facility itself more energy-efficient and environmentally sustainable. Some have even audited every functional area in terms of energy use and environmental impact in order to transform the business toward environmental responsibility.

There is no doubt that the apparel industry is a special case with unique responsibilities based on its *fashion* component that encourages planned obsolescence and stimulates consumption. A mismatch between the number of goods produced and the number consumed has resulted in mountains of products that are sold to consumers at huge discounts, to secondhand or offshore markets, or discarded. The use of toxic chemicals in production and processing of textiles and apparel have adverse environmental effects on the health and safety of factory workers, and energy consumption in production and transportation along every supply chain link is another environmental challenge in the apparel industry. Change is required to identify and reduce these social and environmental impacts. Especially innovative approaches are recommended in the report *The Present and Future Sustainability of Clothing and Textiles in the United Kingdom*.

- Inform consumers about impacts of production.
- Emphasize durability and lengthen product life span and use.
- Decrease production levels by offering apparel for rent or developing networks to pass on clothing after one or two wearings rather than discarding.
- Develop innovative technology to freshen clothing, recycle fibers, and use lower wash temperatures.
- Improve clothing recycling and reuse strategies and infrastructure.
- Develop international trade agreements incorporating environmental and social responsibility standards.[16]

This list can be used by apparel brands, retailers, and suppliers as a framework to develop apparel industry-specific programs that address environmental issues within the context of social responsibility.

Changes in world trade policies, patterns of production and sourcing, and understanding and expectation for environmental sustainability affect the ability of apparel brands and retailers to be socially responsible. Social responsibility is not static, but a dynamic set of policies and practices that are continually improved with the goal of achieving sustainability. We next explore effective action strategies that can form the foundation for constructing a future of social responsibility in the apparel industry.

◉

Identifying New Problems and Solutions

A report, *Beyond Monitoring*, issued in the summer of 2007 by Business for Social Responsibility (BSR) outlines several positive directions for future labor compliance efforts. It acknowledges the successes that have been achieved by the last decade of monitoring, but also recognizes that there is still much to be done.

Beyond Monitoring describes four pillars on which future progress in social responsibility will be built:

1. Internal alignment of purchasing practices with social responsibility objectives
2. Suppliers' ownership of social responsibility in their workplaces
3. Empowerment of workers to be stronger in assuring and protecting their rights
4. Public policy frameworks that ensure wider and more consistent application of labor laws and environmental regulations[17]

We'll explore these four ideas along with three others that contribute to the necessary foundation for institutionalized social responsibility in the apparel industry's future:

5. Involvement of consumers in supporting socially responsible businesses
6. Involvement of investors in financing socially responsible businesses
7. Expanded participation of apparel brands and retailers in integrating social responsibility into their businesses

Purchasing Practices

Professionals in the buying office—including buyers, merchandisers, sourcing specialists, product development specialists, and others who work for apparel brands and retailers—have a role to play in social responsibility. Labor compliance departments realized in the past several years that many of the problems they were trying to fix were caused by their own buying offices. Buyers required suppliers to abide by rules that undermined the activities supporting socially responsible practices (Box 9.3). In 2007, the MFA Forum commissioned a study to identify buyer practices that most significantly undermined suppliers' ability to comply with codes of conduct. Findings from the research that took place in Bangladesh and included 35 interviews that were conducted with representatives from seven international brands, four local offices for the brands, seven buying houses, and 17 suppliers, point to a range of practices contributing to suppliers' lack of compliance.[18]

Box 9.3. An Apparel Intern's Role in Labor Compliance

Recently, a student conducted an independent study focusing on social responsibility. She was interested in understanding how social responsibility was related to the buying function. Buyers often want to make a change in a garment after it is already in production. They call or e-mail the factory and tell the factory management about the needed change and also tell them the original delivery deadline remains in place. Because a factory must often redo work or even start over in some cases, this can create problems meeting the maximum hours of work allowed in a brand's code of conduct. As the student was discussing these issues with her professor, her eyes grew wide and she gasped. She made a connection with the problem and a personal experience. During her internship for a private label manufacturer headquartered in New York City, she had been responsible for doing just that—contacting factories to let them know of required changes and enforcing the original deadlines. She had no idea how her actions were potentially affecting workers in the factory.

Unstable Relationships

Although large brands and retailers are developing long-term relationships with key suppliers, the majority of business is done with suppliers engaged for single orders, with no guarantee of future orders. This means that suppliers cannot anticipate the size of orders or dates the facilities will be needed, and they receive little technical support from the brands or retailers that would allow them to develop their businesses beyond single orders. Improving a factory's record in compliance is not often rewarded with expanded orders either.[19] Current trends among apparel brands and retailers to consolidate their supply chain could change this situation as fewer and larger suppliers are selected as partners, but contract firms with smaller orders will probably still experience difficulties.

Downward Pressure on Prices

The industry trend toward falling prices for apparel is affecting the production and sourcing strategies used globally. According to Nate Herman, Director of International Trade for the American Apparel and Footwear Association between 1998 and 2007, overall apparel prices in the United States have fallen 10 percent, whereas overall consumer products prices have increased more than 25 percent during that period.[20] An article in *The Guardian* from February of 2006 reported that since 1995, women's wear prices had decreased in the United Kingdom by 34 percent, in part because of the increase in budget retailers.[21]

Supply and demand plays a big role in these decreasing prices—there is an oversupply of clothing produced in the world market. But price pressures are also fueled by buyer practices of using counter quotes and open-book costing. Counter quotes refers to the practice wherein the buyer gets a quote for how much a supplier would charge for an order and then takes it to another supplier—sometimes in an entirely different country—to see whether that supplier can beat the first quote. Open-book costing requires that manufacturers show all of the costs associated with the quote they are giving the buyer, such as the labor, materials, overhead, and profit. This practice makes it very easy to request a lower price in one category or another and fuels the competition among suppliers,[22] causing prices that provide little or no profit for the supplier. Just like consumers who are warned to beware of prices "too good to be true," brands and retailers endorsing socially responsible practices should beware of pushing their suppliers for lower prices that negatively affect their labor practices.

At one time, brands and retailers promised to pay for their goods within 30 days of receiving them. Payment terms are now typically 60 days, often making it difficult for a factory manager to meet payroll. Contracts frequently contain clauses that automatically fine manufacturers for delays, even if the delays are caused or agreed upon by the buyer.[23] These practices also affect the ability to sustain socially responsible practices, and apparel brands and retailers must balance the benefits with the potential costs to suppliers and their workers.

Increased Quality Demands

Brands and buyers in developed countries have not coupled their demand for increased quality and value in the products they receive from suppliers with an increase in the prices they pay suppliers of the products. Even if suppliers manage to lower unit costs through increased productivity, they may face uncompensated increased costs.[24] A current trend in the industry toward higher-quality products capable of commanding premium prices[25] may aid brands, retailers, and consumers in understanding that higher-quality costs more. Socially responsible practices coupled with quality can lead to premium prices.

Pressures to Shorten Production Time

Increasingly popular "fast fashion" strategies in apparel shorten lead times that are allowed from time of order to time of delivery. Brands and retailers want to use "real-time" consumer behavior information and sales data to determine what customers might want now or next. As reported in the MFA Forum Study, Zara is one of the most famous retailers known for fast fashion, moving from design concept to delivery in its stores in 30 days. More generally, there has been a decrease from 120 days' lead time to 90 to 100 days for brands and retailers.[26] The crucial question is—what does a factory have to do to produce the same volume of garments, perhaps at higher-quality levels than ever, in three to four weeks less time than before? The answers are extended work hours or forced overtime, home work, unauthorized subcontracting, child labor, and other unfair work practices. Some apparel brands such as the adidas Group and Nike are working with suppliers to implement lean production technology that shortens production time, creating more efficient production systems; however, questions have arisen about the extent that lean production positively influences worker wages and working conditions.

Exacerbating shorter production lead times are problems instigated by buyer actions, such as the late arrival of technical packages or inaccurate detailing of garment measurements, component specifications, and assembly details. Slow approvals for samples and color lab dips and mistakes or lack of authority by inexperienced buyers and mid-level merchandisers also cut into ever-shortening lead times.[27] All of these slowdowns mean the factory has less time to make a garment, sometimes trimming weeks off the time that was supposed to be allowed for production. Some apparel brands such as Gap are examining the critical path of management decisions and processes involved from product concept to delivery in order to identify where it loses time that would be better spent on production. Gap is also developing training programs to raise awareness among designers and merchandisers about the potential impacts of its decisions on workers.

Changes to Orders

Making changes to existing orders is widespread across the apparel industry. Designers and merchandisers change styles to fine-tune them to emerging style trends based on what consumers are buying. The MFA Forum study found that at least 20 percent of orders have one to two changes per order, and that delivery on 25 percent of orders is delayed by two weeks or more. The number of changes can be much higher with fashion merchandise.

Changing orders creates significant impacts on social responsibility because it undermines production planning. Resampling, additional lab dips for color changes, and style changes are made by designers after the supplier has been contracted, while merchandise planners modify volume forecasts depending on sales information at several times during the production cycle. Giving the factory more time because of changes is not always an advantageous solution to the supplier because it may delay the start of its next order.[28] Both brands and retailers and the suppliers benefit from sticking to schedule.

Cancellation of Orders

The most drastic type of change a buyer can make is canceling orders for outstanding merchandise. The MFA Forum study found that brands may pay for the cost of raw materials used in the cancelled order,[29] but it is up to the supplier to get another order to keep the factory running, or the workers will be sent home.

A Future Purchasing Scenario

It is one thing to have a brand find problems in its contract factories that are the fault of the factory. In those cases, the brand is just expected to make sure the factory moves toward compliance with fair labor and environmental practices. If factory management refuses, the brand may elect to end production in the offending factory. But when a problem is found in corporate headquarters in the purchasing function, the blame is the responsibility of brand and retailer management. In addition, design and purchasing cut to the heart of business competition, and socially responsible concerns may moderate the success of the business. Changes are made by designers and buyers to offer customers the right product, at the right place, at the right time, and for the right price. How can apparel brands and retailers do this and not forfeit socially responsible practices at the factories?

Or maybe a better question is this: Are brands and retailers expecting too much of suppliers under the prevailing practices? Production moved from the skilled factory base of the United States to countries that have started production with little money and many unskilled workers. Often factories are offered the lowest possible price to make goods and fined when goods are late or defective, and there is no commitment to production orders in the future. Compliance expectations are established that require significant changes in management processes and attitudes. Many managers have no expertise in human resources.

Beyond Monitoring recommends a structural realignment of the purchasing function with the social and environmental function in businesses,[30] in this case apparel brands and retailers. The goals and incentive systems for buyers and merchandisers, designers, and product developers should be compatible with the socially responsible practices of the business. Instead of rewarding buyers and sourcing professionals solely for negotiating the lowest price and quickest delivery time, the level of compliance in the factories producing goods or other socially responsible actions should be integrated into a reward system. Designers and product developers should be rewarded at least in part for products that have lower impact on the workers and the environment through health and safety measures in the factories and product care requirements, longer life span, and recyclable characteristics. This goal is not unrealistic, as exemplified by Nike's Overtime Task Force, which is charged with evaluating design, merchandising, and product development actions that adversely affect a supplier's ability to comply with established fair working hours and by Patagonia's use of product life cycle analysis to measure the social and environmental impacts of a particular product at each stage of its life cycle.

In addition, information flow and communication need to improve both internally in the apparel business among the functional departments, such as design, buying, and labor compliance, as well as externally between the buyers and suppliers. The balanced scorecard approach is a first step in sharing increased information to (1) evaluate more than price factors when selecting suppliers and (2) provide a guide toward which factories need remediation attention for improved social responsibility. Better metrics and a greater percentage of apparel companies adopting the balanced scorecard approach are needed to fully realize the potential of the scorecard. However, the Clean Clothes Campaign reminds us that "the challenge facing the clothing industry is not to demonstrate to labour rights advocates . . . that they are carrying out more audits, but that workers' lives are improving."[31]

Beyond Monitoring acknowledges that information sharing beyond single buyer and supplier partners is also important. The report identifies the Suppliers Ethical Data Exchange and the Fair Factories Clearinghouse as two information-sharing platforms that have multiple buyer contributors. By pooling data from factory audits, these clearinghouses can potentially eliminate duplicate audits, begin to identify systemic issues surrounding the socially responsible activities industrywide, and then work collaboratively to find solutions.[32]

Supplier Ownership

BSR also recommended in its report that suppliers take ownership for their factory conditions and environmental and labor standards. Supplier ownership of social responsibility can contribute to a virtuous circle wherein multiple stakeholders work together to improve business and sustainability. The policing model of compliance, whereby brands and retailers send in their monitors to catch the factory in the act of breaching the code of conduct, is not the answer to long-term change in factories. It requires a lot of money to be spent on monitoring, with too many factories to enforce compliance only from the outside, and the monitoring does not address the root causes or the "whys" of noncompliance.[33] Without knowing why something is occurring, how can apparel brands and retailers or their suppliers make changes that will prevent the problem in the long run?

Streamlining Monitoring for Compliance

A new initiative of the FLA, called FLA 3.0, is a good example of a new model for sustainable compliance. One of its objectives is to improve the quality of FLA due diligence while streamlining compliance data collection by addressing the problem of "audit fatigue" in supplier factories. Audit fatigue is caused by monitoring production of numerous brands and retailers in one factory by multiple teams during a relatively short period of time. FLA 3.0 recognizes that with all the internal monitoring the FLA brands and retailers have completed in the past decade, they know very well what the problems are in the factories, and rather than waste resources doing more monitoring, they should focus their efforts on making real improvements in critical areas.

Expanding Local Stakeholder Involvement

The second objective is to expand supplier ownership and local stakeholder involvement in improving factory conditions. The traditional monitoring model has been a top-down, corporate-driven one that does not take into account the considerable body of knowledge that suppliers, NGOs, and community stakeholders in producing countries have accumulated about the problems facing workers. With the assistance of these stakeholders, priority issues for brands and retailers and their suppliers can be pinpointed. FLA 3.0 has the potential to greatly improve and sustain the compliance of FLA members' key suppliers and add value to both the members' and the suppliers' businesses.[34]

Raising Public Reporting Standards

The final objective of FLA 3.0 is to raise public reporting standards, particularly for reporting the impacts of production work on the worker and factory compliance. For example, currently the FLA randomly selects factories for independent external monitoring, and that often means that factories are not revisited once they have been monitored and the remediation verified. Consequently, there is a record of how factories performed on compliance at the time when the monitors were there, but not whether the improvements were sustained over time. The FLA 3.0 methodology allows reporting on changes in factories and how they are improving as a result of education and remediation work completed in collaboration with FLA, its members, and factories.

The major steps in FLA 3.0 are as follows (Figure 9.3):

- Factories conduct needs assessment to identify root causes of these priority issues
- Gaps in management systems and activities are identified and training is used to build factory capability for dealing with the problem
- An auditor visits and assesses effectiveness of the capacity building or the impact it had on factory compliance with these issues
- Finally, information about impacts and improvements is made available to the public

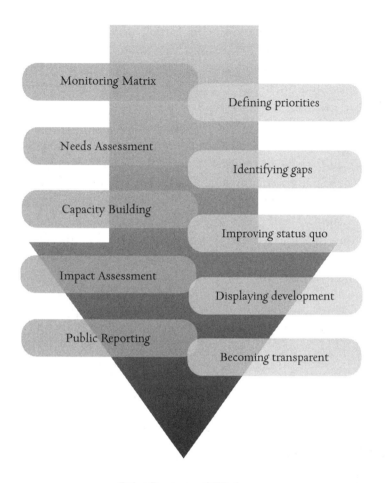

Figure 9.3
FLA 3.0 process.

Pilot Projects of FLA 3.0

FLA 3.0 policies and procedures were piloted in China and Thailand in 2007 with a specific focus on excessive hours of work and grievance systems. One of the initial lessons learned from the pilot project was the importance of trust building. Stakeholders were initially skeptical about their role in the process, but suppliers were especially cautious.

Factories in the pilot did not have the needed policies and management practices to support compliance in either work hours or grievance procedures. Convening a range of relevant local stakeholders, including community members, to participate in the process of compliance building was an obvious way to demonstrate the importance of building trust to improving social responsibility (Figure 9.4).

FLA 3.0 and other capacity building initiatives appear to be good steps for involving suppliers and other local stakeholders in a business's path toward social responsibility by increasing ownership of the process. A very effective way to build ownership and trust is to give external incentives when progress is made. For example, the BSR report suggests reducing the number of audits, providing preferential order opportunities, and conducting long-term planning and order commitment as supplier incentives to improve socially responsible practices. One result will be reduced buyer expenditures on monitoring and greater expenditures devoted to the capacity of factory management and workers for ensuring social responsibility.

Figure 9.4

FLA president Auret van Heerden speaks to suppliers and stakeholders at a meeting in China.

Worker Empowerment

The BSR report *Beyond Monitoring* emphasizes the importance of worker empowerment in the path to sustained social responsibility and its dependence on multi-stakeholder approaches.[35] To involve workers in the solutions by informing them of their rights and encouraging participation in building strategies and networks requires the expertise and collaboration of labor unions, NGOs, and community groups as well as supportive business organizational structures. The report emphasizes that skill development is as important as compliance in addressing worker empowerment. Empowerment is more than knowing one's rights; it is feeling that one will be heard and heeded when one speaks and acts.

Initiatives for Worker Empowerment

Beyond Monitoring identified several new initiatives that serve as models for new worker empowerment efforts. The Ethical Trading Initiative includes labor unions in its dialogues with buyers about codes of conduct. Nike has announced an educational program to be implemented by 2011 in all of the factories to which it contracts work. The program will cover workers' rights and freedom of association, among other topics. Timberland's and Verite's peer-to-peer education project, in which workers share information from nutrition and language to mathematics and labor laws, is another model program. Workers are trained as peer educators and commit to teaching two to three others on these topics. Corroborating this approach, Roseann Casey concluded that education of workers plays a key role in worker empowerment: "Once workers are more aware of their rights, and have reasonable opportunity to recognize these rights, they will be effective as the first line of reporting and accountability."[36]

Labor Unions and Parallel Means of Representation

Two of the ILO labor conventions are fundamental for worker empowerment and addressing labor standards and working conditions—those dealing with the right to organize and bargain collectively. As explained by labor law expert Halton Cheadle and Auret van Heerden, president of the FLA, these conventions "are considered the foundation for many other Conventions in that workers who can organize and bargain collectively can defend their rights and interests, provided of course, that the legal framework by the nation state is in place and maintained."[37] As such, these conventions are termed "enabling rights."[38] Freedom of association and collective bargaining are reflective of human dignity. They enable workers to stand together in defending their economic interests and civil liberties—including the right to life, security, integrity, and personal and collective freedom.[39] Neil Kearney, secretary of the International Textile, Garment and Leather Workers Federation (ITGLWF) and Dwight Justice, with the Multinational Companies Department of the International Trade Union Confederation (ITUC), concur by saying, "Where workers can form independent trade unions and bargain, there may be no need for a code of conduct."[40]

Despite the fundamental importance of freedom of association for ensuring safe and fair workplaces, Casey labeled it as "one of the most divisive issues among workers' rights advocates. Some advocate unions as the only effective vehicle for workers' voice; others point out a negative connotation and perception of unions . . . ineffectiveness and competition between unions have been cited as reasons to consider other alternatives for worker representation." The need to consider alternative methods is especially true in countries where laws do not permit formation of independent unions and the government organizes its own union. A legitimate union has representatives democratically elected by its members, operates independently from the business management, and includes as members workers who have freely affiliated with the organization of their choice.[41] Government control takes away unionization as an option for addressing worker rights and in some of the locations where this has occurred, "parallel means of representation" are being used to assure workers' voices are heard.[42] For example, in China some companies are establishing parallel means of representation such as worker councils or welfare committees as part of implementing their codes of conduct to encourage some form of worker participation. The practice of encouraging parallel means is criticized by some because the efforts may undermine the position of labor unions, so in countries where freedom of association is allowed, labor unions are preferred for worker representation.[43] Despite concerns about parallel means, Reebok has been lauded for its efforts to ensure worker representation through establishment of worker committees.[44]

Brands and retailers cannot organize unions, but they can uphold freedom of association and intervene if there is reason to think their factories are prohibiting this basic worker right.[45] Moreover, the presence of a union in a factory does not necessarily mean that workers are able to exercise their rights to freedom of association. For example, the All China Federation of Trade Unions (ACFTU) is the only union allowed by the Chinese government—formation of independent unions is prohibited.[46]

Accurate figures estimating the number of unionized workers in the apparel industry are not available. However, the rate of unionization is almost certainly below 10 percent in the formal part of the sector and much lower if one takes the informal economy in apparel production, including homeworkers, into account. In some Asian countries such as Cambodia, the Philippines, and Indonesia, unions have made some headway in their organizing drives and in Africa there have been membership gains in Uganda, Lesotho, Swaziland, South Africa, and Malawi. But in the post–Agreement on Textiles and Clothing (ATC) competitive environment, many unions have been scrambling to maintain their membership and in a number of cases are registering real losses. Doug Miller, project coordinator for the Multinationals Department of the ITGLWF, maintains that union membership is so low because sections of the global apparel industry are anti-union and factories participate in "union busting" and "union avoidance." Union busting can range from violence and intimidation to blatant dismissal when workers exercise their right of freedom of association. Union avoidance may involve the establishment of "worker committees," which are established by factory management, are often top-heavy with line managers, and are given credence by inappropriate reference to clauses in codes of conduct that provide for parallel means of representation. Parallel means of independent and free association of workers and collective bargaining is intended for a small range of supplying countries, such as China and Myanmar, for example, where these rights are restricted under law. Additionally, in many countries apparel production is located in industrial parks or export processing zones where national governments, eager to encourage foreign direct investment, have relaxed national labor laws. In most cases, such parks are off-limits to trade union organizers even though they may house suppliers of apparel brands and retailers whose codes indicate respect for the core labor conventions of freedom of association and collective bargaining. As well, many countries do not provide a right for foreign migrant workers to join a trade union. A significant internal challenge for trade unions themselves in some countries is an aging male leadership that can be out of tune with the needs of a young, female migrant workforce.[47] Limits to worker rights and freedom of association frequently surface in urgent appeals by the Clean Clothes Campaign and as third-party complaints on participating companies in the Fair Labor Association.

Worker Empowerment throughout the Supply Chain

Although we often think of worker empowerment in terms of workers in factories in developing countries, worker empowerment is crucial at all levels of global apparel supply chains. Workers are empowered by opening channels of communication within functional areas of the business, such as design and product development, sourcing, and logistics. Fresh eyes can sometimes see the problems with institutionalized approaches that have been accepted and applied for years. It can take empowered employees to ask questions like: Why can't we include a measure of environmental impact in our design process as another criterion to consider? Why do we reward buyers for the lowest price and for canceling orders when we know the impacts of these actions on low-paid production workers in our contract factories? How can we inform consumers about the impact of their product choices on the labor conditions in apparel factories and on the footprint they leave on the environment?

Team approaches to problem solving that are open to fresh ideas, controversy, and bold action have the potential for engaging all employees in the integration of social and environmental responsibility into every aspect of a business. Patagonia is now evaluating its products with a process that identifies environmental and social impacts at each stage in the life cycle and requires input from all functional areas. It started with one product and is integrating the life cycle analysis process into product development until all of its products will have an impact rating. Ratings will be used to decide whether to continue production of a product, change its design to better its rating, or drop the product.[48] Ad hoc teams that cross departmental or functional lines can be formed to address specific problems or to brainstorm broad ideas that can transform the social responsibility approaches of a business. Contests to propose actions that increase social responsibility can engage workers in all departments in the effort.

Involvement of Potential Future Employees

Students in higher-education programs in apparel studies who are future professionals in the apparel industry can be dominant players in the social responsibility movement. They are interested and knowledgeable about the field and braced to make a difference in the world. With an understanding and passion for the significance of socially responsible practices, they can work for change in their own spheres of influence. Businesses can engage local communities in discussions and programs to increase awareness as well as attract socially conscious potential employees. The goal is to multiply the numbers of workers throughout the supply chain who are empowered and dedicated to bringing the social responsibility message to their everyday job responsibilities. Their questioning, decision making, and new approaches will bring incremental change to the apparel industry.

Public Policy Framework

The *Beyond Monitoring* report argues that business and government should collaborate to develop public policy on social responsibility, and that public and private worlds must work together to achieve sustainable social responsibility policy. It outlined the gap between government regulation and enforcement that widened as the apparel industry moved toward global supply chains where it was hard to identify and enforce the labor and environmental practices being used in individual factories and their effects on workers.[49] Codes of conduct, the initial business response to the crisis, have their limitations. The report maintains that new public policy frameworks are necessary to advance the socially responsible movement toward sustainability.

Three methods for companies to engage in the public policy debate and initiatives are identified: (1) fight to integrate social responsibility in international trade agreements, (2) promote social responsibility in home countries through government procurement and bilateral and multilateral agreements, and (3) work with local governments to strengthen enforcement.

Several apparel industry examples illustrate these approaches. For example, the African Growth and Opportunity Act (AGOA) was supported by Nike, Gap, and Levi Strauss as a trade vehicle to draw attention to fair labor practices as a competitive tool for production in a number of African countries. The purpose of AGOA was to provide incentives to sub-Saharan African countries to open their markets to free trade with the goal of achieving economic self-reliance. A socially responsible approach to economic development is evident in the act's specification that a country's eligibility for AGOA benefits hinges on its establishment of and progress toward human rights initiatives. Although none of the African countries met all of the eligibility requirements, in 2007, 26 had made sufficient progress to be both AGOA eligible and eligible for apparel benefits, which means they had in place effective systems for preventing illegal trans-shipment and counterfeit documentation. All of the 26 apparel eligible countries had exported to the United States under AGOA in 2006, but in some cases the exports were quite small.[50] Time will tell whether this model for linking trade policies to social responsibility initiatives is successful.

Another example is the International Labour Organization's Better Factories Cambodia program, which resulted from a labor agreement with the United States that addressed the economic development aspects of garment production while ensuring labor monitoring and reporting.[51] In the program, business and government worked together toward sustainable social responsibility in apparel supply chains.

As explained by Casey, "Governments have numerous roles, ranging from better and more consistent enforcement of the rule of law, or creation of incentives (tax consideration, favored access, protection from litigation, etc.) to encouragement and reward of behavior by buyers, suppliers, and other stakeholders."[52]

These initiatives can serve as models for groups of businesses taking on policy roles through collaboration among themselves and with government agencies. This closes the loop between established labor and environmental laws and enforcement; it closes the loop between regulations and practice. In addition, the frameworks that multi-stakeholder groups have developed can be modified to include the organization and energy of government agencies for enforcement as well as innovative trade negotiations that include social responsibility expectations. For example, perhaps the FLA could be expanded to include government membership in order to identify the successes and challenges of FLA 3.0 and to apply these findings in the trade negotiations related to apparel and footwear production in the future. Large brands and retailers could identify and engage small and medium-sized enterprises (SMEs) in these public/private collaborations as trade agreements are negotiated in countries where production for SMEs makes up a major portion of apparel production.

Involvement of Consumers

Through their purchasing, consumers can pull the economy and effect change in business as well as contribute to the formation of a virtuous circle of business development and social responsibility. How can we harness the power of consumer demand to advance social and environmental responsibility?

One core issue is that it is very difficult for consumers to find information about the socially responsible practices of any given business.[53] Part of the problem is transparency—information is not published at all by many companies.[54] Another part of the problem is clarity and accessibility of information—social responsibility is a complex topic and sometimes improvements are difficult to describe because they are not complete. For example, that there are essentially no 100 percent compliant factories makes for a murky story that is far from the black-and-white solution that consumers might prefer. It is problematic that a business is seen as a self-promoter when it presents information about the social responsibility activities of the company and therefore the authenticity of the information as well as its altruistic motivation are suspect. Businesses have also found it very difficult and time-consuming to (1) track the exact factory at which an apparel product was sewn because of the multiple subcontracts used in any order and (2) develop a reporting strategy that makes their practices transparent and readily available to consumers.

Another issue is providing consumers with information they want and will use in a form and location that is easily accessible and user-friendly. Some consumers want lots of information, others want just a little, and still others do not know what information they should have. Transforming consumer awareness into engagement and social activism in social responsibility is tricky.

Several multifaceted approaches involving a variety of interest groups and action strategies are possible:

⊚ Develop industry-wide reporting mechanisms that present accurate evaluative information about social responsibility practices of individual firms in an accessible format. Perhaps early attempts by the Fair Factories Clearinghouse (FFC) or the Fair Labor Association (FLA) regarding their member companies could be expanded. Currently the FFC does not provide information to the public and the

FLA's reports are dense. Then, public awareness of these reporting venues needs to be increased as well as how to use them, and additional information for consumers needs to be provided through public relations campaigns and at consumer purchase points.

⊚ Initiate consumer awareness campaigns that articulate the main issues simply and in memorable ways. For example, human rights, fair labor, and sustainable design can be illustrated with important subcategories and graphic images that are easily recognizable and can be repeated in many public venues, at individual businesses, and at consumer points of purchase.

⊚ Present local and regional forums for consumers to engage in educational and social activities that inform and promote social responsibility. These could be connected with sports and musical events or stand-alone events such as walks for environment or speakers of broad-based interest.

⊚ Use celebrities, designers, and politicians to spread the message through TV and press spots, national publicity campaigns, runway fashion shows, and challenges for social action.

When the apparel industry standards for social responsibility are agreed upon by most businesses and institutionalized into industry practice, it may be time for product labeling to be introduced that clearly informs consumers about the social and environmental impacts of product materials, production, and distribution. There are examples of product labeling for socially responsible practices, such as no child labor (e.g., Rugmark), fair labor practices (e.g., Timberland), organic cotton and wool (e.g., USDA organic label), and fair trade cotton (e.g., Transfair). Some are business-specific and used as an educational and marketing tool, whereas others cross businesses and industries to distinguish a number of businesses that follow specific guidelines in the sourcing and production of materials and finished products.

Labels can serve as awareness, educational, and marketing tools and can be good for consumers, businesses, and public policy. However, the accuracy of labeling information depends on the integrity of the business and labeling criteria and can only be ensured with a strong system of verification involving evaluation and sometimes certification based on a set of criteria. Perhaps the systems of factory certification and labor compliance program accreditation currently used by SAI and the FLA, respectively, can form the first step toward a widespread labeling effort.

Involvement of Investors

Engaging investors—individuals, organizations, and even government agencies—in the advancement of socially responsible business practices can effect significant positive change. The market valuation of U.S. public corporate stock is largely based on short-term growth. This process sets up investment strategies that may negatively affect social and environmental responsibility goals. Investors should rethink the goals of their investment to factor in the social and environmental impacts of business practices. By procurement and reward actions, investors can effect change in the assessment given responsible social and environmental business practices. An early example was the movement to divest investments in countries with human rights violations in the 1990s.

Additionally, investment firms that screen companies based on social and environmental criteria should make better use of information available that distinguishes socially responsible leaders from companies making less effort in the area. More investment funds could be screened on detailed human rights and labor standards and environmental practices. Perhaps collaboration between investment firms and a multi-stakeholder group might provide the necessary data and research for more detailed screening. For example, the FLA gathers and publishes a considerable amount of data, and involving a socially responsible investment firm with that group could lead to a collaboration resulting in credible information on apparel brands' and retailers' socially responsible practices.

Expanded Participation of Apparel Brands and Retailers

Finally, organized collaboration for social responsibility, such as multi-stakeholder initiatives, can result in positive change. Many large apparel and footwear brands and retailers have addressed human rights, fair labor practices, and environmental stewardship through initiatives, organizational structure, and campaigns to increase awareness of social responsibility issues in employees and consumers. A number of small businesses have been founded with social responsibility visions as the foundation of their mission statements. Businesses that have made some strides in social responsibility need to ensure continuous improvement by examining the role their corporate decisions and purchasing practices play in noncompliance, developing long-term partnerships with suppliers that have strong performance on social responsibility, and having the necessary staff on the ground in production regions.

There are many firms and professionals in the field, both large businesses that have not been the target of activist campaigns or that produce private labels without well-known brands and small and medium sized enterprises (SMEs), that have neither considered nor integrated these issues in their business practices. Industry-wide participation is essential for advancing social responsibility, especially when addressing systemic issues that require industry-wide negotiations and leverage with governments. The circle of businesses working cooperatively and proactively toward social responsibility must be expanded to create a critical mass of apparel brands and retailers that are accountable and responsible for the impacts of their power on employees, workers producing their products, consumers, and other stakeholders.

◉

The Challenge That Lies Ahead

We have painted a picture of the potential future of social responsibility—transforming it from a reaction to negative publicity toward a sustainable institutional goal that is an expectation, a *nontrend*, and an integrated part of all business. Our revised model of socially responsible apparel business in Figure 9.5 includes the stakeholders necessary for realizing this future and the concepts of continuous improvement and sustainability.

Figure 9.5

Dickson, Loker, and Eckman's Model of Socially Responsible Apparel Business.

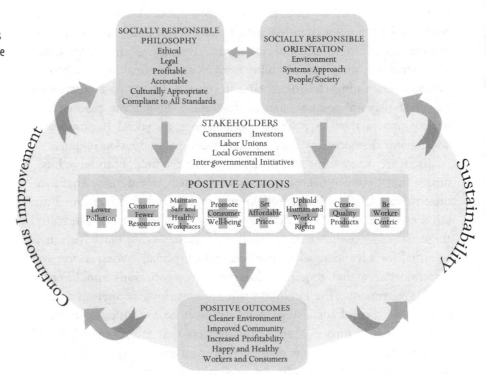

We added positive actions based on the *Beyond Monitoring* report's four pillars on which future progress in social responsibility will be built, including the additional pillars we proposed—consumer and investor involvement and expanded participation of apparel brands and firms.

Aligning the purchasing practices of apparel brands and retailers with socially and environmentally responsible practices by these businesses as well as by their suppliers is highlighted in the positive action statement: "Embrace social responsibility in purchasing and design." "Empower workers" and "Build capacity and supplier ownership for social responsibility in factory management" are included in addition to two action statements that were listed in the original model: "Maintain safe and healthy workplaces" and "Uphold worker rights." The statement "Collaborate with government to influence public policy" addresses the need for public–private dialogue and initiatives to add social responsibility goals to trade agreements.

Involving consumers and investors to advance social responsibility is indicated both as an action, "Inform consumers and investors," and as an outcome, "Engaged consumers and investors." Institutionalized social responsibility addresses the importance for social responsibility to be integrated into all functional areas of a business in everyday activities so that in the future it is an expectation.

Stakeholders form the safety net that is the backdrop for successful and sustainable socially responsible business practices. These include workers and consumers, businesses and governments, labor unions and investors, intergovernmental and nongovernmental organizations—all of the individuals and organizations interested in socially responsible apparel production. This safety net is effective when all of its members work together, adding their expertise within and beyond their spheres of influence. Continuous improvement and sustainability are the broad goals that anchor the model, connecting philosophy and orientation to actions and outcomes with the help of apparel industry stakeholders.

It is not enough to have a model of socially responsible apparel business. Transformational change will be necessary to realize the social responsibility of the future as we have described it, and everyone's help is needed (Box 9.4). Individuals can become change agents by asking questions when they recognize a concern or an opportunity for advancing social responsibility in their personal lives, at work, or in their community. The first step is to describe the problem as you see it. Who is affected? What are the consequences of inaction? What are the opportunities with change? Then identify a strategy. This could mean creating a buzz about the issue through private and public discussion. It could be getting others to help develop a vision. It could be accomplishing small steps toward social responsibility. The important thing is to take action. Be part of the solution. Use your knowledge about the apparel industry and your passion for strengthening it to promote socially responsible business practices until they are expected, untrendy, and institutionalized.

Box 9.4. Transformational Change

Transformational change requires collaboration among stakeholders and effective change strategies. In his book, *Transformational Change*, John Kotter outlines eight steps to transformational change that multi-stakeholder groups, individuals, and businesses can apply in individual actions, specific projects, and long-range endeavors.

- Establish a sense of urgency
- Create the guiding coalition
- Develop vision and strategy
- Communicate the *change* vision
- Empower employees for broad-based action
- Create short-term wins
- Consolidate gains and produce more *change*
- Anchor new approaches in the culture

Kotter, J. P. (1996). *Leading change*. Boston: Harvard Business School Press.

Appendix: Acronyms

Acronyms	Organizations and Concepts | Websites
1%FTP	1% For the Planet | www.onepercentfortheplanet.org/en/
ACFTU	All China Federation of Trade Unions www.china.org.cn/english/2002/Nov/48588.htm
ACTWU	Amalgamated Clothing and Textile Workers Union
ACWA	Amalgamated Clothing Workers of America
AFL-CIO	American Federation of Labor and Congress of Industrial Organizations | www.aflcio.org
AIP	Apparel Industry Partnership
ALGI	A.L.G.I. Group | www.algi.net
ASEAN	Association of Southeast Asian Nations www.aseansec.org
ATC	Agreement on Textiles and Clothing www.wto.org/english/tratop_e/texti_e/texti_e.htm
BSCI	Business Social Compliance Initiative | www.bsci-eu.org
BSR	Business for Social Responsibility | www.bsr.org
CAFTA-DR	Central America-Dominican Republic-United States Free Trade Agreement | www.ustr.gov/Trade_Agreements/Bilateral/CAFTA/CAFTA-DR_Final_Texts/Section_Index.html
CCC	Clean Clothes Campaign | www.cleanclothes.org

CIES	International Committee of Food Retail Chains www.ciesnet.com
COVERCO	Commission for the Verification of Codes and Conduct www.coverco.org.gt
CREA	Center for Reflection, Education and Action www.crea-inc.org
CSCC	Cal Safety Compliance Corporation | www.cscc-online.com
CSR	corporate social responsibility
DOL	U. S. Department of Labor | www.dol.gov
EEC	European Economic Community
EPEA	Environmental Protection Encouragement Agency www.epea.com
ETI	Ethical Trading Initiative | www.ethicaltrade.org
EU	European Union | http://europa.eu
FFC	Fair Factories Clearinghouse | www.fairfactories.org
FLA	Fair Labor Association | www.fairlabor.org
FLSA	Fair Labor Standards Act | www.dol.gov/esa/whd/flsa/
FTA	Free Trade Agreements www.ustr.gov/Trade_Agreements/Section_Index.html
FWF	Fair Wear Foundation | http://en.fairwear.nl/
GATT	General Agreement on Tariffs and Trade www.wto.org/english/tratop_e/gatt_e/gatt_e.htm
GMIES	Groupo de Monitoreo Independiente de El Salvador www.gmies.org.sv
GRI	Global Reporting Initiative | www.globalreporting.org
GSCP	Global Social Compliance Programme www.globalsocialcompliance.com
ILGWU	International Ladies Garment Workers Union
ILO	International Labour Organization | www.ilo.org/
ILRF	International Labor Rights Forum | http://laborrights.org

IPCC	Intergovernmental Panel on Climate Change | www.ipcc.ch
ISO	International Organization for Standardization www.iso.org/
ITGLWF	International Textile, Garment and Leather Workers Federation
ITUC	International Trade Union Confederation | www.ituc-csi.org
JO-IN	Joint Initiative on Corporate Accountability and Workers Rights | www.jo-in.org/
LCA	Life Cycle Assessment
LEED	Leadership in Energy and Environmental Design www.usgbc.org/DisplayPage.aspx?CategoryID=19
MBDC	McDonough Braungart Design Chemistry www.mbdc.com/
MFA	Multi-fiber Arrangement
MSI	multi-stakeholder initiative
MSN	Maquila Solidarity Network | http://en.maquilasolidarity.org/
NAFTA	North American Free Trade Agreement www.nafta-sec-alena.org/DefaultSite/index.html
NCL	National Consumers League | www.nclnet.org/
NGO	nongovernmental organization
NLC	National Labor Committee | www.nlcnet.org/
OTA	Organic Trade Association | www.ota.com/index.html
PCR	post consumer recycled
REACH	Registration, Evaluation, Authorization, and Restriction of Chemicals
SAI	Social Accountability International | www.sa-intl.org/
SGS	Société Générale de Surveillance | www.sgs.com/
SMEs	small to medium sized enterprises
SRI	Socially responsible investing
UDHR	Universal Declaration of Human Rights www.un.org/Overview/rights.html

UN	United Nations | www.un.org/
UNITE HERE!	Merged Union of Needletrades, Industrial and Textile Employees (UNITE) and Hotel Employees and Restaurant Employees International Union (HERE) www.unitehere.org/
USAS	United Students Against Sweatshops www.studentsagainstsweatshops.org/
US-LEAP	U. S. Labor Education in the Americas Project www.usleap.org/
VGCL	Vietnam General Confederation of Labor
WRAP	Worldwide Responsible (Accredited) Production www.wrapapparel.org/
WRC	Worker Rights Consortium | www.workersrights.org/
WTO	World Trade Organization | www.wto.org/

Notes

Chapter 1

1. United Nations Global Compact Web site, www.unglobalcompact.org.
2. Personal communication, Stephen Frost, April 2007.
3. *Sadler Committee Report.* (1832). Retrieved on December 21, 2006, from http://history.hanover.edu/courses/excerpts/111sad.html.
4. Moran, W. (2002). *The belles of New England: The women of the textile mills and the families whose wealth they wove.* New York: Thomas Dunne Books.
5. Although the apparel, textile, and footwear industries are classified as separate industries for government accounting purposes, we use the term apparel industry more simply in this book to encompass the range of business activities required to transform fiber and other raw materials to finished apparel and sport footwear.
6. Von Drehle, D. (2003). *Triangle: The fire that changed America.* New York: Atlantic Monthly Press.
7. Cannarella, D. (1993). The Triangle shirtwaist company fire, 1911. *Piecework,* September/October, pp. 42–45.
8. Von Drehle, D. (2003).
9. Greenwald, R. A. (2003). Labor, liberals, and sweatshops. In D. E. Bender & R. A. Greenwald (Eds.), *Sweatshop USA: The American sweatshop in historical and global perspective* (pp. 77–90). New York: Routledge.
10. Von Drehle, D. (2003).
11. Kheel Center for Labor-Management Documentation and Archives, Cornell University/ILR. The story of the Triangle fire, Part 2. Available from www.ilr.cornell.edu/trianglefire/narrative2.html.
12. Von Drehle, D. (2003), p. 3.
13. Cannarella, D. (1993).
14. Von Drehle, D. (2003), p. 3.
15. Kheel Center for Labor-Management Documentation and Archives, Cornell University/ILR. Guide to the Amalgamated Clothing Workers

Of America Records, 1914–1980, Collection Number: 5619. Available from http://rmc.library.cornell.edu/EAD/htmldocs/KCL05619.html; Ross, R. J. S. (2004). *Slaves to fashion: Poverty and abuse in the new sweatshops*. Ann Arbor: The University of Michigan Press.

16. Ross, R. J. S. (2004).

17. Wallace, B. (1995, August 4). 70 immigrants found in raid on sweatshop: Thai workers tell horror stories of captivity. *San Francisco Chronicle*, p. A12.

18. Associated Press. (1997, December 6). Kathie Lee faces more sweatshop allegations. *Toronto Star*, p. A30.

19. Bourbeau, H. (1998, March 19). U.S. companies under fire for using Chinese sweatshops. *Financial Times,* p. 8.

20. McCool, G. (1998, September 21). Sweatshop watchdog slams Liz Claiborne. *Journal of Commerce*, p. 6A.

21. Gelles, J. (1998, August 9). Wal-Mart said to use sweatshops: Big Retailer says its suppliers not abusive. *Houston Chronicle*, Business p. 2.

22. Rohde, D. (1998, June 12). Factory chief faces charges of labor abuses. *New York Times*, p. B5.

23. Branigan, W. (1999, January 14). Top clothing retailers labeled labor abusers. *Washington Post,* p. A14. Reuters, (2000, March 29). 8 Retailers Settle Suit. *New York Times*.

24. The National Labor Committee Web site, www.nlcnet.org.

25. Personal communication, Marcela Manubens, January 2008.

26. Garcia, M., & Powell, M. (2003, October 29). P. Diddy feels the heat over sweatshop charge. *Washington Post,* p. C3.

27. Hansen, C., & Greenberg, R. (2005, June 17). Human cost behind bargain shopping: Dateline hidden camera investigation in Bangladesh. *Dateline NBC*. Available from www.msnbc.msn.com/id/8243331/.

28. Reidy, C. (2006, January 7). Labor group hits New Balance. *Boston Globe*, p. C9.

29. The National Labor Committee Web site, www.nlcnet.org.

30. Wolensky, K. C. (2003). "An industry on wheels": The migration of Pennsylvania's garment factories. In D. E. Bender & R. A. Greenwald (Eds.), *Sweatshop USA: The American sweatshop in historical and global perspective* (pp. 91–116). New York: Routledge.

31. Wolensky, K.C. (2003), p. 92.

32. Blumenberg, E., & Ong, P. (1994). Labor squeeze and ethnic/racial recomposition in the U.S. apparel industry. In E. Bonacich, L. Cheng, N. Chinchilla, N. Hamilton, & P. Ong (Eds.), *Global production: The apparel industry in the Pacific Rim* (pp. 309–327), Philadelphia: Temple University Press.

33. Bonacich, E., & Waller, D. (1994). Mapping a global industry: Apparel production in the Pacific Rim triangle. In E. Bonacich, L. Cheng, N. Chin-

chilla, N. Hamilton, & P. Ong (Eds.), *Global production: The apparel industry in the Pacific Rim* (pp. 21–41), Philadelphia: Temple University Press.

34. Bonacich, E., & Waller, D. (1994).

35. Nordås, H. K. (2004). *The global textile and clothing industry post the agreement on textiles and clothing.* Geneva: World Trade Organization. Available from www.wto.org/english/res_e/booksp_e/discussion_papers5_e.pdf.

36. Office of Textiles and Apparel Web site, http://otexa.ita.doc.gov/.

37. Fair Labor Association. (2003). *First public report: Toward improving workers' lives.* Washington, DC: Author. Available from www.fairlabor.org/all/transparency/charts_2002/PublicReportY1.pdf.

38. Gap Inc. Web site, www.gapinc.org.

39. Allwood, J. M., Laursen, S. E., de Rodriguez, C. M., & Bocken, N. M. P. (2006). *Well dressed? Report on the present and future sustainability of clothing and textiles in the United Kingdom.* Cambridge: University of Cambridge, Institute for Manufacturing.

40. Hawken, P. (1993). *Ecology of commerce: A declaration of sustainability.* New York: HarperBusiness.; McDonough, W. & Braungart, M. (2002). *Cradle to cradle.* New York: North Point Press.

41. Elkington, J. (1998). *Cannibals with forks: The triple bottom line of 21st century business.* Stony Brook, CT: New Society Publishers.

42. Hawken, P. (1993), p. 167.

43. Adams, R. J. (2002). Retail profitability and sweatshops: A global dilemma. *Journal of Retailing and Consumer Services, 9,* 147–153; Bhagwati, J. (2000, May 2). Nike wrongfoots the student critics. *Financial Times.*; Landsburg, S. E. (2001, July 29). False compassion for the third world. *Pittsburgh Post-Gazette,* p. B-1.

44. Kristoff, N. D., & WuDunn, S. (2000, September 24). Two cheers for sweatshops. *New York Times,* p. 70.

45. Bhagwati, J. (2000).

46. Bhagwati, J. (2000).

47. Adams, R. J. (2002).

48. Adams, R.J. (2002).

49. Adams, R.J. (2002).

50. Maquila Solidarity Network. (2007). 2006 year in review: Heightened global competition tests the limits of CSR initiatives. *Codes Memo,* 21.

51. Waddock, S., & Bodwell, C. (2004). Managing responsibility: What can be learned from the quality movement? *California Management Review, 47*(1), 25–37. Quote from p. 35.

52. Waddock, S., & Bodwell, C. (2004), p. 35.

53. Zadek, S. (2004). The path to corporate responsibility. *Harvard Business Review, 82*(12), 125–132.

54. Waddock, S., & Bodwell, C. (2004).
55. Waddock, S., & Bodwell, C, (2004), p. 32.

Chapter 2

1. As cited in Carroll, A. (1999). Corporate social responsibility. *Business & Society, 38*(3), 268–295.
2. Carroll, A. (1999).
3. Business for Social Responsibility Web site, www.bsr.org.
4. See, for example, Berman, B., & Evans, J. R. (2001). *Retail management: A strategic approach* (8th Ed.). Upper Saddle River, NJ: Prentice Hall. (Quote from p. 474).
5. Littrell, M. A., & Dickson, M. A. (1999). *Social responsibility in the global market.* Thousand Oaks, CA: Sage. (Quote from p. 6).
6. Dickson, M.A., & Eckman, M. (2006). Social responsibility: The concept as defined by apparel and textile scholars. *Clothing and Textiles Research Journal. 24*(3), 178–191.
7. Dickson, M.A., & Eckman, M. (2006), p. 188.
8. American Apparel & Footwear Association, www.apparelandfootwear.org.
9. Province stiffens fines on polluters. (2007, April 26). *ChinaDaily.com.cn.*
10. China sets up special fund to support textile industry. (2007, February 2). *Business Daily Update.*
11. Office of the United Nations High Commissioner for Human Rights, Module: Introduction to human rights, Section: What are human rights? Available from www.unssc.org/web/hrb/details.asp?mod=1&sec=1&cur=1.
12. United Nations Global Compact Web site, www.unglobalcompact.org.
13. Personal communication, Dusty Kidd, 8/27/07.
14. United Nations Global Compact Web site, www.unglobalcompact.org
15. Waddock, S., & Bodwell, C. (2002). From TQM to TRM: Total Responsibility Management approaches. *Journal of Corporate Citizenship,* (Autumn), 113–126.
16. Waddock, S., & Bodwell, C. (2002).
17. Park, H., & Lennon, S. J. (2006). The organizational factors influencing socially responsible apparel buying/sourcing. *Clothing and Textiles Research Journal, 24*(3), 229–247.
18. Personal communication, Daryl Brown, 6/27/07.
19. Maquila Solidarity Network. (2005, January 24). *Gildan agrees to do the right things: MSN suspends campaign.* Retrieved on December 19, 2006, from www.maquilasolidarity.org/campaigns/gildan/index.htm.
20. Waddock, S., & Bodwell, C. (2002), p. 125.
21. Ostapski, S. A., & Isaacs, C. N. (1992). Corporate moral responsibility and the moral audit: Challenges for Refuse Relief, Inc. *Journal of Business Ethics, 11*, 231–239.

22. International Labour Organization Web site, www.ilo.org
23. United Nations Global Compact Web site, www.unglobalcompact.org
24. Elliot, K. A., & Freeman, R. B. (2003). *Can labor standards improve under globalization?* Washington, DC: Institute for International Economics.
25. Waddock, S., & Bodwell, C. (2004). Managing responsibility: What can be learned from the quality movement? *California Management Review, 47*(1), 25–37.
26. FLA (2005). Tracking Chart-PVH-Factory Reference 10008476D. Available from www.fairlabor.org.
27. Waddock, S., & Bodwell, C. (2002).
28. Quoted from www.adidas-group.com/en/sustainability/Overview/our_standards/standards_of_engagement.asp.
29. FLA (2006). Tracking Chart-adidas Group-Factory Reference 010015352E. Available from www.fairlabor.org
30. United Nations Global Compact Web site, www.unglobalcompact.org.
31. Quoted from www.adidasgroup.com/en/sustainability/_downloads/social_and_environmental_reports/connected_by_football_social_and_environmental_report_2005.pdf (p. 23).
32. Waddock, S., & Bodwell, C. (2002).
33. Waddock, S., & Bodwell, C. (2002).
34. Robin, D. P., & Reidenbach, R. E. (1993). Searching for a place to stand: Toward a workable ethical philosophy for marketing. *Journal of Public Policy & Marketing, 12*(1), 97–105.
35. Waddock, S., & Bodwell, C. (2002).
36. Ostapski, S. A., & Isaacs, C. N. (1992). Corporate moral responsibility and the moral audit: Challenges for Refuse Relief, Inc. *Journal of Business Ethics, 11*, 231–239.
37. Personal communication, Dan Henkle, 7/12/07.
38. Gap Inc inspected 98.7% of its garment factories in 2005. (12 December 2006). Available from www.just-style.com.
39. Nike corporate Web site, www.nikebiz.com.
40. Waddock, S., & Bodwell, C. (2002).
41. Quoted from www.adidasgroup.com/en/sustainability/_downloads/social_and_environmental_reports/connected_by_football_social_and_environmental_report_2005.pdf (p. 23).
42. Waddock, S., & Bodwell, C. (2002).
43. Elkington, J. (1997). *Cannibals with forks: The triple bottom line of 21st-century business.* Oxford, UK: Capstone Publishing.
44. Wal-Mart. (2006). *2005 report on ethical sourcing.* Retrieved on December 19, 2006 from http://walmartstores.com/Files/05_ethical_source.pdf.
45. Waddock, S., & Bodwell, C. (2002).
46. Global Reporting Initiative Web site, www.globalreporting.org.

Notes

47. Waddock, S., & Bodwell, C. (2002), p. 124.
48. Personal communication, Auret van Heerden, numerous dates, 2003–2007.
49. Waddock, S. & Bodwell, C. (2002).
50. Quoted from GAP, Inc 2004 Social Responsibility Report. Available from www.gapinc.com/public/documents/CSR_Report_04.pdf.

Chapter 3

1. Hill, C. W. L. (2006). *Global business today* (p. 48). New York: McGraw-Hill.
2. Hill, C. W. L. (2006). (p. 131).
3. United Nations Research Institute for Social Development (2005, January 6). *Conference News: Corporate social responsibility and development: Towards a new agenda?* Report of the UNRISD conference, November 2003, Geneva. Retrieved from www.unrisd.org.
4. Allwood, J. M., Laursen, S. E., de Rodriquez, C. M., & Bocken, N. M. P. (2006). *Well dressed? The present and future sustainability of clothing and textiles in the United Kingdom.* Cambridge: University of Cambridge Institute for Manufacturing.
5. Allwood, J. M., Laursen, S. E., de Rodriquez, C. M., & Bocken, N. M. P. (2006).
6. Costa, J. A., & Bamossy, G. J. (Eds). (1995). *Marketing in a multicultural world: Ethnicity, nationalism and cultural identity.* Thousand Oaks, CA: Sage Publications.
7. Kroeber, A. L., & Kluckhohn, C. (1952). *Culture: A critical review of concepts of definitions.* New York: Random House.
8. Merriam Webster Incorporated (2007). *Merriam Webster dictionary.* Retrieved from www.m-w.com/.
9. Srnka, K. (2004). Culture's role in marketers' ethical decision making: An integrated theoretical framework. *Academy of Marketing Science Review, 01,* 1–32. Available from www.amsreview.org/articles/srnka01-2004.pdf .
10. Hill, C. W. L. (2006), p. 146.
11. Capela, J. J., & Hartman, S. W. (1996). *Dictionary of international business terms.* Hauppauge, NY: Barron's.
12. Anwar, S. A., & Jabnoun, N. (2006, June). The development of a contingency model relating national culture to total quality management. *International Journal of Management, 23*(2), 272–280.
13. Hofstede, G. H. (1980). *Culture's consequences: International differences in work-related values.* Beverly Hills, CA: Sage Publications and Hofstede, G. H. (1991). *Cultures and organizations: Software of the mind.* New York: McGraw-Hill.
14. Hofstede, G. H. (1980 and 1991).

330

15. Triandis, H. C. (2006). Cultural aspects of globalization. *Journal of International Management, 12*, 208–217.

16. Dickson, M. A., & Littrell, M. A. (1998). Organizational culture for small textile and apparel businesses in Guatemala. *Clothing and Research Journal, 16*(2), 68–78.

17. Ferraro, G. P. (2006). *The cultural dimension of international business* (5th ed.). Upper Saddle River, NJ: Pearson Prentice Hall.

18. Ferraro, G. P. (2006), p. 6.

19. Office of the United Nations High Commissioner for Human Rights (2006). *Human rights treaty bodies: Monitoring the core international human rights treaties*. Retrieved from www.ohchr.org.

20. Quoted from International Labour Organization (2007). *International Labour Organization: Promoting decent work for all*. Geneva: ILO. Retrieved from www.ilo.org/global/lang--en/index.htm.

21. Rugmark Foundation Web site, www.rugmark.org.

22. Rugmark Foundation Web site, www.rugmark.org.

23. Doumbia-Henry, C., & Gravel, E., (2006). Free trade agreements and labour rights: Recent developments. *International Labor Review, 145*(3), 185–206.

24. Rugmark Foundation Web site, www.rugmark.org.

25. Yanz, L. (2007, June). Panel discussion at the FLA Stakeholder Forum, Santiago, Dominican Republic.

26. U.S. Department of Labor (2000). *Wages, benefits, poverty line, and meeting workers' needs in the apparel and footwear industries of selected countries*. Washington: U.S. Department of Labor Bureau of International Labor Affairs.

27. Center for Reflection, Education and Action Web site, www.crea-inc.org/.

28. See www.workersrights.org/DSP/WRC_Letter_to_FLA_3-4-06.pdf.

29. Joint Initiative on Corporate Accountability & Workers' Rights Web site, www.jo-in.org/english/index.asp.

30. International Labour Organization (2006, January). *Global employment trends brief*. Geneva: ILO. J. M., Laursen, S. E., de Rodriquez, C. M., & Bocken, N. M. P.

31. Allwood, J. M., Laursen, S. E., de Rodriquez, C. M., & Bocken, N. M. P. (2006).

32. Allwood, J. M., Laursen, S. E., de Rodriquez, C. M., & Bocken, N. M. P. (2006).

33. International Labour Organization. (2006).

34. See, for example, Krueger, A. O. (1993). Virtuous and vicious circles in economic development. *American Economic Review, 83*(2), 351–355, and Masuch, M. (1985). Vicious circles in organizations. *Administrative Science Quarterly, 30*(1), 14–33.

35. Allwood, J. M., Laursen, S. E., de Rodriquez, C. M., & Bocken, N. M. P. (2006).

36.   Allwood, J. M., Laursen, S. E., de Rodriquez, C. M., & Bocken, N. M. P. (2006).

37.   Jorgenson, H. B., Pruzan-Jorgenson, M., Jungk, M., & Cramer, A. (2003). *Strengthening implementation of corporate social responsibility in global supply chains.* Washington, DC: The World Bank.

38.   Ferenschild, S., & Wick, I. (2004, June). *Global fame for cuffs and collars: The phase-out of the WTO agreement on textiles and clothing aggravates social divisions.* Siegburg, Germany: South Wind Institute of Economics and Ecumenism.

39.   Capela, J. J., & Hartman, S. W. (1996).

40.   Ferenschild, S., & Wick, I. (2004).

41.   Allwood, J. M., Laursen, S. E., de Rodriquez, C. M., & Bocken, N. M. P. (2006).

42.   Ferenschild, S., & Wick, I. (2004).

43.   Ferenschild, S., & Wick, I. (2004).

44.   Burtless, G. (2001, Fall). Labor standards and global trade: Workers' rights. *Brookings Review,* 10.

45.   Burtless, G. (2001), p. 10.

46.   Doumbia-Henry, C., & Gravel, E. (2006), p. 189.

47.   Doumbia-Henry, C., & Gravel, E. (2006).

48.   Doumbia-Henry, C., & Gravel, E. (2006).

49.   Doumbia-Henry, C., & Gravel, E. (2006).

50.   Doumbia-Henry, C., & Gravel, E. (2006).

51.   Doumbia-Henry, C., & Gravel, E. (2006). 51

52.   Prasso, S. (2007). *Case study: Bringing labor issues into the Cambodian textile agreement.* Initiative for Policy Dialogue. Retrieved at www2.gsb.columbia.edu/ipd/j_cambodia_bk.html.

53.   Ferenschild, S., & Wick, I. (2004).

54.   Prasso, S. (2007).

55.   Doumbia-Henry, C., & Gravel, E. (2006).

56.   Prasso, S. (2007).

57.   Prasso, S. (2007). p. 4.

58.   Yanz, L. (2007).

59.   Porter, M. S., & Kramer, M. R. (2006, December). Strategy & society: The link between competitive advantage and corporate social responsibility. *Harvard Business Review, 84*(12), 78–92.

60.   Porter, M. S., & Kramer, M. R. (2006).

61.   Porter, M. S., & Kramer, M. R. (2006).

62.   Porter, M. S., & Kramer, M. R. (2006).

63.   Kidd, D. (2006, May 2). *Nike and responsibility: A look into the future.* Presentation made for the Fashioning Social Responsibility lecture series at the University of Delaware.

Chapter 4

1. Von Drehle, D. (2003). *Triangle: The fire that changed America*. New York: Atlantic Monthly Press.

2. Greenwald, R. A. (2003). Labor, liberals, and sweatshops. In D. E. Bender & R. A. Greenwald (Eds.), *Sweatshop USA: The American sweatshop in historical and global perspective* (pp. 77–90). New York: Routledge.

3. Boris, E. (2003). Consumers of the world unite! In D. E. Bender & R. A. Greenwald (Eds.) *Sweatshop USA: The American sweatshop in global and historical perspective* (pp. 203–224). New York, NY: Routledge.

4. Von Drehle, D. (2003).

5. Greenwald, R. A. (2003).

6. Von Drehle, D. (2003).

7. Greenwald, R. A. (2003).

8. Greenwald, R. A. (2003).

9. Bender, D. E., & Greenwald, R. A. (2003). Introduction. In D. E. Bender & R. A. Greenwald (Eds.) *Sweatshop USA: The American sweatshop in global and historical perspective* (pp. 1–36). New York, NY: Routledge.

10. Greenwald, R. A. (2003).

11. Von Drehle, D. (2003), p. 3.

12. Von Drehle, D. (2003), p. 212.

13. Von Drehle, D. (2003).

14. Ross, R. J. S. (2004). *Slaves to fashion: Poverty and abuse in the new sweatshops*. Ann Arbor: The University of Michigan Press.

15. Von Drehle, D. (2003), p. 267.

16. Boris, E. (2003); Ross, R. J. S. (2004).

17. Von Drehle, D. (2003).

18. Greenwald, R. A. (2003).

19. Ross, R. J. S. (2004).

20. Greenwald, R. A. (2003).

21. Infoplease. Fair Labor Standards Act. Available from www.infoplease.com/ce6/bus/A0818152.html.

22. Bender, D. E., & Greenwald, R. A. (2003).

23. Friedman, M. (1970, September 13). The social responsibility of business is to increase its profits. *The New York Times Magazine*.

24. Freeman, R. E., Wicks, A. C., & Parmar, B. (2004). Stakeholder theory and "the corporate objective revisited." *Organization Science, 15*(3), 364–369. (Quote from p. 365).

25. Freeman, R. E., Wicks, A. C., & Parmer, B. (2004), p. 367.

26. Carroll, A. B. (1991). The pyramid of corporate social responsibility: toward the moral management of organizational stakeholders. *Business Horizons, 34*, 39–48. (Quote from p. 43).

27. Freeman, R. E. (1984). *Strategic management: A stakeholder approach*. Mansfield, MA: Pittman Publishing.
28. Freeman, R. E., Wicks, A. C., & Parmar, B. (2004), p. 364.
29. Donaldson, T., & Preston, L. E. (1995). The stakeholder theory of the corporation: Concepts, evidence, and implications. *Academy of Management Review, 20*(1), 65–91. (Quote from p. 67).
30. Freeman, R. E., Wicks, A. C., & Parmar, B. (2004).
31. Clarkson, M. B. E. (1995). A stakeholder framework for analyzing and evaluating corporate social performance. *The Academy of Management Review, 20*(1), 92–117. (Quote from p. 112.)
32. Donaldson, T., & Preston, L. E. (1995).
33. Clarkson, M. B. E. (1995), p. 98.
34. Donaldson, T., & Preston, L. E. (1995), p. 67.
35. Clarkson, M. B. E. (1995), p. 106.
36. Clarkson, M. B. E. (1995), p. 106.
37. Donaldson, T., & Preston, L. E. (1995).
38. Clarkson, M. B. E. (1995), p. 107.
39. Accountability. (2005). *AA1000 Stakeholder engagement standard: Exposure draft*. Available from www.accountability.org.uk/resources.
40. Clement, R. W. (2005). The lessons from stakeholder theory for U.S. business leaders. *Business Horizons, 48*, 255–264.
41. Phillips, R. (2004). Ethics and a manager's obligations under stakeholder theory. *Ivey Business Journal, March/April*, 1–4.
42. Donaldson, T., & Preston. L. E. (1995), p. 87.
43. Business for Social Responsibility Web site, www.bsr.org.
44. Accountability. (2005).
45. Gable, C., & Shireman, B. (2005). Stakeholder engagement: A three-phase methodology. *Environmental Quality Management, Spring*, 9–24.
46. Gable, C. & Shireman, B. (2005), p. 12.
47. De Colle, S. (2005). A stakeholder management model for ethical decision making. *International Journal of Management and Decision Making, 6*(3/4), 299–314.
48. Weiner, E., & Brown, A. (1986). Stakeholder analysis for effective issues management. *Planning Review, 14*(3), 27–31. (Quote from p. 28).
49. Accountability. (2005).
50. Gable, C., & Shireman, B. (2005).
51. Gable, C., & Shireman, B. (2005), p. 17.
52. Business for Social Responsibility Web site, www.bsr.org.
53. Gable, C., & Shireman, B. (2005).
54. Gable, C., & Shireman, B. (2005).
55. Business for Social Responsibility Web site, www.bsr.org.
56. adidas Group. Summary report on worker training strategy workshop. Available from www.adidas-group.com/en/sustainability/_downloads/stake

Notes

holder_reports/Asia_Stakeholder_Report_China_June_2005_English_
version.pdf.

57. Clarkson, M. B. E. (1995); Phillips, R. (2004).
58. De Colle, S. (2005), p. 313.
59. GRI Apparel and Sector Footwear Supplement. Available from www.
globalreporting.org/NR/rdonlyres/D9F94ACE-5598-45A6-ABED-
CE12D44E33A0/0/SS_Draft_ApparelFootwear.pdf.
60. Clarkson, M. B. E. (1995), p. 108.
61. For example, see adidas Group Reports to Download Web page at www.
adidas-group.com/en/sustainability/reporting/reports_to_download/default.
asp, Nike CR Report Web page at www.nikeresponsibility.com/#home/, and
Gap Inc. Social Responsibility Web page at www.gapinc.com/public/Social-
Responsibility/socialres.shtml.
62. Fair Labor Association, Tracking Charts Web page. Available from www.
fairlabor.org/pubs/tracking.
63. Clement, R. W. (2005).
64. Donaldson, T., & Preston, L. E. (1995), pp. 79–80.
65. Bendell, J. (2005). In whose name? The accountability of corporate social responsibility. *Development in Practice. 15*(3&4): 362–374. (Quote from p. 372).
66. Clement, R. W. (2005).
67. Hart, S. L., & Sharma, S. (2004). Engaging fringe stakeholders for competitive imagination. *Academy of Management Executive, 18*(1), 7–18.
68. Business for Social Responsibility Web site, www.bsr.org.
69. Business for Social Responsibility Web site, www.bsr.org.
70. Bendell, J. (2005), p. 364.

Chapter 5

1. World Bank Web site. Defining civil society. Available from http://web.
worldbank.org/WBSITE/EXTERNAL/TOPICS/CSO/0,,contentMDK:2
0101499~menuPK:244752~pagePK:220503~piPK:220476~theSitePK:228717,0
0.html.
2. United Nations Global Compact Web site, www.unglobalcompact.org.
3. Capela, J. J., & Hartman, S. W. (1996). *Dictionary of international business
terms* (pp. 335–336). Hauppauge, NY: Barron's Educational Series, Inc.
4. *Bangladesh: Garment workers riot against new pay deal.* (2006, October 10).
Available from www.just-style.com; *Bangladesh: Garment worker killed in factory riots.* (2007, May 21). Available from www.just-style.com.
5. Reebok, (2005). *Our commitment to human rights: Reebok human rights report
2005.* (Quote from p. 36).
6. UNITE HERE! Web site, www.unitehere.org.
7. Change to Win Web site, www.changetowin.org.

8. Solidarity Center Web site, www.solidaritycenter.org/

9. International Textile, Garment and Leather Workers Federation Web site, www.itglwf.org.

10. International Federation of Free Trade Unions Web site, www.icftu.org/default.asp?Language=EN.

11. Heerden, A., & Baumann, D. (2005). The expiration of the Multifibre Arrangement (MFA) and its consequences for global labor standards. *Fair Labor Association Annual Public Report 2005*. Available from www.fairlabor.org.

12. Heerden, A. (2004). Freedom of association: Year two featured code provision. *Fair Labor Association Year Two Annual Public Report*. Available from www.fairlabor.org

13. Infoplease. Fair Labor Standards Act. Available from www.infoplease.com/ce6/bus/A0818152.html.

14. Ross, R. J. S. (2004). *Slaves to fashion: Poverty and abuse in the new sweatshops.* Ann Arbor: The University of Michigan Press.

15. Fair Labor Association. About the Fair Labor Association. Available from www.fairlabor.org/about.

16. http://harkin.senate.gov/issue/i.cfm?guid=c428ce18-3f51-404c-bdof-9576acf46004

17. Berlau, J. (1997, Nov. 24). The paradox of child-labor reform. Retrieved on 1/29/08 at http://findarticles.com/p/articles/mi_m1571/is_n43_v13/ai_20027231.

18. United States Senate. 110th Congress, 1st Session, S. 367 (2007, January 23). Available from http://frwebgate.access.gpo.gov/cgi-bin/getdoc.cgi?dbname=110_cong_bills&docid=f:s367is.txt.pdf.

19. Senate. (2007, January 26). *Cracking down on sweatshop abuses.* Text of the statement by Senator Dorgan introducing his Decent Working Conditions and Fair Competition Act.

20. American Apparel and Footwear Association Web site, www.appareland footwear.org.

21. Rosen, J. (2007, January 24). Senate sweatshop bill gains bipartisan support: Legislation aims to stop companies from profiting from unfair labor practices abroad. *McClatchy Newspapers.*

22. Heerden, A., & Baumann, D. (2005).

23. China Labour Bulletin. (2007, June 29). National People's Congress approves new Labour Contract Law: China Labour Bulletin welcomes the new law, but cautions that without determined enforcement, labour abuses are unlikely to decline. *China Labour Bulletin Press Release.*

24. International Labour Organization. Better Factories Cambodia. Available from www.ilo.org/public/english/dialogue/ifpdial/publ/cambodia11.pdf.

25. *SWITZERLAND: ILO asks Cambodia to clarify accusations.* (2007, January 26). Available from www.just-syle.com.

26. International Labour Organization Web site, www.ilo.org.

27. Maquila Solidarity Network Web site, www.maquilasolidarity.org.
28. International Labor Rights Forum Web site, www.laborrights.org/.
29. Greenhouse, S. (2005, September 14). Suit says Wal-Mart is lax on labour abuses overseas. *The New York Times*, p. 3.
30. www.usleap.org/.
31. Sweatshop Watch Web site, www.sweatshopwatch.org/index.php?s=1.
32. Play Fair 2008 Web site, www.playfair2008.org.
33. Oxfam International Web site, www.oxfam.org.
34. Human Rights First Web site, www.humanrightsfirst.org.
35. Powell, J. E. (1969) *Freedom and reality* (p. 22). New Rochelle, NY: Abington House.
36. Dickinson, R. A., & Carsky, M. L. (2005). The consumer as economic voter. In R. Harrison, T. Newholm, & D. Shaw (Eds.), *The ethical consumer* (p. 28). London: Sage.
37. Golodner, L. F. (1997, October 6). *Apparel industry code of conduct: A consumer perspective on social responsibility*. Paper presented at the Notre Dame Center for Ethics and Religious Values in Business. Available from www.nclnet.org.
38. Golodner, L. F. (1997).
39. National Consumers League Web site, www.nclnet.org.
40. Bowden, C. (2001, July/August). Keeper of the fire. *Mother Jones*, pp. 68–73.
41. National Labor Committee mission statement. Available from www.nlcnet.org/aboutus.php.
42. Wick, I. (2005). *Workers' tool or PR ploy, 4th ed., A guide to international labor practice*. Bonn: Friedrich-Ebert-Stiftung. Downloaded on 11/28/05 from www.cleanclothes.org
43. Featherstone, L. (2003). Students against sweatshops: A history. In D. E. Bender, & R. A. Greenwald (Eds.) *Sweatshop USA: The American sweatshop in global and historical perspective* (pp. 247–264). New York: Routledge.
44. United Students Against Sweatshops Web site, www.studentsagainstsweatshops.org/.
45. Fair Labor Association Web site, www.fairlabor.org.
46. Casey, R. 2006. Meaningful change: Raising the bar in supply chain workplace standards. *Corporate Social Responsibility Initiative, Working Paper No. 29.* Cambridge, MA: John F. Kennedy School of Government, Harvard University. (Quote from p. 32).
47. Featherstone, L. (2003).
48. Worker Rights Consortium Web site, www.workersrights.org.
49. Coleman, L. (2006, January 26i). Whose sweat are you wearing? *The Georgetown Voice.* Retrieved on 7/5/07 from www.georgetownvoice.com/2006-01-26/news/whose-sweat-are-you-wearing.

50. Freeman, R. E., Wicks, A. C., & Parmar, B. (2004). Stakeholder theory and "the corporate objective revisited." *Organization Science, 15*(3), 364–369.

51. Dow Jones Sustainability Indexes. Available from www.sustainability-indexes.com/.

52. FTSE Group Web site, www.ftse.com/About_Us/index.jsp

53. White, A. L. (2006). *Invest, turnaround, harvest: Private equity meets CSR.* Retrieved on 7/5/07 from www.bsr.org/meta/Private_Equity.pdf (Quote from p. 5).

54. *US: Limited Brands sells majority stake in flagship chain.* (2007, July 9). Available from www.just-style.com.

55. White, A. L. (2006), p. 11.

56. Power, G. (2005, April 9). *The new frontier in responsible business: The UN perspective.* Presentation made at the Haas School of Business, University of California at Berkeley. Retrieved on 7/5/07 from www.haas.berkeley.edu/responsiblebusiness/conference/documents/UNGlobalCompactGPower.ppt#1.

57. Social Investment Forum. (2003). *2003 report on socially responsible investment trends in the United States.* Retrieved on 7/5/07 from www.socialinvest.org/areas/research/trends/sri_trends_report_2003.pdf.

58. SocialFunds.com. (2000, July 13). *Human rights compel social investors.* Available from www.socialfunds.com/news/article.cgi/307.html.

59. Calvert Online. Issue Brief: Human Rights. Available from www.calvert.com/sri_IBHumanRights.html.

60. Calvert Online. Issue Brief: Labor and Workplace Safety. Available from www.calvert.com/sri_IBLaborWorkplaceSafety.html.

61. Odell, A. M. (2007, August 30). *Green outsourcing: Companies demanding more environmentally sound suppliers.* Available from www.socialfunds.com/news/article.cgi/2360.html.

Chapter 6

1. Excerpt from McCaffety, J. (2005, August 1). Price of a cheap suit: Companies spend millions to assess overseas suppliers. So why are they still missing so many problems? *CFO Magazine.*

2. Howard, R. (1990). Values make the company: An interview with Robert Haas. *Harvard Business Review,* Sept–Oct, 133–144. (Quote from p. 135).

3. Esbenshade, J. (2004). *Monitoring sweatshops: Workers, consumers, and the global apparel industry.* Philadelphia: Temple University Press.

4. Zadek, S. (2004). The path to corporate responsibility. *Harvard Business Review, 82*(12), 125–132.

5. Clean Clothes Campaign. (2005). *Looking for a quick fix: How weak social auditing is keeping workers in sweatshops.* Retrieved on 11/23/05 from www.cleanclothes.org. (Quote from p. 12).

6. Levi Strauss Web site, www.levistrauss.com.

7. Emmelhainz, M. A., & Adams, R. J. (1999). The apparel industry response to "sweatshop" concerns: A review and analysis of codes of conduct. *The Journal of Supply Chain Management, 35*(3), 51–57.

8. International Labour Organization Web site, www.ilo.org.

9. International Labour Organization Web site, www.ilo.org.

10. Maquila Solidarity Network. (2007). 2006 year in review: Heightened global competition tests the limits of CSR initiatives. *Codes Memo,* 21.

11. Dickson, M. A., & Kovaleski, K. (2007, November 8). *Implementing labor compliance in the apparel industry.* Paper presented at the annual meeting of the International Textile and Apparel Association, Los Angeles, CA.

12. Esbenshade, J. (2004).

13. Clean Clothes Campaign. (2005).

14. Esbenshade, J. (2004).

15. Clean Clothes Campaign. (2005), p. 18.

16. Harvey, P., Collingsworth, T., & Athreya, B. (2002). Developing effective mechanisms for implementing labor rights in the global economy. In R. Broad (Ed.), *Global backlash* (pp. 228–235). Lanthan, MD: Rowman & Littlefield Publishers.

17. Esbenshade, J. (2004).

18. Casey, R. 2006. Meaningful change: Raising the bar in supply chain workplace standards. *Corporate Social Responsibility Initiative, Working Paper No. 29.* Cambridge, MA: John F. Kennedy School of Government, Harvard University.

19. Clean Clothes Campaign. (2005).

20. Esbenshade, J. (2004).

21. Clean Clothes Campaign. (2005).

22. Clean Clothes Campaign. (2005).

23. Esbenshade, J. (2004).

24. Clean Clothes Campaign. (2005).

25. Esbenshade, J. (2004).

26. Clean Clothes Campaign. (2005).

27. Verité Inc. Web site, www.verite.org.

28. Ethical Trading Initiative. (2002, March 7). ETI Members' Roundtable 2: Issues affecting women workers. Available from www.ethicaltrade.org/Z/lib/2002/03/rt2-wom/index.shtml#verite.

29. Esbenshade, J. (2004).

30. Harvey et al. (2002).

31. Casey, R. (2006), p. 22.

32. Dickson, M. A., & Kovaleski, K. (2007).

Notes

33. O'Rourke, D. (2003). Outsourcing regulation: Non-governmental systems of labor standards and monitoring. *Policy Studies Journal, 31*(1), 1–29.
34. Clean Clothes Campaign. (2005).
35. Casey, R. (2006), p. 3.
36. Ethical Trading Initiative. (2006, November 16). *Getting smarter at auditing: Tracking the growing crisis in ethical trade auditing.* Available from www.ethicaltrade.org.
37. Clean Clothes Campaign. (2005).
38. Ethical Trading Initiative, (2006).
39. Clean Clothes Campaign. (2005).
40. Niemi, W. (2004, September 27). The next chapter: How to incorporate labor rights needs. *Footwear News.*
41. Locke, R., Qin, F., & Brause, A. (2006). Does monitoring improve labor standards?: Lessons from Nike. *MIT Sloan Working Paper No. 4612-06.* Retrieved on 7/25/07 from http://ssrn.com/abstract=916771.
42. How China's labor conditions stack up against those of other low-cost nations. (2006, November 27). *BusinessWeek*, Online Extra.
43. Clean Clothes Campaign. (2005).
44. Maquila Solidarity Network. (2007). *Emergency assistance, redress and prevention in the Hermosa Manufacturing case.* Retrieved on 8/11/07 from http://en.maquilasolidarity.org/sites/maquilasolidarity.org/files/Hermosa ReportFinal_1.pdf.
45. Ethical Trading Initiative. (2006).
46. Clean Clothes Campaign. (2005).
47. O'Rourke, D. (2003).
48. Clean Clothes Campaign. (2005), pp. 59–60.
49. O'Rourke, D. (2003).
50. Ethical Trading Initiative. (2006).
51. Clean Clothes Campaign. (2005).
52. Esbenshade, J. (2004).
53. Excerpt from Brown, J. S. (2001). Confessions of a sweatshop inspector. Downloaded from www.albionmonitor.com/0108a/sweatshopsinspect.html.
54. Clean Clothes Campaign. (2005).
55. Clean Clothes Campaign. (2005).
56. Ethical Trading Initiative. (2006).
57. As quoted in Clean Clothes Campaign. (2005), p. 50.
58. Clean Clothes Campaign. (2005).
59. Ethical Trading Initiative. (2006); Clean Clothes Campaign. (2005).
60. Clean Clothes Campaign. (2005), p. 24.
61. Secrets, lies and sweatshops. (2006, November 27). *Businessweek.*
62. Fooling the Auditors. (2006, November 27). *Businessweek Online.*
63. Casey, R. (2006); Clean Clothes Campaign. (2005).

64. Clean Clothes Campaign. (2005), p. 74.
65. Casey, R. (2006), p. 40.
66. Casey, R. (2006), p. 28.

Chapter 7

1. Zadek, S. (2004). The path to corporate responsibility. *Harvard Business Review, 82*(12), 125–132.
2. Mamic, I, (2003). *Business and code of conduct implementation: How firms use management systems for social performance*, Geneva: International Labour Organization.
3. Dickson, M. A., & Kovaleski, K. (2007, November 8). *Implementing labor compliance in the apparel industry*. Paper presented at the annual conference of the International Textile and Apparel Association, Los Angeles, CA.
4. Mamic, I. (2003) and Dickson, M. A., & Kovaleski, K. (2007).
5. Mamic, I. (2003).
6. Dickson, M. A., & Kovaleski, K. (2007).
7. Personal communication, Doug Cahn, April 2006.
8. Mamic, I. (2003).
9. Fair Labor Association (2007). 2007 annual report Available from www.fair labor.org/pubs/reports.
10. Mamic, I. (2003).
11. Fair Labor Association. (2007).
12. Personal communication, Bill Anderson, April 2007.
13. Mamic, I. (2003).
14. Dickson, M. A. & Kovaleski, K. (2007).
15. Mamic, I. (2003).
16. Mamic, I. (2003). (p. 90).
17. Clean Clothes Campaign. (2005). *Looking for a quick fix: How weak social auditing is keeping workers in sweatshops*. Retrieved on 11/23/05 from www.cleanclothes.org.
18. Dickson, M. A., & Kovaleski, K. (2007).
19. Global Reporting Initiative Web site, www.globalreporting.org/Home
20. Dickson, M. A., & Kovaleski, K. (2007).
21. Freeman, B. (2006). Substance sells: Aligning corporate reputation and corporate responsibility. *Public Relations Quarterly*, Summer, 12–19, p. 17.
22. Nike. (2005/2006). *Innovate for a better world: Nike FY05–06 corporate social responsibility report*. Available from www.nike.com/nikebiz/nikebiz.jhtml?page=24.
23. Dickson, M. A. (2006, June 14). *The complexity of sourcing in a global market*. Paper presented at the Multi-Stakeholder Forum, Fair Labor Association, Bamberg, Germany.

24. Mamic, I. (2003).

25. Hurley, J., & Faiz, N. (2007). *Assessing the impact of purchasing practices on code compliance: A case study of the Bangladesh garment industry.* Available from www.mfa-forum.net/.

26. Roner, L. (2007, Oct. 3). Wal-Mart's ethical sourcing: Green does not mean ethical. *Ethical Corporation.* Available from www.laborrights.org/press/Wal-Mart/ethicalsourcing_ethicalcorp_100307.htm, and Gap Inc. SR report 2006.

27. Zadek, S. (2004).

28. Clement, R. W. (2005). The lessons from stakeholder theory for U.S. business leaders. *Business Horizons, 48,* 255–264.

29. Fashioning an Ethical Industry (Fashioning). (2007). *Factsheet 10: Multi-stakeholder initiatives.* Available from http://fashioninganethicalindustry.org/resources/factsheets/#.

30. Fashioning. (2007).

31. Dan Henkle, SVP of social responsibility for Gap as quoted in Chelan, D. (2007, January). How Gap manages social compliance. *Apparel Magazine, 48*(5), 32–34. 31

32. Fashioning. (2007).

33. Ethical Trading Initiative (2006, November 16). *Getting smarter at auditing: Tracking the growing crisis in ethical trade auditing* (p. 15.). Available from www.ethicaltrade.org.

34. Clean Clothes Campaign Web site, www.cleanclothes.org.

35. Ethical Trading Initiative, www.ethicaltrade.org.

36. Wick, I. (2005). *Workers' tool or PR ploy: A guide to international labor practice* (4th ed.). Bonn: Friedrich Ebert Stiftung.

37. Casey, R. 2006. Meaningful change: Raising the bar in supply chain workplace standards. *Corporate Social Responsibility Initiative, Working Paper No. 29.* Cambridge, MA: John F. Kennedy School of Government, Harvard University. (Quote from p. 31).

38. Maquila Solidarity Network (2004, Jan/Feb). *2003 year end review: Emerging trends in codes and their implementation.* Available from http://en.maquilasolidarity.org/.

39. Van der Zee, B. (2006, December 14). Ethical living. *The Guardian,* p. 18.

40. Greenhouse, S. (1997, February 1). Voluntary roles on apparel labor prove hard to set", *New York Times,* p. 1.

41. Fair Labor Association Web site, www.fairlabor.org.

42. Green, P. (1998, November 6). Industry to oversee textile factories. *Journal of Commerce,* p. 8A, and Greenhouse, S. (1998, July 3). Anti-sweatshop coalition finds itself at odds on garment factory code. *New York Times,* p. A16.

43. Clean Clothes Campaign. Sweatshop Agreement. Part 2: Documents. Available from www.cleanclothes.org/codes/AIP-2.htm.

44. FLA Charter as amended February 2007. Available from www.fairlabor.org/about/charter.

45. Dickson, M. A. (2006). *Backgrounder: Labor and corporate responsibility—The role of monitoring companies in labor enforcement.* Columbia University, Initiative for Policy Dialogue. Available from www2.gsb.columbia.edu/ipd/j_labor_corporateresponsibility.html.

46. Fair Labor Association (2007).

47. O'Rourke, D. (2003). Outsourcing regulation: Non-governmental systems of labor standards and monitoring. *Policy Studies Journal, 31*(1), 1–29.

48. Fair Labor Association Web site, www.fairlabor.org.

49. Dickson, M. A., & Eckman, M. (2008). Media portrayal of voluntary public reporting about corporate social responsibility performance: Does coverage encourage or discourage ethical management? *Journal of Business Ethics, 83,* 725–743.

50. Fair Labor Association Web site, www.fairlabor.org.

51. Dickson, M. A. (2006); Wick, I. (2005).

52. Fair Labor Association (2007).

53. Fair Labor Association Web site, www.fairlabor.org.

54. Casey, R. (2006), (p. 31).

55. Mandle, J. R. (2000). The student anti-sweatshop movement: Limits and potentials. *Annals of the American Academy of Political Science and Social Science, 570*(1), 92–103.

56. Bohnett, T. (2006, October 16). Just don't do it. *The Daily Princetonian.*

57. Wick, I. (2005).

58. Hemphill, T. A. (2004). Monitoring global corporate citizenship: Industry self-regulation at a crossroads. *The Journal of Corporate Citizenship*, Summer.

59. O'Rourke, D. (2003).

60. Casey, R. (2006). (p. 32).

61. Fair Wear Foundation Web site, http://en.fairwear.nl.

62. Fashioning. (2007).

63. Wick, I. (2005).

64. Social Accountability International Web site, www.sa-intl.org.

65. Dickson, M. A. (2006).

66. Social Accountability International Web site, www.sa-intl.org/.

67. Casey, R. (2006).

68. Clean Clothes Campaign. (2005).

69. Clean Clothes Campaign. (2007, October). Urgent appeals. Available from www.cleanclothes.org/news/newsletter24-08.htm.

70. O'Rourke, D. (2003).

71. Esbenshade, J. (2004). *Monitoring sweatshops: Workers, consumers, and the global apparel industry.* Philadelphia: Temple University Press.

72. Wick (2005).

73. Worker Rights Consortium Web site, www.workersrights.org.
74. O'Rourke, D. (2003).
75. Wick, I. (2005).
76. Worker Rights Consortium Web site, www.workersrights.org.
77. United Students Against Sweatshops Web site, www.studentsagainstsweat shops.org/.
78. Worker Rights Consortium Web site, www.workersrights.org/.
79. Maquila Solidarity Network (2004, January/February).
80. Wick, I. (2005).
81. O'Rourke, D. (2003).
82. Business for Social Responsibility Web site, www.bsr.org/.
83. Business for Social Responsibility. (2007). *Our role in designing a sustainable future: BSER annual report 2007.* Available from www.bsr.org/about/bsr-report.cfm.
84. Business for Social Responsibility Web site, www.bsr.org.
85. Business Social Compliance Institute Web site, www.bsci-eu.org/.
86. Clean Clothes Campaign. (2005).
87. Business Social Compliance Institute Web site, www.bsci-eu.org/.
88. Fashioning. (2007).
89. Clean Clothes Campaign. (2005).
90. CIES Web site, www.ciesnet.com/.
91. Clean Clothes Campaign. (2005).
92. Clean Clothes Campaign. (2005), (p. 72).
93. Joint Initiative on Corporate Accountability and Workers Rights Web site, www.jo-in.org/english/about.asp.
94. Worldwide Responsible Accredited Production. About WRAP. Available from www.wrapapparel.org/modules.php?name=Content&pa=showpage&pid=.
95. Worldwide Responsible Accredited Production Web site, www.wrapapparel.org/.
96. Worldwide Responsible Accredited Production Web site, www.wrapapparel.org, and Maquila Solidarity Work (2003, January 20). Codes memo. Available from http://en.maquilasolidarity.org/en/resources/codesmemo?page=1.
97. Dickson, M. A. (2006).
98. Worldwide Responsible Accredited Production Web site, www.wrapapparel.org/.
99. Clean Clothes Campaign Web site, www.cleanclothes.org.
100. Clean Clothes Campaign. (2005).
101. Casey, R. (2006). (p. 33).
102. 1% For the Planet Web site, www.onepercentfortheplanet.org.
103. GreenBlue Web site, www.greenblue.org.
104. See MBDC Web site, www.mbdc.com.

105. Organic Exchange. Introduction to the Organic Exchange. Available from www.organicexchange.org/intro.php.
106. Organic Trade Association Web site, www.ota.com/index.html.
107. Dickson, M. A., & Kovaleski, K. (2007).
108. Clean Clothes Campaign. (2005).
109. Dickson, M. A., & Kovaleski, K. (2007).
110. Casey, R. (2006). (p. 31).
111. Ross, R. J. S. (2004). *Slaves to fashion: Poverty and abuse in the new sweatshops.* Ann Arbor: The University of Michigan Press.
112. Ross, R. J. S. (2004).
113. Zadek, S. (2004).
114. Freeman, B. (2006). Substance sells: Aligning corporate reputation and corporate responsibility. *Public Relations Quarterly*, Summer, 12–19. (Quote from pp. 15–16).

Chapter 8

1. Brown, M. S., & Wilmanns, E. (1997). Quick and dirty environmental analyses for garments: What do we need to know? *Journal of Sustainable Product Design, 1*(1), 28–34.; Fletcher, K. T. & Goggin, P. A. (2001). The dominant stance on ecodesign. *Design Issues,17*(3), 15–25; Allwood, J. M., Laursen, S. E., de Rodriguez, C. M., & Bocken, N. M. P. (2006). *Well dressed? Report on the present and future sustainability of clothing and textiles in the United Kingdom.* Cambridge.: University of Cambridge, Institute for Manufacturing.
2. United Nations Global Compact Web site, www.unglobalcompact.org.
3. The Brundtland Report, Report on the World Commission on Environment and Development, 1987. Available from www.un.org/esa/sustdev/publications/publications.htm#climate.
4. The Rio Declaration on Environment and Development at Earth Summit, 1992. Available from www.un.org/documents/ga/conf151/aconf15126-1annex1.htm
5. The Kyoto Protocol, 1997. Available from http://UNFCCC.int/2860.php.
6. Intergovernmental Panel on Climate Change and its award of the 2007 Peace Prize. Available from www.ipcc.ch/.
7. Walsh, J. A. H., & Brown, M. S. (1995). Pricing environmental impacts: a tale of two T-shirts. *Illahee* 11:3&4, 175–187.
8. Choinard, Y. (2005). *Let my people go surfing* (p. 212). New York: The Penguin Press.
9. Hawken, P. (1993). *The ecology of commerce* (p. 131). New York: HarperBusiness.
10. Rivoli, P. (2005). *The travels of a T-shirt in the global economy.* Hoboken, NJ: John Wiley & Sons.

11. Fletcher, K., Dewberry, E., & Goggin, P. (2001). Sustainable consumption by design. In Cohen, M. J. & Murphy, J. *Exploring Sustainable Consumption: Environmental Policy and the Social Sciences* (pp. 213–224). Amsterdam: Pergamon.

12. McDonough, W., & Braungart, M. (1998). The next industrial revolution. *The Atlantic Monthly, 282*:4, 82–92.

13. Choinard, Y. (2005), p. 212.

14. International Organization for Standardization Web site, www.iso.org.

15. McDonough, & Braungart (1998).

16. Brown, M. S., & Wilmanns, E. (1997); Fletcher & Goggin (2001); Allwood et al. (2006).

17. Brown, M. S., & Wilmanns, E. (1997); Allwood et al. (2006).

18. Sustainable Textile Standard at www.GreenBlue.org/activities_stm/html; Brown, M.S., & Wilmanns, E. (1997).

19. Sustainable Textile Standard at www.GreenBlue.org/activities_stm/html; Brown, M. S., & Wilmanns, E. (1997); Allwood et al. (2006); Fletcher & Goggin (2001).

20. Brown, M. S., & Wilmanns, E. (1997).

21. Fletcher, K. (2005). Fashion, gear and clothing: Toward an ecology of clothing. *Fourth Door Review, 7*, 67–71.

22. McDonough, W. & Braungart, M. (2001, November/December). Available from green@workmag.com.

23. EPEA Web site, www.EPEA.com.

24. United States Department of Agriculture. National Organic Program. Available from www.usda.gov/wps/portal/!ut/p/_s.7_0_A/7_0_1OB?navid=ORGANIC_CERTIFICATIO&parentnav=AGRICULTURE&navtype=RT.

25. Ingeo Web site, www.ingeofibers.com.

26. Climatex Web site, www.climatex.com.

27. Trigema Web site, www.trigema.de.

28. Ecocircle Web site, www.ecocircle.jp.

29. Polartec Web site, www.maldenmills.com/fabrics/technologies.php.

30. Alabama Chann.l Cotton series. Available from http://alabamachanin.com/Collections/SS08/SS08Title.htm.

31. Urban Outfitters Web site, www.urbanoutfitters.com; What Goes Around Comes Around Web site, www.nyvintage.com/history/history.html; Undesigned by Carol Young Web site, www.undesigned.com.

32. McDonough, W., & Braungart, M. (2002). *Cradle to cradle.* New York: North Point Press.

33. www.levistrauss.com/Citizenship/Environment, Nike Corporate Web site. Nike Responsibility. Available from www.nikebiz.com/responsibility/.

34. Loker, S. (2008). A technology enabled sustainable fashion system: Fashion's future. In Ulasewicz, C. & Hethorn, J. (Eds.). *Sustainable Fashion, Why Now?* New York: Fairchild.

35. Hawley, J. M. (2006). Textile recycling: A system perspective. In Y. Wang, (Ed.). *Recycling in textiles* (pp. 7–24). Cambridge, England: Woodhead.

36. Sustainable Packaging Coalition Web site, www.sustainablepackaging.org.

37. Timberland. About Us. Available from www.timberland.com/corp/index.jsp ?page=pressrelease&eid=850000724.

38. Franklin Associates (1993). Resource and environmental profile analysis of a manufactured apparel product: Woman's knit polyester blouse. Washington, DC: American Fiber Manufacturers Association. Retrieved from www. fibersource.com/f-tutor/LCA-Page.htm, November 1, 2007.

39. Allwood et al. (2006).

40. Allwood et al. (2006); Fletcher & Goggin (2001).

41. Dombek-Keith, K. (2008). *Eco-friendly apparel design: Altering users' experiences with their clothing to promote eco-friendly behaviors.* Unpublished masters' thesis, Cornell University, Ithaca, NY; Energy Star, Clothes Washers Web page, Available from www.energystar.gov/index.cfm?c=clotheswash. pr_clothes_washers; Walsh, J. A. H. & Brown, M. S. (1995).

42. Hawley, J. M. (2006).

43. Shaw Floors Web site, www.shawindustries.com.

44. Dombek-Keith, K. (2008).

45. Issey Miyake and Dai Fuiwara at the Vitra Design Museum Berlin. (2000). Museum Publication. Features Miyake's APOC designs–A Piece of Cloth—that address environmental issues through versatility and customer involvement.

46. Chen, C., & Lewis, V. D. (2006). The life of a piece of cloth. *The International Journal of Environmental, Cultural, Economic & Social Sustainability,* *2*(1), 198–207.

47. Fiber News. (2007). Cargill, Teijin form joint venture for NatureWorks. Available from www.fibersource.com/f-info/More_News/Cargill-100307. htm.

48. Fiber News. (2007).

49. Franklin Associates (1993).

50. Walsh & Brown (1995).

51. U.S. Green Building Council. (2008). Leed rating systems. Available from www.usgbc.org/LEED.

52. www.timberland.com.timberlandserve/timberlandserve_index.jsp

53. Porter, M. E. (1990). *The competitive advantage of nations.* New York: Free Press.

54. Choinard, Y. (2005).

55. Porter, M. E., & Kramer, M. R. (2006). Strategy and society: The link between competitive advantage and corporate social responsibility. *Harvard Business Review,* (December), 78–92.

56. Maggie's Functional Organics. Maggie's story. Available from www.maggiesorganics.com/achievements.php.

57. Alabama Chanin Web site, www.alabamachanin.com.

Chapter 9

1. Allwood, J. M., Laursen, S. E., de Rodriquez, C. M., & Bocken, N. M. P. (2006). *Well dressed? The present and future sustainability of clothing and textiles in the United Kingdom.* Cambridge: University of Cambridge Institute for Manufacturing.

2. Dickson, M. A. (2006, June 14). *The complexity of sourcing in a global market.* Paper presented at the Multi-Stakeholder Forum, Fair Labor Association, Bamberg, Germany.

3. Allwood, J. M., Laursen, S. E., de Rodriquez, C. M., & Bocken, N. M. P (2006).

4. International Labour Office (2006, January). *Global employment trends brief (p. 6).* Geneva: International Labour Organization.

5. Allwood, J. M., Laursen, S. E., de Rodriquez, C. M., & Bocken, N. M. P (2006).

6. International Labour Office. (2006).

7. SÜDWIND (2004). *Global game for cuffs and collars.* Mosel, Germany: South Wind Institute of Economics and Ecumenism.

8. Fair Labor Association. (2004, October 26). FLA Board of Directors Adopts Resolution on the Elimination of Apparel Quotas. Available from www.fairlabor.org/all/news/docs/MFA_resolution.pdf.

9. Fair Labor Association. (2006). 2006 annual public report. Available from www.fairlabor.org.

10. Cheadle, H., & van Heerden, A. (2007). Retrenchment and plant closures: Challenges for worker rights and industrial relations. In *Fair Labor Association 2007 Annual Report.* Available from www.fairlabor.org/pubs/reports/.

11. The MFA Forum Web site, www.mfa-forum.net.

12. Doumbia-Henry, C., & Gravel, E., (2006). Free trade agreements and labour rights: Recent developments. *International Labor Review,* 145(3), 185–206.

13. Doumbia-Henry, C., & Gravel, E. (2006).

14. Doumbia-Henry, C. & Gravel, E. (2006).

15. International Labour Office. (2006, p. 5).

16. Allwood, J. M., Laursen, S. E., de Rodriquez, C. M., & Bocken, N. M. P. (2006, pp. 3–4).

17. Business for Social Responsibility. (2007). *Beyond monitoring: A new vision for sustainable supply chains*. Available from www.bsr.org.

18. Hurley, J., & Faiz, N. (2007). *Assessing the impact of purchasing practices on code compliance: A case study of the Bangladesh garment industry*. Available from www.mfa-forum.net/.

19. Hurley, J., & Faiz, N. (2007).

20. Personal communication, Nate Herman, May 2007.

21. Beckett, A. (2006, February 28). Going cheap. *The Guardian*, p. 6.

22. Hurley, J., & Faiz, N. (2007).

23. Hurley, J. & Faiz, N. (2007).

24. Hurley, J. & Faiz, N. (2007).

25. Personal communication, Paula Zusi and Al Shapiro, November 2007.

26. Hurley, J., & Faiz, N. (2007).

27. Hurley, J., & Faiz, N. (2007).

28. Hurley, J., & Faiz, N. (2007).

29. Hurley, J., & Faiz, N. (2007).

30. Business for Social Responsibility. (2007).

31. As cited in Labour Behind the Label (2006). *Let's clean up fashion: The state of pay behind the UK high street* (p. 18). Available from www.labourbehindthe label.org/resources.

32. Business for Social Responsibility. (2007).

33. Business for Social Responsibility. (2007).

34. Fair Labor Association Web site, www.fairlabor.org.

35. Business for Social Responsibility. (2007).

36. Casey, R. 2006. Meaningful change: Raising the bar in supply chain workplace standards. *Corporate Social Responsibility Initiative, Working Paper No. 29*. Cambridge, MA: John F. Kennedy School of Government, Harvard University. p. 39.

37. Cheadle, H., & van Heerden, A. (2007, pp. 98–99).

38. Clean Clothes Campaign. (2005). *Looking for a quick fix: How weak social auditing is keeping workers in sweatshops*. Retrieved on 11/23/05 from www.cleanclothes.org.

39. As cited in Labour Behind the Label (2006, p. 21).

40. Kearney, N., & Justice, D. (2003). The new codes of conduct: Some questions and answers for trade unionists. In I. Wick, (2005). *Workers' tool or PR ploy: A guide to international labor practice* (4th ed.). Bonn: Friedrich-Ebert-Stiftung.

41. Personal communication, Doug Miller, September 2007.

42. Casey, R. (2006, p. 22).

43. Clean Clothes Campaign. (2005).

44. Oxfam International. (2006). *Offside! Labour rights and sportswear production in Asia*. Available from www.oxfam.org/en/policy/briefingnotes/offside_labor_report.

45. Personal communication, Doug Miller, September 2007.
46. Clean Clothes Campaign. (2005).
47. Personal communication, Doug Miller, September 2007.
48. Brown, M. S. & Wilmanns, E. (1997). Quick and dirty environmental analyses for garments: What do we need to know? *Journal of Sustainable Product Design*, 1(1), 28–34.
49. Business for Social Responsibility. (2007).
50. Office of the U.S. Trade Representative. (2007). *2007 Comprehensive Report on U.S. Trade and Investment Policy toward Sub-Saharan Africa and Implementation of the African Growth and Opportunity Act.* Available from www.agoa.gov/.
51. Better Factories Cambodia Web site, www.betterfactories.org/.
52. Casey, R. (2006).
53. Dickson, M. A. (2005). Identifying and profiling apparel label users. In R. Harrison, T. Newholm, & D. Shaw (Eds.), *The ethical consumer* (pp. 155–171). Thousand Oaks, CA: Sage.
54. Dickson, M. A., & Kovaleski, K. (2007, November 8). *Implementing labor compliance in the apparel industry.* Paper presented at the annual conference of the International Textile and Apparel Association, Los Angeles, CA.

Credits

Chapter 1

Figure 1.1: AP Photo.
Figure 1.2: Courtesy of the adidas Group.
Figure 1.3: © Ryan Pyle/Corbis.
Figure 1.4: Photography by Lewis W. Hine. Courtesy of the Library of Congress.
Figure 1.5: © Corbis.
Figure 1.6: Courtesy of the Catherwood Library Kheel Center.
Figure 1.7: Illustrated by Lindsay Lyman-Clarke.
Figure 1.8: Illustrated by Lindsay Lyman-Clarke.

Chapter 2

Figure 2.2: Illustrated by Lindsay Lyman-Clarke.
Figure 2.3: © Marsha Dickson.
Figure 2.5: © University of Delaware Social Responsibility Project.

Chapter 3

Figure 3.1: Courtesy of Fairchild Publications, Inc.
Figure 3.2: Adapted from Srnka. K. (2004). Culture's role in marketer's ethical decision making: An integrated theoretical framework. Academy of Marketing Science Review, 1, 4, p. 17.
Figure 3.3: Courtesy of Molly Eckman.
Figure 3.4: © University of Delaware Social Responsibility Project.
Figure 3.5: © Pascal Deloche/Godong/Corbis.
Figure 3.6: © University of Delaware Social Responsibility Project.
Figure 3.7: Illustrated by Lindsay Lyman-Clarke.
Figure 3.8: Illustrated by Lindsay Lyman-Clarke.

Chapter 4

Figure 4.1: Copyright © 2008 The President and Fellows of Harvard College.
Figure 4.2: AP Photo.
Figure 4.3: Courtesy of The New York State Archives.
Figure 4.4: Adapted from Gable, C., & Shireman, B. (2005). Stakeholder engagement: A three-phase methodology. Environmental Quality Management, Spring, p. 15.
Figure 4.5: Adapted from Colle, S. (2005). A stakeholder management model for ethical decision making. International Journal of Management and Decision Making, 6(3/4), 299–314.

Credits

Chapter 5

Figure 5.1: © RAFIQUR RAHMAN/Reuters/Corbis.
Figure 5.2: © University of Delaware Social Responsibility Project.
Figure 5.3: Courtesy of the adidas Group.
Figure 5.5: Courtesy of Better Factories Cambodia.
Figure 5.6: Courtesy of The Associated Press.

Chapter 6

Figure 6.1: © University of Delaware Social Responsibility Project.
Figure 6.2: © University of Delaware Social Responsibility Project.
Figure 6.3: © Marsha Dickson.
Figure 6.4: © Marsha Dickson.
Figure 6.5: © Marsha Dickson.

Chapter 7

Figure 7.1: Courtesy of Puma.
Figure 7.2: Mamic, I, (2003). Business and code of conduct implementation: How firms use management systems for social performance, Geneva: International Labor Organization.
Figure 7.3: Courtesy of adidas Group.
Figure 7.4: Courtesy of Nike.
Figure 7.5: Zadek, S. (2004). The path to corporate responsibility. Harvard Business Review, 82(12), 125–132.

Chapter 8

Figure 8.1: © Suzanne Loker. Illustrated by Lindsay Lyman-Clarke.
Figure 8.2: Garment by Natalie Chanin.
Figure 8.3: Courtesy of The Timberland Company.
Figure 8.4: © Katie Dombek-Keith.
Figure 8.5: Garments by Katie Dombek-Keith. Photographer, Shai Eynav.
Figure 8.6: © Van Dyk Lewis and Connie Chen.

Chapter 9

Figure 9.1: © Marsha Dickson.
Figure 9.2: © Marsha Dickson.
Figure 9.3: Courtesy of the Fair Labor Association.
Figure 9.4: Photograph by Helena Perez. Courtesy of the Fair Labor Association.
Figure 9.5: Illustrated by Lindsay Lyman-Clarke.

Back cover photos

© University of Delaware Social Responsibility Project.

Index

Index

Index